TAONGA TUKU IHO

AN ILLUSTRATED ENCYCLOPEDIA OF

TRADITIONAL MĀORI LIFE

A note about the Original Encyclopedia

An Illustrated Encyclopedia of Māori Life was first published by A.H. and A.W. Reed in 1963 and was reprinted every two to three years until the early 1980s. Although the exact details of its prinitng history are no longer known, a likely estimate of the total number printed is in excess of 30,000 copies. The original text was written by A.W. Reed and the line illustrations were drawn from books illustrated by Dr. Terry Barrow, Russell Clark, Harry Dansey, W. Dittmer, S.M. Mead, L.C. Mitchell and Dennis Turner — it is worth noting that these graphic illustrations are as alive and informative today as they were some 50 years ago.

The author, A.W. Reed, researched and wrote over 200 books from 1934 up until his death in 1979. At the time of writing, 22 of them (each one updated in text as well as design) remain in print. No other New Zealander has achieved this longevity with so many titles.

Ray Richards (1921–2013)
Lifetime Achievement Award 2001
Former vice-chairman and publisher, A.H. and A.W. Reed

TAONGA TUKU IHO

AN ILLUSTRATED ENCYCLOPEDIA OF TRADITIONAL MĀORI LIFE

A.W. REED
Edited by Buddy Mikaere

This edition published in 2022 by White Cloud Books, an imprint of Upstart Press Ltd.

26 Greenpark Road, Penrose, Auckland, 1061, New Zealand

www.upstartpress.co.nz

First published in 1963 by A.H. & A.W. Reed as *An Illustrated Encyclopedia of Maori Life*

ISBN: 9781990003721

A catalogue record for this book is available from the National Library of New Zealand

Cover design: Nick Turzynski, redinc. book design, www.redinc.co.nz

Illustrations on page 33: Anna Egan-Reid

Cover photograph: Karetao (Jumping Jack), reproduced with permission courtesy Te Papa, Wellington, New Zealand

10 9 8 7 6 5 4 3 2 1

Printed by: Dongguan P&C Printing Technology Co., Ltd, China

INTRODUCTION

Tēnā rā koutou

For the second time in the past twenty years I have been given the privileged task of reviewing and revising again the *Illustrated Encyclopedia of Traditional Māori Life* now nearly sixty years since it was first published. In the earlier editions I was saddened by the way the text reminded me of how so much had been lost — the "old" Māori way of life, concepts and modes of thinking. But while that still holds true, what is different today is the revival of interest in *Te Ao Māori* – the Māori world and the active pursuit by many, of the information set out here.

I believe that has been sparked by a tremendous push across the whole Aotearoa community to learn *te reo* — a direct outcome of *te wiki o te reo Māori* — Māori language week. Media, national media in particular, has been supportive of the use of *te reo*, to the extent that use of the language is now an expectation rather than an occasional offering. So it is only natural that there should be a spill over into learning about other aspects of Māori culture and for many, getting to grips with the cultural foundations of the language has become a worthy pursuit. *Mihi aroha ki a koutou.*

Taonga Tuku Iho is the perfect accompaniment to this drive for the acquisition of aspects of a culture that is found nowhere else in the world and which is what makes us who live in this country, so unique. This is <u>our</u> Aotearoa culture and <u>our</u> shared heritage.

So it is inevitable in such a general work that there are references to post-contact Māori life, but I have endeavoured to keep the flavour of the original by retaining the focus on traditional or pre-contact Māori life.

The intention of the original publication was to provide a universal reference for the average reader and for this reason I have retained the English language headings.

Like many with an abiding interest in Māori history I have an admiration for the work of the twentieth-century ethnologist Elsdon Best, who spent much of his life observing and recording life amongst the Tūhoe people of the Urewera. While it is fashionable in some quarters to demean Best's work, nevertheless a great debt is owed to him because the fine body of work he left behind, and on which this publication relies quite heavily, is a genuine taonga (treasure). *Nā mihi ki a koe, e pā!*

So too should I acknowledge the other kaumātua, scholars, ethnologists and writers whose works and recorded knowledge and observations underpin the entries in this book: Johannes C. Anderson, Dr Terry Barrow, J. Herries Beattie, Bruce Biggs, Sir Peter Buck, William Colenso, James Cowan, T.W. Downes, Roger Duff, Raymond Firth, Hare Hongi, Sir Apirana Ngata, W.J. Phillips, Nepia Pohuhu, Andrew Sharp, Percy Smith, Rev Richard Taylor, Te Matorohanga, Dr A.P. Thomson, Edward Tregear, A.P. Vadya, H.T.Whatahoro. Nā mihi nui ki a koutou hoki.

I also have to acknowledge the use of works by Peter Bellwood, Dr Lyndsay Head, J.P. Johanson, Professor Margaret Orbell, Joel Polack, P.M. Ryan, Edward Shortland, James Stack, H.T. Taiaroa, William A. Taylor, and Harrison Wright.

I am especially grateful to Dr Lyndsay Head, formerly of the Māori Department, University of Canterbury, for her advice and assistance in helping me resolve some of the contradictory aspects of several entries. Another delight in editing this book has been my re-acquaintance with the line drawings and illustrations of Dr Terry Barrow, Russell Clark and Dennis Turner. We have become so used to photographs and modern graphics that black and white ink illustrations have taken on a somewhat quaint appearance. In my opinion they possess an innocent and attractive charm for that very reason. I think that the drawings of Dennis Turner, especially, retain a freshness of interpretation that gives us an insightful window into traditional Māori life. The illustration on page 80 of Māori children playing on a wet day is my personal favourite.

I should also acknowledge the contribution made by A.W. Reed and A.H. and A.W. Reed publishers for their original concept for this book and the generous philanthropic gesture that saw the royalties paid to the Māori Education Foundation, which subsequently became the National Kohanga Reo Trust. The Reed connection lives on in that without the efforts of the late Ray Richards, who was vice-chairman and publisher of the A.H. and A.W. Reed company during some of its most progressive publishing years, the revised editions over the years would not have come to fruition.

It is my hope that the new reader will enjoy this book and find sufficient in its contents to excite further interest and inquiry.

E iti noa ana, nā te aroha — A small gift, given in love.

Naku na

Buddy Mikaere
Manaia, Coromandel
April 2022

A

ACTION SONGS or *waiata ringa* are a central feature of any Kapa Haka performance. The body movements of the performers are used to supplement the telling of the story behind the lyrics, and are a development that has sprung from the traditional *haka waiata.*

The actions that accompany the songs have become largely standardised and the six illustrations reproduced here are typical of the movements incorporated into many songs. In traditional times, movements of the body, arms and fingers accompanied the dances of the women. But in the modern version the movements are used to convey definite emotions or ideas. In fact this is the dominant characteristic of the modern action song: using the actions to convey and interpret the mood and meaning of the words.

With their seamless incorporation of the old and the new in music, dance and poetry, action songs now form a major part of any Māori cultural entertainment.

Dances, songs.

'Haere mai e hoa mä'
(Welcome friends)

'Kia kaha'
(Be strong)

'Hoatu i taku ringa'
(I give you my hand)

'Ka karanga ki te Matua'
(Call to the Lord above)

'Kei te moe taku tinana'
(My body is sleeping)

'Ko te reo o Wharepunga'
(The voice of Wharepunga)

Typical movements in the modern action song, with their meanings.

ADZES (*toki*). These were the most common tools for working timber. They were normally made from hard, fine-grained stone such as basalt or argillite that were easily flaked and shaped. Highly prized *toki* were fashioned from greenstone (nephrite). Adze blades were roughly blocked out, flaked, chipped and bruised with round granite hammer-stones, and rubbed to a smooth surface on sandstone; greenstone blades were worked to a smooth surface by sandstone cutters and finally polished by hand. The adze blade was lashed to a wooden handle, often with a step against which the blade rested, helping to hold it firmly in position.

Large adzes attached to heavy wooden handles and suspended on swings or mounted on tensioned 'bows' were used to fell trees. Experts were adept in using the adze with which they roughed out canoes and shaped timbers used in *whare*, houses or buildings. The adze

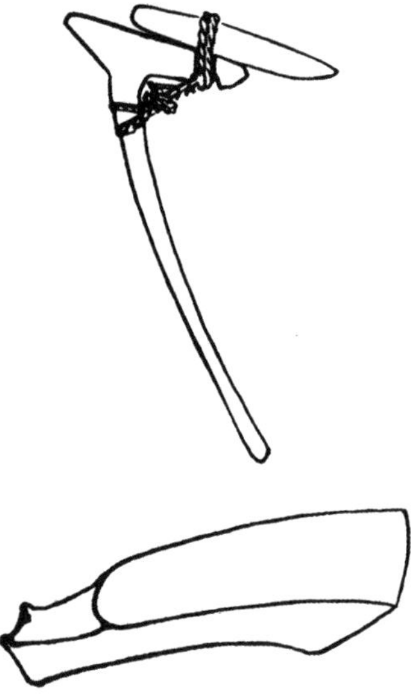

Top: A stone adze head lashed to a wooden handle.

Above: A stone adze blade of early manufacture. These early adzes were made with a 'tanged' step and end nodes which made it easier to lash the adze to a wooden handle.

enabled them to produce a smooth surface on a plank with a characteristic pattern that resembled that on the trunk of the *mamaku*, black tree fern.

Canoes, drills, sandstone, trees.

AGRICULTURE. When Māori first came to Aotearoa they found themselves in a colder climate where vegetable foods did not grow with the same profusion as in their tropical homelands. Berries could be obtained in the season but the only article of diet that grew in profusion throughout the year, and which became a staple, was *aruhe*, the rhizome or root of the bracken fern.

Fortunately the Māori migrants brought some food plants with them and were able to supplement their diet with edible root crops such as *kūmara*, *taro*, and *uwhi*, yam. They also cultivated the hue, gourd plant. The *kūmara* was the only food plant to flourish but it needed careful attention. Climate and soil conditions in the warmer parts of the country suited *kūmara* cultivation, and the plant ing, tending, harvesting, and storing of the tubers occupied much of the people's time, especially in densely populated, warm, fertile areas such as the Tāmaki (Auckland) isthmus.

Although gardening was an activity in which all joined; men and women had their own special tasks in the plots of land devoted to culti vation. The usual mode of gardening was slash and burn with the ash from the burnings applied to the land as fertil iser. The men prepared the ground by loosening long sods of earth with pointed digging sticks called *kō*. Subsequently the soil was broken up by women with smaller implements and kept weeded. Sand and gravel were brought in baskets and scattered over heavy clay soil to break it up and in some areas to extend the growing season. Gravel and small stones retained daytime heat, promoting soil warmth and allowing earlier planting.

Windbreaks of sticks or low stone walls were built to protect young plants. Gardening work was performed with care, with the plants placed in neat rows. Individual *kūmara* plants would have their own growing mound or ridge. After one or two seasons the fertiliser in the soil would be exhausted and the gardens would be moved to a new location with the former garden land left fallow.

The work involving *kūmara* cultivation was so important that it was surrounded by religious

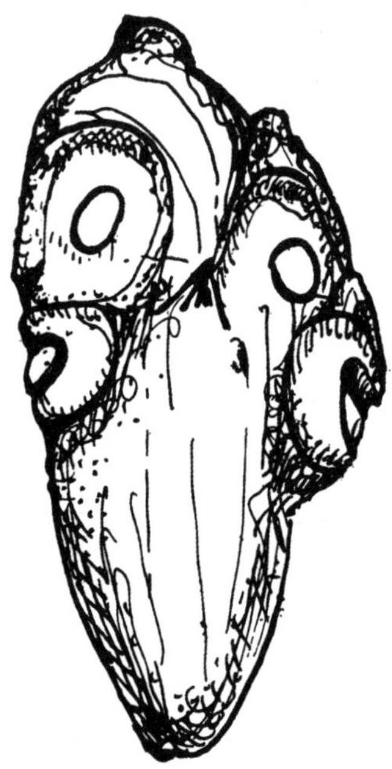

A stone *kūmara* god.

ceremony; workers were *tapu* at planting time, and various rituals, *karakia*, invocations, and *waiata*, songs were employed to ensure fertility and vigorous growth.

The times for planting and harvesting were marked by the first appearance of particular star constellations in the night sky. As Rongo was the god of the moon as well as of agriculture and of peaceful arts, the phases of the moon were also very carefully observed because they dictated what work would be done in the gardens. 'Planting by the moon' is a practice still followed by some Māori gardeners today.

Stones, sometimes roughly shaped into images and which contained the *mauri*, the life essence of a growing crop, were placed in the kūmara plantations. The stones would also become a temporary residence for an *atua*, god, whose *mana* served to protect the *mauri*.

Prior to harvesting, *rua*, pits, lined with fern, were prepared for the proper storage of the valuable tubers. The pits were 'lipped' to prevent groundwater entering and roofed so that rainwater could be kept out as well. Special storage *rua* were sometimes dug into the sides of banks or hillsides, the entrances being fitted with a wooden door.

Cultivations, gourds, implements (agricultural), kūmara, months, moon, nights of the moon, pits, Rongo, stars, taro, yams.

AHI, see FIRE.

AHU, see MOUNDS.

ĀHUA. A word frequently used in ritual, it has the meaning of appearance, character, form or semblance. A Māori person may accept the *āhua* of a gift by touching it and returning the physical object to the donor, thus accepting it in spirit. Similarly, when food offerings are made to the *atua*, gods, they take the *āhua* and leave the food untouched. At times the *āhua* may be a material representation of a material or immaterial object. The word is also used for personality, as when a branch or twig of *karamū* is applied to the body of a sick person. The *āhua* of the sick person then enters the branch, which is carried to the *tohunga*, who, from a distance, is able to tell when the patient will recover. In such cases there is a distinction between *āhua*, personality, and *wairua*, soul or spirit.

Ariā, wairua, theft.

AHUREWA, see ALTARS.

AITUĀ. Misfortune, or unlucky omen.

Omens

AKA, see VINES.

ALBINOS *(rako)*. There were few real albinos, but, as happens in all races, fair-skinned, red-haired types were sometimes seen. Albino birds were *tapu*, and misfortune would come to anyone who touched or killed them.

Urukehu.

ALPHABET. When the Māori alphabet was recorded in written form, 15 letters or phonograms were needed: the consonants *h, k, m, n, p, r, t, w*, the nasal sound *ng*, the aspirated *w*, which is written *wh*, and the vowels *a, e, i, o, u*. Every syllable in a Māori word ends in a vowel. When a word is divided at the end of a line it is important that the division should come after the vowel, never after a consonant. No two consonants ever come together.

With modern written and printed Māori a distinction is made between long and short vowels by use of a macron (e.g. Māori) to denote a double vowel or by writing the double vowel itself (Maaori) although this is often thought to make the written language look ungainly. The macron method is generally preferred, and is used in the authoritative *A Dictionary of the Māori Language* (Williams). Modern printing techniques and electronic dictionaries and spell checks make use of the macron a relatively straightforward task.

Language, pronunciation.

ALTARS or SHRINES *(ahurewa, tūāhu)*. In every *kāinga*, village, there was a *wahi tapu*, sacred place, which was used by the *tohunga*, priestly expert, as a place to perform sacred or divinatory rites. More particularly it was known as the *tūāhu*. It could be located anywhere, in or outside the *pā*, but was usually in a secluded space in the forest or amongst bracken. Frequently it was placed close to the communal latrine, which was also a *tapu* place, surrounded by religious restriction. The site of the *tūāhu* was simply marked with stones or wooden pegs.

No one but the *tohunga* entered the *tūāhu* enclosure. In the space there was usually a mound, and poles or rods used for divination and other rites. *Tūāhu* in Te Waka a Māui, the South Island, were often fenced in and sometimes contained a wooden image. Offerings were made to the gods in the *tūāhu*, and were placed on the ground, on stones, or on an elevated platform. Ceremonial fires were kindled here, and the place was under the guardianship of the primal *atua* Tāne, Rongo and Tupai.

Ahurewa was another word used in the broad sense of an altar. It was seldom if ever located outside, but was usually at the base of the rear post in the *whare wānanga*, house of learning. It was at this spot that ceremonies were performed over the pupils of the school, and the small stones used in many of the rites were kept in this place.

Magic, sacred stones, whare wānanga.

A *tohunga* at a sacred fire on the *tūāhu*, which is indicated by the vertical stones.

AMO, see LITTERS.

ANCESTORS (*Ngā tipuna, Ngā tūpuna*). Great respect was paid to ancestors, whose spirits were called upon in time of stress. They could be relied upon to come to the aid of mothers in labour, and of men in battle.

When a whānau grew large and strong enough to take a tribal name, it usually adopted that of its first male forbear, prefixing it with *Āti, Ngāi, Ngāti*, or in some cases *Whānau*. *Ngā* means 'the' (plural); *Āti*, 'offspring'; *Ngāi* and *Āti* are variants of *Ngāti* while *Whānau* means 'family'. Well-known examples of such tribal names are *Āti Awa, Ngāi Tahu, Ngāti Tūwharetoa* and *Whānau A Apanui*. (Apanui's family).

Families, tribes.

ANA, see CAVES.

ANCHORS (*punga*). Stone anchors were most often dumb-bell in shape with the anchor rope tied round the 'waist'. Large stones, pierced with one or more holes through which the anchor rope was threaded, were also used. In some other cases smooth, heavy stones enclosed in a woven net served as anchors.

Rakiura, Stewart Island.

ANIMALS. The only land animal native to New Zealand was the *pekapeka*, bat. The other animals of pre-Pākehā days were the *kurī*, dog, and the *kiore*, rat, both of which were brought here by Māori. In the early days of Pākehā settlement Māori called all introduced mammals kurï or kararehe. The horse became *kurī waha tangata* (literally, man-carrying dog).

Bats, dogs, rats.

ĀNIWANIWA, see RAINBOWS.

Two men carrying the anchor stone of a canoe. The anchor rope is threaded through the hole by which it is being carried.

ANKLETS, see ORNAMENTS.

AO. Cloud, day, world.

Light.

AO MĀRAMA. The world of light. Light came into the world when Tāne pushed apart the primal parents, Rangi and Papa. Mārama is a name for the moon and for heavenly light. Rarohenga, the Māori under world, has light, but this does not have its source in sun, moon, and stars, therefore the world of men is dis tinguished by being called Te Ao Mārama.

Separation.

AOTEA. One of the famous ancestral canoes. Its captain was the explorer Turi. Aotea made landfall at Whangaparāoa, on the east coast of Te Ika a Māui, the North Island, near Cape Runaway. The canoe followed the coastline north and was either taken across the short canoe portage at Tāmaki (Auckland), or sailed round North Cape, and down the west coast of Te Ika a Māui. Turi finally made his home at Pätea. His descendants claim that Aotea brought gods, the kūmara and other plants and animals to Aotearoa. The descendants of the canoe are the Ngāti Ruanui, Ngā Rauru and Āti-hau tribes of Taranaki and Whanganui.

Kurahaupo.

AOTEAROA. The Māori name for New Zealand. According to tradition, Kupe and Ngāhue sailed from Hawaiki in their canoes and discovered a new land far to the south. This is reckoned to have occurred about 1000 years ago. Landfall was made somewhere in the far north of the country, but the first indication of land was the white cloud that shrouded it. Hine-te-aparangi, Kupe's wife, is said to have cried, '*He ao! He ao!*' (A cloud! A cloud!); this was later changed to *Aotea* (white cloud) and then, according to some, changed to *Aotea-roa* (long, white cloud), presumably because of the size of the country when its full extent was realised.

Aotearoa has therefore become 'Land of the long, white cloud' the popular name for New Zealand. But the name is one of the unsolved puzzles of Māori lore, because it violates the rule that a noun is never followed by more than one adjective and for that reason Aotearoa probably indicates a relatively modern (and romantic) origin. There are quite a number of other feasible translations. These include: the long, clear day, the long, white world, the long, bright world, the land of long-lingering daylight, the land of shimmering twilight, the big, glaring light, the continuously clear light, the land of abiding day, the long-lingering day, the long, bright land, and the long, bright day.

Kupe, Māui.

APA. In some late collected traditions Apa were celestial beings likened to angels and who were said to guard the door to the twelfth or topmost heaven or overworld.

Overworlds.

ARAI-TE-URU. An early migration canoe that sailed down the east coast of Te Waka a Māui and was wrecked at Moeraki. The canoe was petrified in the form of a reef, and the round boulders that strew the nearby beach are believed to be the *hue*, calabashes, and *kūmara,* tubers, of the canoe. Some Ngāi Tahu traditions claim descent from this canoe. Arai-te-uru was also the name of one of the *taniwha*, monsters, which is said to have accompanied the Takitimu migration canoe to Aotearoa. The home of the *taniwha* is the southern head of the entrance to the Hokianga Harbour.

ARAWA, TE. One of the principal migration canoes, it was commanded by Tama-te-kapua. The famous *tohunga,* priest, Ngatoro-i-rangi, was also among the crew, having been tricked into boarding Te Arawa when it left the Hawaiki homeland. Te Arawa also made landfall at Whangaparāoa on the east coast. There they met the crew of the Tainui waka. Tainui's crew tricked them into believing that they (Tainui) had arrived first, so forcing Te Arawa to move on. (Like many migration stories, this one is also told from the opposite perspective.)

The final resting-place of the Te Arawa waka was at Maketū in the Bay of Plenty, where it was burnt by the chief Raumati following a tribal squabble. The crew settled around Rotorua and parts of the Bay of Plenty where they were first known as Ngā Oho. Subsequently they increased and became a confederation of related tribes and took their name from the ancestral canoe, becoming generally known as the Arawa people. The following tribes, located at Maketū, Mātātā, Rotorua and Taupō, are just some of those descended from Te Arawa: Arawa, Ngāti Pikiao, Ngāti Rangitihi, Ngāti Rangiwewehi, Ngāti Whakaue, Tuhourangi, and Ngāti Tūwharetoa.

Tides.

ARERO, see TONGUES.

ARIĀ, see MEDIUMS. Also a form of incantation.

ARIKI, see CHIEFS.

ART. There are six Māori decorative arts. They

are *moko,* body and face tattoo, *tuhi* or *kōwhaiwhai*, panel or rafter painting, *tāniko,* weaving of cloak borders, *raranga*, the plaiting of coloured elements in baskets and mats, *tukutuku,* lattice-work house panels and *whakairo*, carving in wood, bone, and stone. Of these, the last is considered the most important.

Māori developed a type of curvilinear art, radically different from most other Polynesian art forms. It is seen in the *kōwhaiwhai* painted rafter patterns of houses, in *moko* and in *whakairo,* wood carving in particular. Such designs were gracefully executed and, in the carving of the *tauihu*, bow, and *taurapa*, stern, pieces for canoes, were transformed into delicate filigree that would test the skill of modern artists with razor-sharp steel tools.

In the curves and loops of the Māori version of the curvilinear art form there is a clear link to the plants of the forests, particularly the graceful spirals of the fern frond, which is the most common pattern invoked as a decorative motif. Others say that the spiral motif represents the web of a spider.

The spiral designs of Māori traditional art are what set it apart from its origins. The *koropepe* or small, single spiral is used extensively as a decorative element in *whakairo* and *moko* work, while the large, double spiral is a device used on larger works such as carved war canoes.

Finely detailed carving work also appears on *waka huia,* carved boxes, and on the handles of tools and weapons of wood, stone, bone, and greenstone. Māori artisans achieved a very high degree of sophistication in this type of carving work despite using only stone chisels and adzes.

The carved *pou whakairo*, carved representations of the human figure, represent the pinnacle of the carver's art. Various tribal groups developed their own carving styles and schools of carving and the work they produced ranged from a heavily ornamented baroque style to work best described as starkly minimalist.

While the shape of most *pou* is often stylised the details are usually intricate and suggest aggressive or intimidating movement. This is because the intent was to portray ancestral figures as the gods they had become and to surround them with *mana*, prestige, and authority, a reflection of the identity and power of the descendants who had made them.

Woodwork on the scale practised by Māori was found nowhere else in Polynesia and this probably reflects the relative richness of the stone and timber resources found here.

In *kōwhaiwhai, whakairo* and *moko*, traditional Māori art tended to fall within a range of fixed patterns and themes with any differentiation arising from the skill of the artist rather than innovation. This was because the range of materials and tools, while rich in comparison with other parts of the South Pacific, nevertheless also limited what could be done. The relative isolation of Aotearoa meant that there were no opportunities to exchange ideas with artists in other lands. But within these parameters there is evidence of a keen observation of nature and small echoes of the ancient Polynesian art tradition to which Māori belonged.

The Polynesian characteristic use of rectilinear patterns appears best in the textile arts. Basket weaving, *tāniko* patterns, and the *tukutuku*, decoration on the panelled walls of houses, resulted in the traditional rectilinear form, but it was employed with imagination and a fine sense of symmetry and contrast. In *tukutuku* design the yellow stalks of *toetoe* were sometimes ornamented with a spiral pattern applied by wrapping strips of *harakeke*, green flax, round the rods and holding them over the fire. When the *harakeke* was removed, the exposed parts formed a black spiral pattern round the stalk.

Traditional Māori art is not representational in the Western sense, although motifs such as the *ngārara,* lizard, and the *pakake,* whale, were depicted in a lifelike style on the bargeboards of houses. But their function was usually magical rather than decorative. The *ngārara* was a symbol of fear and also guardianship while the *pakake* represented wealth and plenty, particularly in terms of food.

As a general observation Māori art clearly evolved away from its Polynesian origins and shows a sufficient separateness in its design elements to support a thesis that the separation was of a reasonably lengthy duration.

Baskets, canoes, carving, caves, cloaks, houses, painting, tāniko, tattooing, weaving.

ARUHE, see FERN ROOT.

ASTRONOMY. The movements and position of the stars were studied and, combined with other knowledge about bird movements, weather patterns, wind and currents, enabled Māori and other Pacific peoples to navigate canoes across the ocean.

Another reason for needing to possess an intimate knowledge of the stars was because they acted as the seasonal 'clock', announcing the coming of the seasons and therefore whether it was time to plant, time to harvest, or whether it was the season for the collection of particular foods. For example, the appearance of the stargroup Matariki, the Pleiades, just before sunrise (about June) signalled the beginning of the Māori year.

While the majority of ordinary people knew something of the subject, experts, known as *tohunga kokorangi*, were responsible for preserving the greater body of knowledge, much of which has unfortunately been lost.

Experts, stars.

ATA, see SOUL. The *ata* was the divine shape or spirit of man.

ĀTAHU, see LOVE CHARMS, MAGIC.

ĀTEA (or **WĀTEA**), see SPACE.

ATUA, see GODS.

AURORA AUSTRALIS ***(Tahu-nui-a-rangi)*****.** In legend, the mysterious, glowing, southern lights were said to be the reflection of the fires of a party of ancient explorers wandering lost in the cold lands of the south and unable to return. The Māori name for the phenomenon literally means: the great glowing, setting on fire, or the burning of the sky.

AUTE. The paper mulberry tree provided *tapa*, 'bark cloth', a material used throughout Polynesia. The tree was brought to Aotearoa by the first Māori but apparently did not flourish in the colder climate. While there is some evidence that a few trees survived, these are believed to have died out shortly after the arrival of the Pākehā. There are traditions that a substitute for *tapa* was found in the inner bark of the *houhere*, lacebark tree, but because the *harakeke*, flax plant, provided an abundance of leaves and fibre for the making of cloaks, mats, baskets, and ropes 'bark cloth' fell out of use. Examples of *tapa* cloth from *aute* bark have been preserved.

Cloaks.

AUTUMN ***(ngahuru)***, see SEASONS.

AWE, see SOULS. *Awe* is a lofty conception of the soul.

AXES ***(toki)*****.** Although this word is sometimes used for a hewing tool, for Māori it was an unusual implement. As with Western axes, the blade was set at right angles to the handle but an edge was only put on one side. A few examples of blades ground on both faces have been preserved, but it is not known exactly how they were used. The usual cutting tool was the adze.

Adzes.

B

BABIES *(tamaiti)*. A newborn baby was shaken vigorously to expel fluid from its mouth and nostrils in the belief that its voice would be nasal if it were not subjected to this treatment. The mother would constantly *mirimiri,* massage, the child's limbs to make them supple and shapely.

In some districts the baby was placed in a basket-like cradle suspended from the roof of a *whare*, house, and, by means of a cord attached to it, swung to and fro by the mother.

Infants were weaned when they were able to turn over by themselves, but sometimes not until they were able to walk. The mother rubbed her breasts with a bitter juice to wean the baby quickly.

Usually only the parents were encouraged to hold the baby in the belief that it would help strengthen the bond between them.

A charm was frequently recited over a male child to make him a brave warrior, while girls were dedicated to Hine-te-iwaiwa, the deity who oversaw domestic duties.

Baptism, birth, lullabies, mana.

BAILERS *(tā)*. *Tatā*, canoe bailers, were made of wood in the form of an oval scoop, with a handle projecting forward from the back rim and over the body of the scoop. The back rim and handle were often elaborately carved in the form of a stylised human face.

BALLS, see POI.

BAPTISM *(tohi, tūā, iriiri)*. As in Christian baptism, the Māori baptismal ceremony was designed to dedicate the infant to the gods, as well as to confer a name upon it. The rite was performed shortly after the umbilical cord came away. The ceremony described here was that carried out by the Tūhoe people of the Urewera. It differed greatly according to the status of the child. If it were the child of an *ariki*, senior chief, the ceremony was usually longer and more elaborate.

The child was taken to a stream by its parents and grandparents and given to the officiating *tohunga*, priest, who stood waist-deep in the stream and sprinkled the child's head with a twig which he dipped in the water, subsequently immersing himself and the baby completely. He faced the rising sun and chanted *karakia*, incantations, and then declared the baby's name. The name was conferred after, instead of during the rite, as is the Christian practice.

The infant was given to the father, who handed it to the mother, and the procession returned to the village where the participants were greeted with shouts and songs and tears. In the case of the child of an *ariki*, valuable gifts were presented.

The ceremony concluded with the lifting of the *tapu*, again achieved by the use of water and the reciting of *karakia*. In some cases the *tohunga*

The *tohunga* stands waist deep in the stream, baptising the infant by sprinkling water with a branch of *karamū*.

also touched the child's head with a captive bird that was then released.

One final act relating to the baptism ceremony involved the burial of the *iho*, umbilical cord, (sometimes known as the *pito*) in a hole, under a post, or in a hollow tree, which thereafter acquired a degree of *tapu*. In a similar rite, the *whenua*, placenta, of the child was also buried. By doing this it was said that the child was bound to the land – the Māori word *whenua* having the dual meaning of placenta and land.

The following extracts from a long *karakia* used at the baptism of a boy, and a further one at the baptism of a girl, show the list of the skills thought necessary of boys and girls respectively.

Boy: Proceed you
To become angry
To become bold
To kill men
To enter forts
To slay sentries
To stand firm in battle
To bear weapons
To bear spears
To bear stone clubs
To bear double-handed clubs
Give these
To strengthen growth.
Proceed you
To produce food, for yourself
To build a large house, for yourself
To build a war canoe
To welcome visitors
To make nets, for yourself
To net fish, for yourself
Give these
For the upgrowth
For this male child.

Girl: Sprinkle with the water of Tū
Proceed you – navel cord
To prepare food, for yourself
To weave garments, for yourself
To weave fine cloaks, for yourself
To welcome visitors
To carry firewood on the back, for yourself
To dig for shellfish, for yourself
Give these
To help growth
For this first-born girl.

In the case of boys, the child was usually dedicated to Tū-matauenga, the god of war, or to Rongo, the god of peace.

Birth names, Rongo, Tū-matauenga, water.

BARK *(haiko, kiri)*. A kind of cloth was formerly made from the bark of the *aute*, and from the inner bark of the *houhere*, lacebark tree. Baskets for containing birds preserved in their own fat or for carrying water were made of bark from the *tōtara* tree. Bark was also used in thatching and the making of torches.

Aute, baskets, thatch, torches.

BASKETS *(kete)*. *Kete* or kits, baskets, were mostly practical objects and little time was spent on ornamentation. The only type on which considerable trouble was expended were the small baskets used for holding valuable objects.

These *kopa* were usually small, closely woven receptacles with a flap cover and were worn slung from the shoulder or tied round the waist. The various types of basket were woven from flax or *tī*, cabbage tree leaves, the latter being the more durable.

Kono or *rourou*, small baskets or dishes, were quickly plaited from *harakeke*, green flax leaves. Sufficient cooked vegetables and relishes of meat were placed in them for one to four persons to eat. *Tapu* persons and *ariki* ate from baskets reserved for their individual use. The plaited container was burnt after use.

For *kete* baskets intended for permanent use, the flax leaves were scraped and beaten to make the strands pliant, and then sun-dried or hung over a fire, so that the leaves would not shrink. These baskets were neatly plaited and turned inside out so that the protruding ends would not appear. Plaited loop handles were fastened to the sides.

In Te Waka a Māui, the South Island, containers for *tītī*, muttonbirds, were made from the large float bladders of the bull kelp. *Pātua* were open baskets resembling the woven willow baskets of the Pākehā in shape. They were made from large sheets of the bark of the *tōtara* (and occasionally of other trees), bent into shape and tied at two projections at the top, these being connected with a wooden carrying handle.

Elaborate kits with woven geometrical patterns are a modern innovation.

Bowls, coffins, food, kelp, meals, plaiting, stars.

BASKETS OF KNOWLEDGE. The *kete ō te wānanga*, the three 'baskets' of knowledge, were said to have been collected by the god Tāne. They contained the sum of sacred or occult knowledge. Students were trained in the *whare wānanga*, house of learning, for the various grades of *tohunga*, and it was this knowledge that was imparted to them.

The *kete aronui*, the first basket to be opened, contained the lore of the *kauwae runga* (upper jaw), dealing with the myths of creation and all knowledge that benefits human beings.

The *kete tuauri* dealt with occult matters of a more practical nature – the practice of ritual, and the memorising of invocations, chants and charms.

The *kete tuateu* was 'black magic' or *mākutu*, a powerful force exercised by evil priests. This knowledge was of matters harmful to people.

Magic, mākutu, schools of learning, stones (sacred), Tāne, gods (wars of), tohunga, whare wānanga.

BATS *(pekapeka)*. *Pekapeka* were the only true native mammals of New Zealand. Although they were small it is said that they were eaten. They were captured when the entrance to their holes in hollow trees was blocked up and the creatures stupefied with smoke. It is possible that the flesh provided a 'relish' in the food basket. In ancient legend, the fantail sent the bat to guide Mataora from Rarohenga, the underworld, to the Ao Mārama, World of Light (men).

BEATER, FERN ROOT *(patu aruhe)*. The *patu aruhe* was used to pound *aruhe*, fern root, on a stone. The fern root was then roasted and the hard outside layer scraped off. It was the remaining woody pith that was eaten.

Fern root.

BELTS *(tātua)*. Men's belts were woven from fine strips of dried flax leaves, and were sometimes ornamented with strips that had been dyed black. *Tātua pūpara* were doubled-over belts with the edges joined loosely, providing pockets 75–100 millimetres deep to hold small articles.

Women wore a different type of belt. It was made of plaited strands of *harakeke*, flax dyed in several colours, and sometimes mixed with fragrant grasses. Some men and women were tattooed round the waist to give the appearance of a belt.

Plaiting, travellers.

BEDS, see MATS.

BERRIES. Several kinds of berries were used as food, chiefly *hīnau, tawa, karaka* and *tutu*.

The edible flesh of the *hīnau* berries was separated from the stones by pounding and sifting before being mixed with water and boiled. The berries could also be made into large cakes. These cakes were oily and early Pākehā travellers found them inedible, but to Māori they were a valuable food supply because they could be stored for long periods of time.

Only the kernels of the *tawa* berry were used. After cooking in an oven they were dried and kept in store for future use. Placing them in water in a wooden bowl or trough and dropping in heated stones could boil the berries. The boiled nuts were then pounded before being eaten.

The berries of the *tutu* provided a luxury article of diet. Ripe berries were placed in a finely woven conical bag lined with *toetoe* plumes that trapped the highly poisonous seeds. The juice dripped into a bowl and could be drunk or set into a jelly.

Karaka, poisons, rats, tawa.

BETROTHAL. A marriage proposal was a very formal matter for families of rank. The young man would approach the young woman's parents. They in turn would ask her if she agreed, and if so the matter was then debated at length by the *whānau,* family group, until a decision was reached.

On other occasions a group of young men might visit a *whānau*, especially where there was a *puhi*, a virgin. They would be entertained with games and feasts, and would then lay claim to the girl of their choice. If a suitor was rejected and felt the rejection keenly, he might organise a raiding party and take her by force. Betrothals were confined to high-ranking families, where political motives were often the first consideration.

In the case of many high-ranking children, betrothals were entered into during infancy. These betrothals were called *taumau*, and were often celebrated at the feast following a *tohi*, baptismal ceremony, when a male elder would propose a betrothal between the baptised child and a female of appropriate rank.

The parents of the child seldom refused the proposal, particularly when a person of influence made it. Refusal would have been an insult to the speaker and to his tribe if he were a visitor, creating a strained relationship that might eventually lead to conflict. On the other hand an alliance of this kind could bind two *iwi*, tribes, or *hapū*, sub-tribes, firmly together.

Such a ceremony might take place a few years after the *tohi* rite and would be between children of equal rank. The girl might remain in her own home, or be taken into the family into which she would ultimately marry. Elaborate ceremony and ritual practices would be observed at the time of the betrothal, and valuable presents exchanged. When the young couple reached marriageable age, the presents were shown on the *marae* and might then be given to the couple.

BIRDS *(manu)*. There are many stories and legends about birds, reflecting the intimate knowledge that Māori had of them. These stories and legends were not only a convenient way of storing detailed knowledge of their habits and songs, but also helped preserve the many myths that explain the origin and the characteristics of the different species. Birds were the children of the *atua*, god, Tāne, and he provided forest trees for their homes and fruits for their sustenance.

The following lists record the Māori and Pākehā names of the principal birds. Many birds are known only by their Māori name.

akiaki:	red-billed gull
amokura:	red-tailed tropic bird
hakoakoa:	seahawk
hihi:	stitchbird
huia:	huia
kahu:	harrier
kākā:	kaka or parrot
kākāpō:	kakapo or ground parrot
kākāriki:	red-fronted parakeet; yellow-fronted parakeet
kakī:	black stilt
kaoriki:	little bittern
karakahia:	grey duck
kārearea:	New Zealand falcon or bush hawk
karoro:	black-backed gull
kāruhiruhi:	pied shag
kawau:	black shag
kawau-pākau:	white-throated shag
kea:	kea or mountain parrot
kererū:	pigeon
kiwi:	kiwi
kiwi-pukupuku:	little grey kiwi
koekoeā:	long-tailed cuckoo
kohutapu:	shore plover
koitareke:	native quail
kōkako:	blue-wattled crow; orange-wattled crow

korari: mottled petrel or rain-bird
koreke (koriki): native quail
korimako: bellbird
kororā: little blue penguin
kōtare: sacred kingfisher
kōtuku: white egret or heron
kōtuku-ngutea: royal spoonbill
kūaka: common diving petrel; bartailed godwit
kūkū: Chatham Island pigeon
kuruwhengi: shoveller
matata: fern-bird
mātirakahu: Chatham Island rail
mātuhi: bush wren
matuku-hūrepo: brown bittern
matuku-moana: white-faced heron or reef heron
miromiro: white-breasted tit
moa: moa
moeriki: Dieffenbach's rail
moho-pererū: banded rail
mohua: yellowhead
ngirungiru: yellow-breasted tit
ōi: sooty shearwater or muttonbird; grey-faced petrel
pakahā: fluttering shearwater
papango: New Zealand scaup or black teal
pararā: broad-billed prion
pārekareka: spotted shag
pārera: grey duck
pāteke: brown duck
pīhoihoi: New Zealand pipit
piopio: North Island thrush; South Island thrush
pīpipi: brown creeper
pīpīwharauroa: shining cuckoo
pitoitoi: robin
pīwakawaka: black fantail; pied fantail
poaka: white-headed stilt
pōpokotea: whitehead
pūkeko: swamp hen
pūtangitangi: paradise duck
pūteketeke: crested grebe
pūweto: spotless crake or swamp rail
riroriro: grey warbler
ruru: New Zealand owl or morepork
tāiko: black petrel
takahē: takahe or notornis
tākapu: gannet
taonui: flesh-footed shearwater
tara: black-fronted tern
tara-iti: fairy tern
tara-nui: Caspian tern
tarāpunga: black-backed gull; red-billed gull
tātāeko: whitehead
tauhōu: silvereye, waxeye or blight bird
tawaki: crested penguin
tētē: grey teal
tīeke: saddleback
tīrairaka: fantail
tītī: sooty shearwater or muttonbird
tītitipounamu: rifleman
titiwainui: fairy prion
tīwaiwaka: fantail
tīwakawaka: fantail
tokoeka: South Island kiwi
tōrea: pied oyster-catcher
tōrea-pango: black oyster-catcher
toroa: wandering albatross; black-browed mollyhawk
toroa-pango: light-mantled sooty albatross
totorore: Antarctic prion
toutouwai: North Island robin; South Island robin
tūī: tūī or parson-bird
tūturiwhatu: New Zealand dotterel
tuturuatu: sand plover
weka: weka, buff woodhen; North Island woodhen; South Island woodhen
weka-pango: black woodhen
weweia: New Zealand dabchick
whēkau: laughing owl
whio: blue duck or whistling duck

Albinos, eels, eggs, hokioi, huia, mauri, Whiro.

BIRDS, HUNTING. Māori were skilled hunters of birds because in a land without large land animals, birds were an important supply of meat. Birds were caught by spear, snare, hand, the use of decoys, and in some cases by nets. Climbing high trees was a dangerous occupation, and gave rise to the proverb: *He toa piki rakau he kai na te pakiaka* — A tree-climbing expert is food for roots. The first bird caught at the start of a season was given as an offering to Tāne as propitiation for the killing of his children.

Snares were skilfully constructed and used in a number of different ways. Individual snares, sometimes several at a time, were set close together, fastened to a cord, or placed on perching rods, and set on a treetop or at the ends of branches where the birds congregated to eat berries. They were examined frequently, mostly by men, but trees that were easy to climb were sometimes tended by women. Snares for pigeons and some other birds were usually made of the leaves of the *tī*, cabbage tree, because they were stronger and had a longer life than *harakeke*, flax leaves. Before use they were placed in the smoke of a fire to give them more durability.

The nooses of the snares were hung down from either side of the branches, or perching rods, and were connected to a long cord that extended to the hunter's platform. When the bird settled in the noose the hunter pulled the cord and the bird's legs were caught against the perch. It was then seized and killed by crushing its head with the teeth. The dead bird was dropped to the ground. Great care was taken to see that feathers were not scattered about lest newcomers be frightened away. It was thought that the birds might then desert that part of the forest permanently.

It was also done to ensure that Tāne was not offended by the careless taking of his charges. If several birds were caught simultaneously, the hunter kept all the cords taut and killed the birds one after the other. An individual perch and snare was termed a *mutu* (the word is also used as a verb), and was attached to a branch. Platforms, which were used both for snaring and spearing, were sometimes built at heights of 20–25 metres up among the branches.

Māori were familiar with the habits of birds and put this knowledge to good use. The *kahikatea*, white pine, and miro trees were selected principally for setting snares, but they were also placed in *rimu*, *mātai*, *maire*, *kōtukutuku*, (fuchsia), and other trees. Even berry-less trees were used when they were close to fruiting trees. The *miro* was selected because pigeons grew fat on the berries, but *kōwhai* trees, on which they also fed, were avoided, because the leaves made them thin and the flesh distasteful.

The *miro* berries made the birds thirsty, and snares were set by the edge of a nearby stream. Access to the stream would be blocked off and snares placed in the few open places, close together, so that the birds were forced to thrust their necks through nooses in order to drink. In this way they could be caught without the hunter having to attend the snares all the time. The nooses were attached to a rod that spaced them evenly, and to encourage the birds to perch in the right position.

If there was no water in the vicinity, shallow wooden troughs, a few centimetres wide and a metre or so in length, were put in the branches of the tree or erected on posts, and filled with water. These troughs were termed *waka*. The troughs would be put into the trees and left for a time so that the birds became accustomed to them. Eventually they would then be set with snares along the trough edges.

Slip nooses on the end of poles were used for catching *ruru*, owls, *kākāriki*, parakeets, *weka*, woodhens, and sometimes *kākā*, brown parrots. *Pārera*, ducks, were caught on lakes and streams by snares set on a cord and suspended above the water, hanging down in such a way that the birds entered them as they swam on the surface.

The making of bird spears was a tedious process, for they were often as long as 10 metres but needed to be light and slender. They were used mainly for killing pigeons. The spears were tipped with barbed points made of hardwood, bird bone or whalebone or, sometimes, human bone. The hunter constructed a platform high in the branches of a tree, and began his patient vigil. The spear rested against a branch, and when the

Left: A *kākā* on a carved perch, which is lashed to the branch of a tree. *Right*: A bird-hunter on a platform built in the tree top, about to kill a pigeon with his long spear.

bird was within reach it was dispatched with a quick thrust.

Much ingenuity was shown in catching the *kākā*. Ordinary snares could not be used, because the birds would tear them to shreds with their strong beaks. Instead, the *kākā* were lured to the hunter in several ways. A captured *kākā* was kept on a perch in the village until the hunter was ready to take it to the place where the birds were to be caught. Over time such a bird would have become tame and be known as a *mōkai*, which means pet as well as prisoner. If the *mōkai* was taken on to the tree platform, the fowler teased it so that its cries attracted others, or it was given bones that it crushed, thus attracting the attention of other *kākā*. When the inquisitive birds came close they were struck with a stick, or captured with a noose set on the end of a rod. A more usual plan was for the bird to be tethered on the ground to a cord fastened to a bone ring on its leg. The hunter was concealed in a rough shelter, and was able to catch or kill the birds as they flew down to join the captive. A simpler method that did not require the use of a decoy was to place a perch, or *pae*, in a slanting position, close to a stream. When the birds had eaten, they descended the stick, and the concealed hunter caught them by hand, killing them with a spear, or by striking them with a heavy stick.

Decoy calls to attract *tūī* were made by blowing on the edge of a leaf held in the hands. In frosty weather *tūī* and *kererū*, pigeons, were easily taken by hand. One man carried a torch to provide light in order to see the birds, while others lifted them from the branches where they were perched, stiff with cold and unable to make a quick escape. *Tūī* were also taken by tying forked branches of the

Bird hunters. The hunter sheltering under his cloak is tying up a *kiwi*.

pōporo shrub together, as their legs were caught in this rudimentary type of snare.

Hihi, stitchbirds, and *tīeke*, saddlebacks, were caught at night. A net was suspended above the ground and the light of torches lured the birds to it. As they flew towards them they were blinded by the light and blundered into the nets. *Tītī*, muttonbirds, were taken in the same way, as well as being caught by hand in burrows. Young *tītī* chicks were pulled from their burrows by inserting a long, forked fern stick down the burrow and into the wool down of the chick's fledgling feathers.

Ground birds were caught in traps known as *puaka*. A clearing was made in the undergrowth, with entrances at several points, and a loop snare was set at each entrance. Suitable bait was placed on the cleared ground and small birds such as robins were caught as they entered.

Robins were also caught in nets made of bent *pirita*, supplejack, vine and a mesh of flax-leaf strips, which were propped up with sticks. A club was struck against a piece of timber, and as the birds were attracted by the sound and came under the net, the supporting stick was jerked away by the cord attached to it, and the net fell over the robin.

Dogs were used to hunt larger ground birds such as the *kiwi* and *kākāpō*. The *weka*, another flightless bird, was attracted by berries scattered over the ground, and caught by means of a spring trap or snared with a loop suspended from a long stick.

Ducks were also hunted with dogs, and were driven in large quantities into nets suspended immediately above the water of a lake. This more often happened at the time of the annual moult when the ducks were unable to fly.

Another method employed by skilled hunters required them to tie bundles of rushes to their heads and paddle quietly in the water with their bodies concealed beneath it. When an unsuspecting duck drew near, the hunter pulled it under the water by its legs, killed it, and tucked it into his belt. There was no noise or commotion, and the hunter could gather quite a number of birds in this way without being detected.

The balance of nature was not normally upset by any of these hunting methods, but if by any chance the birds became scarce, a protective *rāhui*, or ban, would be proclaimed until the bird population increased again. The *rāhui* was not only used in the case of birds but also when other food resources, such as shellfish, became depleted.

Ladders, muttonbirds, snares, spears, whare, women.

A *tūī* alights on a branch on which a snare has been placed.

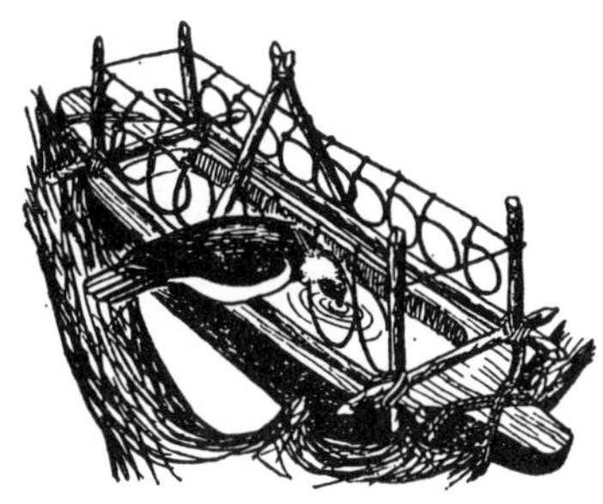

In this picture the *kererū* has put its head through a noose in order to drink. When it withdraws it, the bird will be caught.

BIRDS, PRESERVING *(huahua)*. After a successful hunting season, many birds were preserved for future use. They were plucked, the bones removed, packed in baskets, and placed under water until they were ready for cooking. A number of birds were roasted at the same time. Two stout stakes with a number of notches in them were placed firmly in the ground. The birds were spitted on slender rods that were held horizontally by notches in the stakes. Thus the framework would hold many birds at the same time. A big fire was lit in front of the rack, and as the fat dripped from the roasting fowls, it fell from layer to layer and was finally caught in a long, slightly tilted, wooden trough, from which it ran into a wooden bowl. The fat was kept heated by hot stones. When cooked, the birds were packed tightly into *hue*, calabashes, or vessels made from wood or bark, and the hot fat poured over them until they were covered, and thus preserved. In the far south *tītī*, muttonbirds, were treated in the same manner, but were packed in *pōhā*, containers, made from the float bladder of the giant bull kelp.

Calabashes, kelp.

BIRTH. Childbirth came easily to Māori women. Instances have been recorded of women who gave birth to their babies while travelling, and who were able to continue the journey with the child in the course of an hour or so. In important families elaborate preparations were made for the coming event, and a special *whare kōhanga*, nest-house, was constructed for the occasion. It was a temporary structure, and was burnt when finished with. Because the mother was 'unclean' during the birth period, and the rules of *tapu* had to be observed, segregation was necessary. The *whare kōhanga* might simply be a shelter or windbreak, or a more elaborate house without windows, but amply ventilated and heated. The expectant mother went there with two attendants, and the only visitors allowed were the husband, close relatives, and the *tohunga*, who played an important part in all the ceremonies connected with birth and baptism. After the baby was born the *rangatira* (chiefly) mother would remain in the *whare kōhanga* for about a week until the *tohi* rite was performed, when she would be greeted by her people, and presents would be brought to the infant.

Elaborate ceremonies were observed among the aristocratic families, the rites being supposed to have originated with the first act of conception and birth when Tāne formed the first woman, Hine-ahu-one and mated with her. There were other rites that were designed to cause conception; and there were trees and other objects with the same reputed power.

When labour commenced, the woman knelt on the ground with her knees well apart. An assistant squatted behind her, and pressed down against the mother's abdomen. In other cases two women would face each other, squatting and taking hold under the armpits. The assistant would then use her knees and inner thighs to help express the baby. If the woman were alone, she would sometimes lash a horizontal rod to two saplings and press against it to aid delivery. Again, two stout posts were sometimes planted in the *whare kōhanga*, one to give aid in the birth of a boy and the other of a girl. The *iho* or umbilical cord was cut with a flake of obsidian and buried or concealed, frequently on the tribal boundary.

Babies, baptism, magic.

BOILING, see COOKING.

BONES *(wheua, koiwi, koroiwi)*. Desecration of the

bones of enemies by using them as weapons, flutes, and implements, was an act of *utu*, vengeance, which most often led to war as the desecrators could not help but boast of what they had done. Great efforts were made to keep the bones of *rangatira* and *ariki* safe. They were often kept in small huts on the top of poles, where they would be safe from dogs and rats. In other cases they might be placed in a hiding place such as a cave. The mana of a chief remained in his bones, which at certain seasons were taken to the cultivations as a fertilising agent, and at other times to the *tūāhu* to help in the performance of religious ceremonies.

The bones of whales were used in the making of fighting weapons such as *hoeroa*, a curved bone staff, and *kotiate* and *wahaika*, short hand-clubs. Whale teeth, particularly those of the sperm whale, were made into pendants.

Burial, clubs, flutes, necklaces, Rātā, tattooing, teeth, whales.

BOUNDARIES. Violation of tribal and other boundaries often caused quarrels and violence, leading to war. Not only were tribal boundaries recognised and carefully marked, but the rights of *hapū*, sub-tribes, and *whānau*, families, were also jealously observed.

Tribal boundaries were defined by natural features, such as prominent trees, hills, valleys, streams, and lakes, most of which were named. The locations and names were taught to young people and were an important part of their knowledge, for any ignorance and transgression might have serious consequences. There was little difficulty in recognising the more fruitful areas where berries, fish, birds, eels and rats were plentiful, but more remote and wilder areas that were seldom visited might cause differences of opinion.

Where natural features could not define the boundaries, large stones were placed in position, or posts were set up and consecrated with religious ceremonies.

The lands that were possessed by the *hapū* were well defined, and similarly those of the *whānau*. Although it is usually said that there were no personal possessions in the communal life of the Māori, this was not strictly the case. In the areas of cultivation, the plots were planted in strips separated by narrow paths that were separated by stones. Each strip was reserved for and cultivated by a *whānau*. Spells were cast on the stones so that misfortune visited anyone who had the temerity to remove them, or to change their positions.

Cultivations, tribes.

BOWLS *(kumete)*. In Aotearoa the art of pottery was not known to Māori but there were a few bowl-like vessels. These were normally made of wood, or from a *hue*, gourd, cut in half and perhaps ornamented with a design in black. Although small, bowl-shaped containers were made from soft pumice, few stone bowls were in use because the process of manufacture was so laborious. Māori were content with mostly using baskets and wooden bowls. The latter were usually circular or oval in shape, occasionally rectangular, with lugs for carrying at the sides.

Baskets, cooking, gourds.

BOXES *(waka huia)*. A great deal of care was devoted to the making of wooden boxes, which were elaborately carved, and usually fitted with a lid. They were used to contain articles of adornment, including the prized tail feathers of the *huia* bird, which gave rise to the name *waka huia*. The boxes could be stored by being suspended from house rafters by means of cords attached to the projections on the sides. Sometimes the *waka* were plain on top, and in all such cases the more intricate carving appeared on the under-surface, for it was the base that was seen from below.

Feathers.

BOYS. From an early age boys were usually dedicated to Tū, the god of war, or to Rongo, the god of agriculture. They were taught games to fit them for future life. There were many forms of athletic training and even the milder games such as tī rākau were designed to promote mental and physical agility. Before being entrusted with weapons, they practised with reeds and flax stalks. But wounds were sometimes inflicted even with these light weapons. The throwing of darts and spears was practised assiduously, and when the boys were divided into opposing groups, the darts were parried with sticks, or caught in the hand. Wrestling was a favourite sport for embryo *toa*, warriors, to whom experienced fighters gave instructions.

Baptism, children, darts, games, spears, stick games, tama, warriors.

BRACELETS.

Ornaments.

Boys at play with staves.

BREAST ORNAMENTS.

Necklaces.

BREATH. Breath-holding was a favourite game among children. Long jingles were repeated quickly without taking breath. One such jingle recorded amongst the Tūhoe people runs as follows:

Ka tahi tī, ka rua tī, ka haramai, te pati tore, ka rauna, ka rauna, ka noho, te kiwikiwi, he pō, he wai, takitaki, nō pī, nō pä, ka huia mai, kai, ana, te whetü, kai ana, te marama, ko te tio, e rere, rā runga, rā te pekapeka, kōtore, wīwī, wāwā, heke, heke, te manu, ki ō, tau tihe.

BULLROARERS (*pūrerehua*). The bullroarer, which is a toy for the children of other cultures, was forbidden to Māori tamariki, children, because it was used for ritual purposes by tohunga. The sounding piece of the bullroarer was a thin, flat piece of wood, usually of matai timber, about 45 centimetres in length. It was attached to a handle by a metre-length cord, and swung vigorously to produce the characteristic roaring sound.

BULLRUSHES, see REEDS.

BURDENS (*wahanga, pīkaunga*). The word pīkaunga in its shortened form pīkau was a word appropriated by rural Pākehā at one time but which has since dropped out of usage. The pīkaunga was a back load, and was carried with two plaited shoulder straps. There were several ways of carrying loads; on the shoulder, slung over one shoulder and under the other, and in the arms. Burdens were never carried on the head, for it was the most *tapu* part of the body. *Rangatira*, chiefs, would likewise sometimes attribute tapu status to their backs which meant they could not carry loads, that work then being assigned to slaves or commoners.

Baskets, belts.

BURIAL. After death the body of a rangatira, chief, was placed in a sitting position and tied with cords before it became rigid. It was placed in this manner in the porch of the house, or of the principal building in the village. Sometimes the body might be laid out in a reclining position with the head raised. In either case the body was clad in a valu able cloak, the face was painted with kököwai, red ochre and oil, the hair oiled and adorned with feathers and the ears ornamented with the white down of the albatross. Weapons and heirlooms belonging to the dead chief were

The bones of a chief being taken for burial by canoe.

placed beside the body, and relatives brought other prized heirlooms and placed them there. The number of slaves who were killed after his death might gauge the importance of a chief, and it was not unusual for a widow to commit suicide. During the period that the body was lying in state, the *tangi*, funeral, was held, and relatives and friends came from a distance to join the mourners.

Some days elapsed before the body was buried. It was carried in a litter, and placed in a cave, a hollow tree, a crevice in the rocks, in the branches of a tree, or on a platform. Lesser men and women were buried in swamps and sand dunes. In the case of important chiefs, heirlooms such as ornaments and weapons, which might be recovered in later years, were placed beside the body in honour of the dead. Cremation was rarely used and then only where there was no convenient burial place or it where was necessary to destroy the bodies of dead comrades killed on a far battlefield lest enemies desecrate the bones. Burial in a sitting position was the fate of the lesser persons in Māori society.

Those who touched the body, or bore it to its last resting-place, were extremely *tapu*, and elaborate ceremonial rites were required to bring them back to their normal condition.

The corpse of a dead chief might be placed in a *waka tupāpaku*, cenotaph, made from half of an upended canoe hull, and erected in a place where it was not so likely to be raided by enemies.

Kawhena, coffins, which were also monuments to the dead, were erected in villages. When the body had decayed, the bones were exhumed or recovered, and frequently painted with *kōkōwai* in a ceremony known as the *hahunga*. This was a much more *tapu* procedure than the actual burial. It was a time of reunion, and recollection of the deeds, sayings, and character of former friends, for some years had usually elapsed before the bones were recovered. *Tapu*-removing ceremonies were again observed, and there was much mourning, feasting and the presentation to guests of generous gifts of food. The bones were bundled up and wrapped in cloaks, and concealed in caves and hollow trees, and other convenient hiding places, after which the *whakanoa* rite was performed over the workers. Sometimes the teeth were removed from the skull and used as necklaces or pendants.

Coffins, death, tangi, tombs, whakanoa.

BUTTERFLIES *(pūrēhua)*. Through their random flutterings they were sometimes regarded as being the *wairua*, souls of the dead.

Souls.

C

CABBAGE TREES *(tī* or *tī-kouka)*. The *tī-kouka* or cabbage tree grows freely in all parts of Aotearoa. It was said to have been planted in some places because it was a regular source of food known as *kāuru*.

In preparing *kāuru*, both the pith of the young trunks and the carrot-shaped taproots were used. Gathering took place in October just before the trees flowered. The outer portion of the trunk was chipped off and the roots and stems were steamed in large ovens to crystallise their sugar content. The cooked *kāuru* was then pulled apart, dipped in water and chewed.

Young *tī* leaves from the heart of the plant were eaten as a vegetable.

The mature leaves were more durable than flax, and were used for many purposes such as making ropes and sandals, snares, baskets, etc.

Sledges, snares, torches.

CALABASHES *(hue, ipu)*. The calabash was made from the dried, empty shell of the *hue* or gourd, one of the few useful plants to survive the journey to Aotearoa. In the absence of pottery the calabash served as a handy household vessel for carrying water. Sometimes the *hue* would have the top sliced off to make bowls.

The *hue* was also used to store birds, preserved in their own fat. Large gourds were fitted with a wooden mouthpiece into which melted fat was poured after the birds had been placed inside.

For storage purposes, the *hue* were often circled with two bands, joined by strips of plaited flax leaves, which kept them evenly spaced, and helped protect the vessel. Three or four wooden legs were attached to the bands so that the *hue* could be stored standing upright.

These containers, often carved and ornamented with feathers, served as the centrepieces at *hākari*, ceremonial feasts, or made impressive presents to visitors.

Ipu, preservation of food, gourds, water.

CANNIBALISM. Māori practised cannibalism in a tradition found throughout the Pacific. Eating one's enemies was regarded as an especially satisfying way of celebrating victory in battle, even more so when an element of *utu*, revenge, was involved. Slaves were sometimes killed for food and eaten at feasts to mark important occasions.

The practice of *kai pirau*, the exhuming of partially decomposed bodies that were then cooked and eaten, was also known. In such cases an overwhelming desire to express *utu* was the usual motivation. Women and children were seldom permitted to join in feasts of human flesh.

CANOE RACING *(waka hoehoe)*. From an early age children played in small canoes, and trained themselves to take part in the *waka hoehoe*, which, like all water-borne activities, was always a popular sport. Canoe hurdling made the racing even more exciting. Stout stakes were driven into the bed of a river with their ends projecting above the water, and a crosspiece lashed to them. The paddlers urged the canoe up to the hurdle, sliding the curved prow over the horizontal bar. Great speed was necessary to get the shallow dugout canoe right over the bar and into the water on the far side.

CANOES *(waka)*. While there is still debate about whether Māori came to this country through a series of deliberate journeys or whether they represent the survivors of accidental voyages, driven here by wind and storm, there is no dispute that *waka* were involved. Māori are believed to have settled Aotearoa travelling in *waka* from the islands of eastern Polynesia.

They probably came in ocean-going vessels, similar to the double-hulled sailing *prau* that are still found in northern parts of the Pacific (Micronesia), or in single canoes fitted with stabilising outriggers.

The double-hulled *prau* were connected by a platform on which a small shelter or cabin was built. The canoes were equipped with one or two masts and the typical Polynesian lateen or triangular sail. The hulls were shallow in draught, reflecting the paucity of suitable building timber on the islands, but were able to be built up by the addition of several topstrakes to improve their seaworthiness.

Because ocean voyaging was always hazardous, it was normal practice to observe the proper rituals and protocols to ensure a safe journey. An on-board *tohunga* ensured that all such measures were properly observed and that the gods were appropriately propitiated.

It is said that some canoes were *tapu* and were prevented from carrying cooked food for this reason. (Cooked food was an item that removed *tapu.*) The crew was restricted to eating sun-dried fish, *kūmara*, *taro* and breadfruit. Drinking water was carried in *hue*, gourds.

Although the double-hulled *waka* was used in Aotearoa, mainly in Te Waka a Māui, the South Island, the plentiful supply of large trees meant that a new development in canoe building took place. Tall *tōtara* and *kauri* trees enabled Māori to build longer, deeper canoes requiring only a single topstrake. The increased width of these vessels also meant that they did not need an outrigger for stability. As ocean-going voyaging declined, single-hulled canoes without outriggers became the standard coastal vessel.

Small, unornamented canoes were used on rivers and lakes. These were normally wide and shallow in draught and were often poled rather than paddled.

Māori canoe building reached its peak with the imposing *waka taua*, war canoe. These vessels – which also doubled as deep-sea fishing craft – were works of art and the result of years of labour.

Ritual and ceremony to ensure success surrounded their construction. The tree to be used for the building of a *waka* was carefully selected. It had to have a clean, straight bole and be growing in a position where it could be easily felled

A race in small dugout canoes.

Hurdling in a small *waka*.

and dragged to a suitable site for the shaping of the hull.

A *tohunga tārai waka* was put in charge of the work. He would undertake a placatory ceremony to Tāne, the forest god, because building the waka meant the death of one of his children. The ceremony was also intended to protect from misfortune all those engaged in the *waka* building.

Using stone adzes to slowly peck away at the trunk and small fires to burn out the scarf, the tree was felled and roughly shaped. The real work of the *tohunga* began at this stage, as he marked the parts which required gouging and smoothing to make the sides symmetrical, directing the workers where to employ their adzes. Most of the people were then assembled to drag the log from the forest to a more suitable work site – usually close to water and the village. This was achieved through the use of log rollers and ropes.

It was normal to put the incomplete log in the water to check which way 'up' it floated – that would determine where the 'top' of the canoe would be – before the proper work began. A shelter was usually built over the canoe as it began to take its final shape, and although men were allowed to watch, women were not tolerated. At this stage particularly, all workers were *tapu*.

Chipping, scraping and burning helped hollow out the hull and smooth off splinters and jagged edges. Thwarts, lashed from one top edge to the other, braced and helped stabilise the canoe. The decking was made from long rods with regular spaces to allow access to the hull for bailing. Any holes in the hull were caulked with mud and flax fibre before the whole was painted with a coat of *kōkōwai*, red clay ochre mixed with shark oil. The flax cordage, which lashed the topstrake of the *waka* to the hull, was decorated with small tufts of white *toroa*, albatross feathers.

In other cases the *waka* might be made in three parts. The large, middle section was hollowed from a single tree trunk, and separate bow and stern pieces were attached to it with a carefully fitted mortise and tenon joint.

These end pieces were swept upwards, improving the appearance and performance of the canoe. The *tauihu* with its forward-thrusting head, and the *taurapa* that towered above the canoe stern in an intricate pattern, were amongst the finest examples of *whakairo*, wood carving.

When construction was completed, the *waka* then had the *tapu,* religious restrictions covering its construction, removed, at a special ceremony – it was given a name, usually that of a warrior ancestor of the tribe, and launched. The launch was sometimes accompanied by the killing of a

A Tahitian voyaging canoe with a double hull, and furled sails. The ancestors of the Māori probably voyaged to New Zealand in canoes of this type. The canoes were often of different lengths.

A fishing canoe. Although it has carved bow and stern pieces, it is much less ornate than a *waka taua*.

slave who would then form part of the celebratory feast.

These vessels could be very large – over 25 metres – and could carry crews numbering over one hundred. Two such canoes were sometimes lashed together and a triangular lanteen-rigged sail used in favourable conditions but whether lashed together in tandem or as single units, *waka* were powered by their paddlers – working together to rhythmic chanting and sending their vessels across the water at a surprising speed. The weight and size of the *waka* meant that the timing of the paddling was all-important if inertia was to be overcome and speed maintained.

The *pōtēteke*, watch-captain or fugleman, had the responsibility for maintaining the stroke. He did this with the aid of a *hoe*, paddle, or *taiaha*, striking spear. He used the implement to beat the time on the gunwales and encouraged his crew with a *haka*, war dance, designed to focus their effort and drive the *waka* forward. The noise, synchronised action and demonstration of paddling power was also designed to intimidate

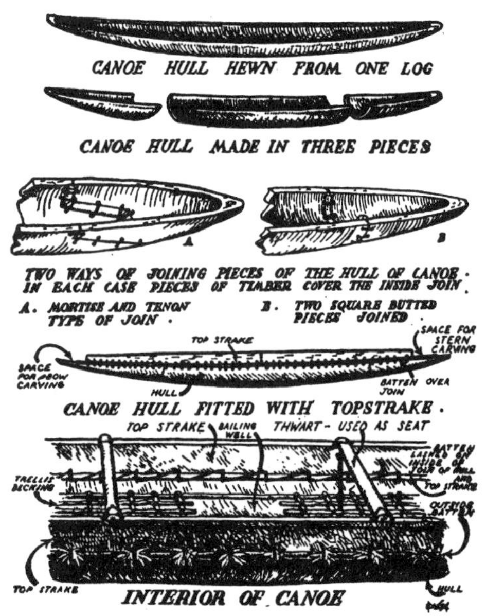

Details of the construction of a canoe.

Smoothing the bow and stern portions of the hull of a large canoe before they are lashed to the main body. The condition of the tree trunk in the background shows the difficulty of felling a large tree with primitive tools.

any foes who might be watching. In traditional Māori society the *waka taua* filled the role of a war machine.

Other chants were used when canoes had to be hauled overland, something which happened frequently because of the great distances that could be saved. The most famous portage was at Onehunga on the Tāmaki (Auckland) isthmus where a narrow strip of land separates the Waitematā and Manukau Harbours or the east and west coasts of Te Ika a Māui, the North Island. Early Pākehā travellers reported that the Onehunga portage was worn so smooth by frequent usage that it resembled a road. Other frequently used portages were found at Mahia and at Kenepuru and other places in the Marlborough Sounds.

The main migratory canoes and their captains were:

Aotea (Turi)
Te Arawa (Tama-te-kapua)
Horouta (Pawa)
Kurahaupo (Ruatea)
Mahuhu (Rongomai)
Mamari (Nukutawhiti)
Mataatua (Toroa)
Nukutere (Porourangi)
Poutini (Tama)
Pukateawainui (Ruaeo)
Tainui (Hoturoa)
Takitimu (Tamatea)
Tokomaru (Whata)

Anchors, bailers, canoe races, coffins, fishing, genealogies, paddles, Rātā, sails, songs, storms, tribes, water games.

CAPES.

Cloaks.

CARVING, WOOD *(whakairo rākau).* The term *whakairo* was used for all decorative work, including the carving of wood, bone, stone, and gourds, and for tattooing, painting, and weaving. Woodcarving was known as *whakairo rākau.* While there are many stories to explain the origins of woodcarving, the best known involves a man known as Rua-te-pupuke. He is sometimes depicted as a traveller in search of a lost son or as a human child of the god Tangaroa. Rua visits the house of Tangaroa under the sea and finds that the *poupou*, human figures, on this house are carved, unlike the houses where he comes from where the figures are painted. Furthermore the figures inside the house can speak. Rua sets the house on fire and steals some of the outside *pou.* In this way the knowledge of carving comes to the world of men although the ability of the *pou* to speak is lost. These miraculous origins show how important this distinctive art form was to Māori.

The intention of the *pou* was to portray ancestral figures in a stylised form that enhanced their power and authority and thereby added to the prestige of their descendants. Other figures, such as fish, birds and lizards, were portrayed in a more naturalised form.

Whare were decorated with carved *amo,* bargeboards, and *poupou,* the large supporting wall slabs inside the house. Human figures appeared on these slabs while at the outside apex of the *amo*, bargeboards, was the *tekoteko*, a figure or head. The bases of the supporting ridge posts were *poupou* carved in the round. The entire post was often carved in this manner. The porch and doors of *pātaka*, food stores, were also elaborately carved in great detail. The intention was to demonstrate prosperity and fertility.

Whakairo rākau, the whole art and design of Māori carving, was curvilinear in form. Spirals were known throughout Polynesia, but Māori art was predominantly curvilinear in contrast with the art of tropical Polynesia, which was mostly rectilinear. It was a development that occurred far from other influences. The skill employed in cutting delicate tracery in wood with primitive stone and greenstone implements is almost beyond belief. The stern and bow pieces of canoes, in particular, demonstrate the degree of skill, as also does the delicate carving that frequently appears on weapons and implements.

One of the outstanding forms of *whakairo rākau* was the spiral that appeared in both double and single form. The best examples are found on the *tauihu*, decorative bow pieces, of *waka.* Small spirals were used on the images of human figures. The other distinctive feature of Māori carving is the series of parallel ridges that enclose what have been termed beaded lines. A characteristic example is the *rauponga*, fern tree leaf, which depicts the midrib of the leaf and the branching pinnae, with the intervening spaces filled with beaded lines.

Carvings were usually painted with *kōkōwai,* clay earth with a high iron oxide content to which was added shark oil. The red 'paint' this produced was smeared on liberally, red being the sacred colour of all Polynesia.

The materials that were available in Aotearoa influenced the art of carving. Timbers such as *kauri* were soft yet durable, easily split and free from knots, while greenstone and fine-grained rock made excellent adzes, gouges, and chisels.

The *tohunga whakairo* was the expert in carving, which was such a *tapu* operation that even the use of discarded chips for cooking fires was prohibited.

Adzes, art, bailers, canoes, chisels, houses, lizards, manaia, marakihau, paddles, pāua, spirals, storehouses, tekoteko, tongues.

CATERPILLARS. One of the few insect pests was the *anuhe*, caterpillar, which ate young *kūmara* plants, and also fed on the *pōhue,* convolvulus. A favourite child's game was to hold the *anuhe* by its tail, upright in the fingers and to ask it questions such as '*Kei hea tō whaea?*' (Where is your mother?); in its wriggling the *anuhe* would answer by pointing its head.

Cultivations, kūmara.

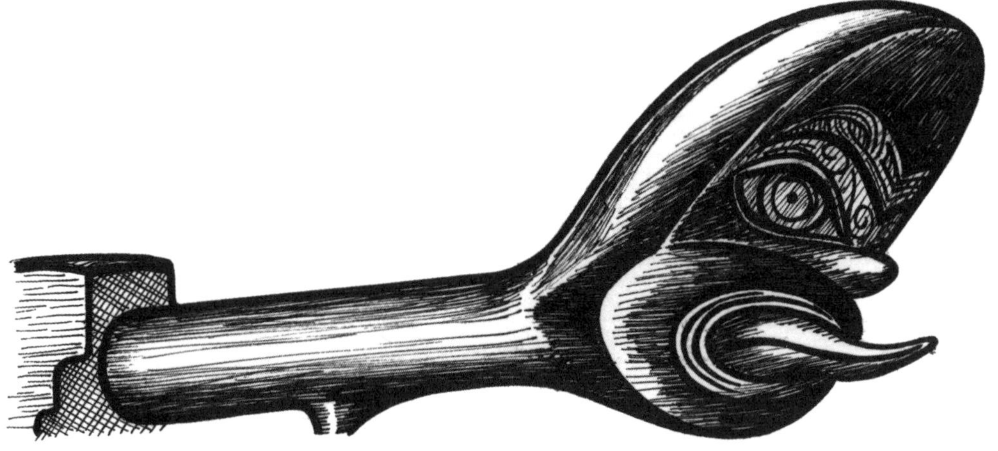

FIG. 1: Figurehead of the *pākurakura* (armless type), for a fishing vessel.

a. b. c.

FIG. 2: (a) *Ngututa*. (b) *Koruru*. (c) *Ruru*.

a. b. c.

FIG. 3: (a) *Tekoteko*. (b) *Manaia*. (c) *Marakihau*.

FIG. 4: This is a typical *raparapa* design, in which a head and a hand have been used for decoration. The upper lip has been extended to form the fifth finger of the stylised hand.

Figures 1 to 4 are reproduced from *The Art of Maori Carving*, by S.M. Mead, with the author's permission.

CAT'S CRADLE *(whai)*. A popular game played by adults as well as children, and a favourite with women. Māori were very dextrous in manipulating the string, and made intricate figures that often required the use of toes and teeth as well as fingers. Some designs required the co-operation of two or more persons.

The game is also called *māui*, because it was invented by the demi-god of the same name. People unfamiliar with the game find it difficult to visualise the legendary events, stars and constellations that were made with the string. A favourite contest was for two players to sit or stand back to back making the same figure. It was a race to see who could finish it first.

A competition to see who can first complete the figure.

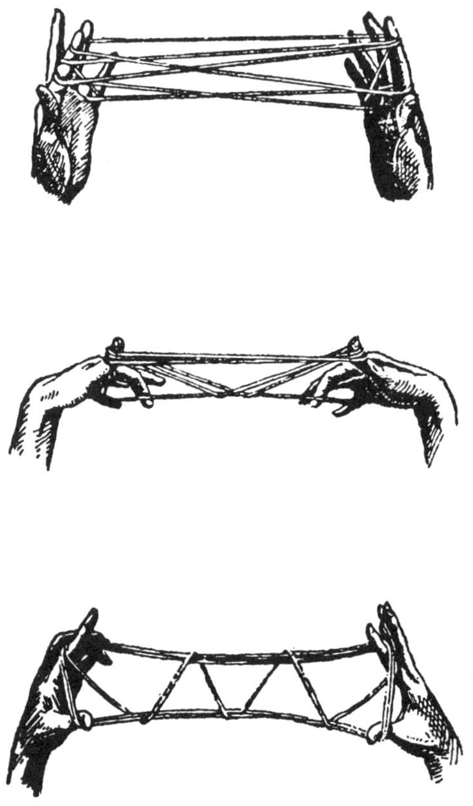

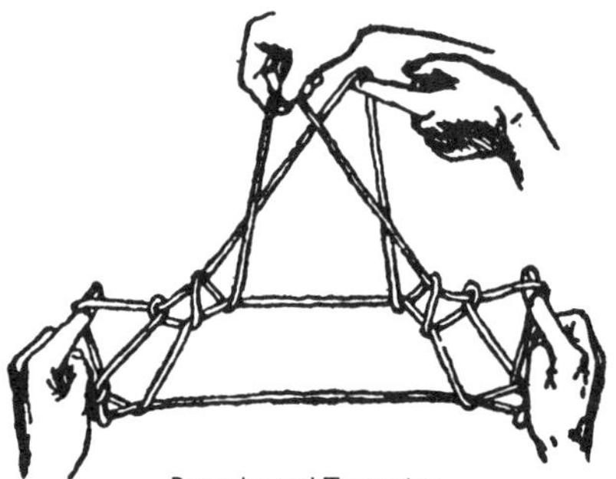

Ruapehu and Tongariro.

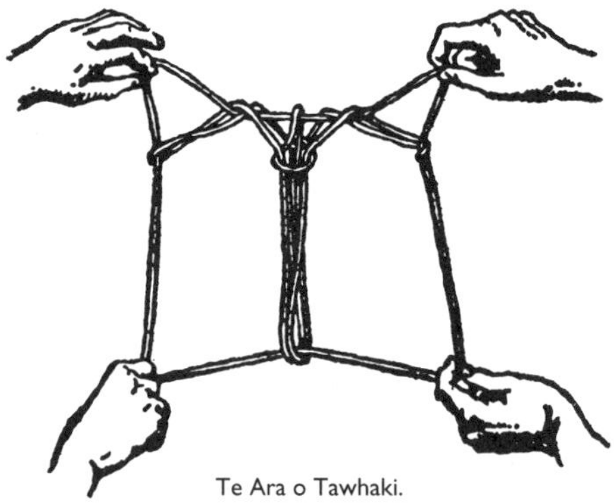

Te Ara o Tawhaki.

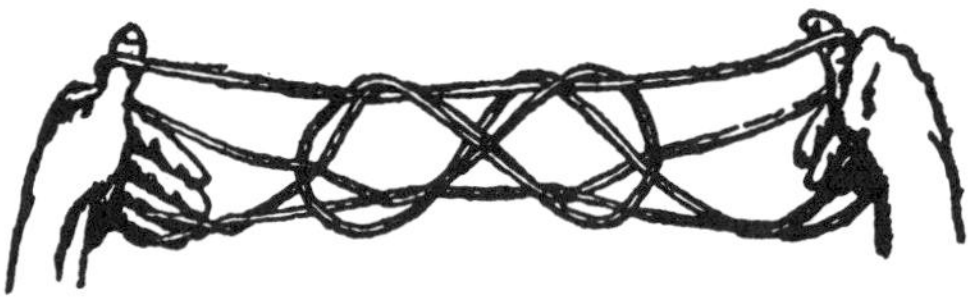

Three movements in the figure called Mouti.

Kōura - the Crayfish.

Various designs used in the game Cat's Cradle, by two or four players.

CAVES *(ana)*. It is possible that caves were used occasionally as dwellings but there are few recorded traditions to support their permanent use as shelters. Rock overhangs and caves were certainly used as temporary shelters but the principal uses to which they were put were for burial or storage purposes. In the latter case, *rua* or *ana*, caves, were excavated in earth and soft rock, and served the same purpose as store pits.

The roof and walls of rock overhangs were also used as an artistic surface. Drawings on overhangs, particularly in the inland parts of Te Waka a Māui and rock carvings in the central Te Ika a Māui and on Rēkohu, or Wharekauri, the Chatham Islands, have been found.

Burial, pits, painting.

CEREMONIES. All facets of traditional Māori life were subject to accompanying rites and ceremonies. The *tohunga* was the presiding expert at the crises of birth and death, of war and peace and at planting and harvesting times. He (female *tohunga* were very rare) used *mākutu* or black magic, healed the sick, blessed the household endeavours and the efforts of the hunters, sought to reveal the future, made people and objects *tapu* and removed *tapu* as appropriate. The tohunga made offerings to the gods. Through him the gods made themselves known to men.

The training of a *tohunga* was arduous because *karakia,* ritual incantations, had to be repeated without mistake or pause otherwise the efficacy of the *karakia* was lost. Improperly conducted ceremonies could bring suffering and ill fortune to those who participated.

Baptism, birth, magic, cultivations, death, divination, birds (hunting), mākutu, offerings, peace, planting, sickness, tapu, thunder, warfare, war parties, water, weaving.

CHALLENGES *(wero)*. The challenge was an important part of the preparations for war, when *hapū*, sub-tribes or clans, gathered together to face a common enemy, or to begin a raid. As the *hapū* gathered together and approached the *pā* from where the call to advance forward had come, the hosts faced the newcomers. One *toa*, soldier, ran forward carrying a spear, which he cast at the advancing *taua*, war party, and returned. Another followed him, and then a third who was noted for his fleetness of foot. The final challenger danced a *haka,* war dance of defiance, cast a spear and then ran back to his own people. Up to this time the advancing *taua* had seemingly taken no notice of the challengers, but at the last challenge a young warrior darted forward from their ranks and tried to overtake the fleeing challenger and trip him up. If he succeeded it was regarded as a propitious omen for the coming fray but in most cases the *wero* was designed to show off the battle-readiness of either side.

In other instances the purpose of the *wero* was to ascertain whether visitors from another *iwi* had friendly intentions. In these cases the challenger would lay down a small token such as a small bunch of leaves. Accepting the token meant the visit was a peaceful one, while a pursuit of the challenger meant the visitors had come to fight.

The *wero* became a ritual part of a formal reception to visitors, and is still practised in a modified form today.

Dances, weapons.

CHANTS. *Karakia* or incantations were often chanted, whether they were the little nonsense rhymes or charms of young children, or the very formal invocations used by *tohunga,* priests. In addition, many songs of love, joy, abuse, derision, thanksgiving, etc., were chanted by individuals or united with others in a chorus.

Charms, divination, karakia.

CHAPLETS *(pare)*. *Pare* made of *kawakawa* leaves or seaweed were worn as a sign of mourning, and by those who carried the bones of the dead for interment. Widows in particular frequently wore *pare* for a considerable time after the death of their husbands.

A widow wearing a chaplet of leaves or seaweed.

Hair, widows.

CHARMS (*karakia*). The word *karakia* was a generic term that described the use of words to invoke supernatural help in a wide range of situations – these could be termed charms, incantations and spells. Charms especially could be childish jingles used in playing games such as dart flying:

Fly forward, my dart, like a meteor in the sky.
A dart of Tuhuruhuru cannot be passed.
Fly straight forward, rise and fall over the mountains.
May this dart be lucky.

Such charms were frequently used by children and adults, and in every conceivable context. The words were often irrelevant, and were only the outward expression of the charm. They were used to avert evil, to encourage the performance of a task, and to seek the assistance of the gods.

In a more practical sense, hunters used many *karakia*. By them birds could be brought down to drink where they were easily caught. Spells were used extensively in fighting illness. Many *karakia*, called *hoa rākau*, were addressed to weapons, or to the gods to give strength to the weapon and the wielder. In warfare there were charms to render pursuer and pursued fleet of foot, to cause the enemy to lose strength, to draw in land and sea in order to make a journey shorter, to draw it out in order to discourage others. Even the passage of the sun in the heavens could be delayed by reciting powerful *karakia*. All such charms and spells were based on a belief in sympathetic magic, even when they were in the form of prayers addressed to the gods. There was seldom any entreaty or direct request, and often the words had little reference to the matter at issue. There was a further complication, in that most of the examples that have been preserved were of great antiquity, and contain obsolete sacerdotal expressions which defy translation because knowledge of the oblique references made in the *karakia* have been lost. However, it was not so much the words of the *karakia* that were important but the attempt to refer to and recreate the circumstances of a previously similar situation where success had been achieved.

The following 'romantic' example was collected by James Cowan who said; 'This, as given by the old folks of Arahura (Greymouth), is the song of the axe that Raureka taught the Ngāi Tahu; she murmured it as she chipped at the stem of the *tī*, cabbage tree.'

I stretch forth my axe
To the head of the tree,
How it moves,
How it resounds, O children!
Because of my desire
For the lofty sons of Tāne.
Tāne, the Tree-God, towering above me –
Tāne, felled and lying at my feet.
See how the chips fly from my axe!
Uncovered to the world are Tāne's children,
Once pillared lofty in the forest shades,
But now all stripped and prone,
Laid bare to the morning light,
The light of Tāne's day.

The *tohunga* were familiar with the widest variety of *karakia*, and their closely guarded repository of knowledge contained powerful invocations that called upon the full resources of the gods.

But there is a world of difference between the frivolous jingles of children and the elaborate forms of incantation known to the *tohunga*, priests. Such incantations, used in birth, baptism, betrothal, and marriage ceremonies, at the death of chiefs, and in time of war and on other important occasions, are sometimes survivals from the days when the gods performed their titanic deeds during the creation. Tupai recited such a *karakia* when Tāne mated with the woman he had created:

Here am I, a man, a divine one, O Hine, ē, ī!
Here is a divine man, for you, O Hine, ē, !
Here am I, a husband of yours, O Hine, ē, ī!
Here am I, a lover, a lover embracing, of yours, O Hine, ē, ī!
Let your body closely adhere to this male,
Concentrate your thoughts on this your lordly husband, O Hine, ē, ī!
'Twas Hine-one, towards those other sons, O Hine, ē, ī!
Be bound by your eyes, be bound by the mouth,
Bound by your body, to this man of yours –
A man desired, a man most suitable,
A man embracing of yours, is this man,
This Tāne-nui-a-rangi –
This Tāne-matua of yours, O Hine, ē, ī!

In recording an example of a *karakia* addressed to Io, the supreme god, early ethnographer S. Percy Smith wrote (*The Lore of the Whare-wānanga*)): 'I have attempted, with the aid of the Scribe, to render these exceedingly difficult, cryptic and elliptical compositions, in a form from which a slight understanding of the meaning may be gathered, with, however, very little satisfactory result. No one who has not tried it knows how difficult it is to render this class of composition into understandable English.'

When powerful invocations were used, the whole *karakia*, or at least a complete section, was recited in a single breath and had to be repeated without any mistakes. If an error was made, or the words forgotten, it was an *aituā*, an omen of bad luck, and the culprit was in danger of losing his life at the hand of the gods. In lengthy or intricate *karakia* an assistant, who carried on the words without a pause as soon as the priest stopped for breath, helped the *tohunga*.

Choking, demons, fishing, hand games, karakia, kites, kūmara, mauri, Rātā, tohunga.

CHIEFS *(ariki)*. The chief or chieftainess of a tribe was the first-born male, or sometimes female, of a senior or leading family. Those with the greatest *mana* were able to trace their descent through a line of successive first-born sons of noble birth. Such lines of descent indicated the status of the *ariki*. There was no natural or elected leader in a tribe, for there might be several *ariki*.

In addition to the privilege of birth, the *mana* of the *ariki* was dependent on his character, bravery, wisdom, and natural gifts of leadership. The *ariki* was frequently a *tohunga*, but whether or not he had attained knowledge of supernatural affairs, his person, and especially his head, was highly *tapu*. He was regarded as the *taumanu* or resting-place of the gods. His people guarded him, and when he travelled he had a retinue of followers, but there was no servility in their attitude toward him. The affairs of the tribe or *hapū*, sub-tribe, were not directed by the chief nor even by a council of *rangatira*, for every man of good standing had the right to speak in open conference. Nevertheless, in time of war, or when any difficult enterprise was undertaken, the qualities of leadership usually came to the fore, and the *ariki* led his people by strength of character as well as by dignity of birth.

Baptism, burial, farewell speech, mana, puhi, rangatira, tohunga.

CHIEFTAINESS. A first-born female of noble birth was an *ariki*, and commanded respect and admiration. She took her place in tribal discussions, and her sex did not deprive her of the privilege of chieftainship.

Chiefs, puhi.

CHILDBIRTH, see BIRTH.

CHILDREN *(tamaiti,* child; *tamariki,* children). Māori children were well treated by adults to such an extent that they might be regarded as being spoilt. They were seldom checked or punished and for that reason were very precocious; on the other hand they possessed a natural courtesy and sophistication, and were easily trained. Training in domestic arts for girls, and in warfare for boys, was severe, and at such times they were treated like adults.

But they had a great deal of freedom when young. They went naked until the age of eight, ten, or even twelve, and enjoyed many games, such as kite flying, wrestling, running, swinging, skipping, tree-climbing, sailing tiny canoes made of flax leaves, top-spinning, etc.

Boys, games, girls.

CHISELS *(whao).* Although fine carving could be done by means of small *toki*, adzes, when handled by skilled craftsmen; intricate and delicate work needed the use of small chisels and gouges. They varied in length from tiny 1.5 centimetre-long tools to 20 centimetres, and in weight from a few grams to half a kilogram. *Whao* were made of basalt, greenstone and other hard materials. Some were used in the hand, but mallets were generally required to tap the *whao.*

CHOKING *(natia, taronatia).* The most common cause of choking was the swallowing of a fish bone. This *karakia,* collected by Sir George Grey in the 19th century, was used to help the removal of fish bones from the throat. On the last line the 'patient' was slapped on the back to aid the expulsion.

The incantation,
For starting the choking,
For commanding the choking.
Serve you right for choking,
Because you ate standing,
Because you ate hurriedly,
Because you ate like a girl.
How many of my sons
Were swallowed by you?
There was Nini, there was Nana,

Children playing in the *kāinga*. The elevated store house at the right is a *pātaka*.

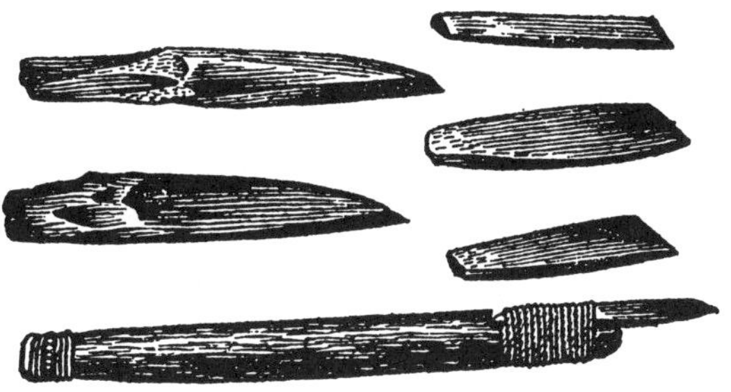

Chisels and small adze blades.

There was Te Patahi o Wahieroa,
Eaten to go within.
Vomit them forth,
Come out!

CLIMBING *(whakaeke rākau)*. Tree-climbing was a favourite pastime for boys. Large climbing poles were set up in some villages, and the boys practised on these. They became skilful at ascending straight, limbless trees such as *kauri* rickers. An interesting method was the *tapaka* form of climbing, in which a cord was looped round the trunk, with the climber holding both ends. The cord was jerked upwards as the climber made his way up the tree, sometimes using foot loops as well. *Tapaka* is a method of climbing still found throughout the Pacific.

Trees of small girth were climbed without assistance. Large trees with no branches near the ground could be ascended by means of a pole, or by several poles, one above the other, lashed to the trunk.

The boyish pastime had a practical purpose in training for the serious adult role of bird hunting. That job was a hazardous one and required skill and daring.

Birds (hunting), ladders.

CLOAKS *(kākahu, korowai)*. *Aute*, paper mulberry bark, provided sufficient covering in the tropical climate of the Pacific islands but in the temperate climate of Aotearoa, Māori needed further

Tree-climbing by means of ropes looped round hands and feet.

protection against the elements. In any event the *aute*, though introduced, did not flourish, and the nearest substitute – the inner bark of the *houhere*, lacebark tree – was only used occasionally.

The dried leaves and fibre of the ubiquitous *harakeke*, flax, became the basis for all clothing, including *kākahu* and *korowai*, capes and cloaks. The explorer, Captain James Cook, who was an acute observer, made the following observations:

> Their common clothing are very much like square thrumbed mats, that are made of rope yarns, to lay at the doors or the passages into houses to clean one's shoes upon. Besides the thrumbed mats they have other much finer clothing, made of the same plant after it is bleached and prepared in such a manner that it is as white, and almost as soft as flax, but much stronger.

Although cloaks were worn in cold weather,

A group of men wearing different types of cloak as described in the text.

they were loose-fitting and coarse in texture and were not much protection against the cold. The coarse fibres of rain cloaks, closely woven from *kiekie* and *tī* leaves, were waterproof, and could be thrown off quickly when the wearer entered a *whare*. The garments were rectangular in shape and worn draped around the body, leaving the arms free. Longer cloaks were fastened at the shoulder with a bone, wood, or greenstone pin. The shorter capes, which came only to the waist and were worn with a *maro*, or mat, were usually tied at the neck.

In battle or for work purposes cloaks were usually discarded. Though warriors often fought naked, they might sometimes wear a closely woven cloak, often soaked in water, as a protection against spear thrusts.

Cloaks and capes were worn by both sexes. Although there is no special term for either garment in the Māori language, the common word *kākahu* applied to the better type of cloak and *kahu* to those of lesser quality.

Superior cloaks were works of art which were highly prized, and to which much careful preparation was devoted. The foundation material was not dyed, but ornamental *tāniko* borders were woven with patterns in colour, and there was a loose fringe of thrums. The better cloaks were trimmed with feathers and dogskin. In some cases whole skins of birds were attached to the cloak, and dogskins sewn together, but usually the feathers were inserted and secured

A cloak with pompoms.

individually, or narrow strips of dogskin sewn to the flax foundation. *Kiwi* feathers, and the brilliant red feathers from under the wings of the *kākā*, made highly prized garments. Other cloaks were decorated all over with loosely hanging thrums, for the feather cloaks were a rare luxury.

Usually only the more important members of the tribe possessed a number of ornamental *kākahu*, and on ceremonial occasions they might wear several at a time.

The following are some of the principal types of cloak:

kahu-huruhuru: a feather cloak.
kahu-kekeno: a sealskin cloak.
kahu-kererū and *kahu-kūkupa*: a cloak covered with pigeon feathers.
kahu-kiwi: a cloak covered with *kiwi* feathers.
kāhu-koka: a rough outer-garment of undressed *harakeke*, flax, or *kiekie* leaves.
kahu-kura: a brilliant red cloak of *kākā* feathers, or a coarse flax cape coloured with red ochre.
kahu-mamae: a garment sent to distant relatives of one who has been killed in order to keep resentment alive.
kahu-mōtea: a cloak of mourning.
kahu-tāniko: a cloak of fine *harakeke* fibre with an ornamental border.
kahu-toroa: a cloak covered with *toroa*, albatross down.
kahu-waero: a cloak covered with the skin and hair of dogs' tails.
kahu-wai-a-rangi: a cloak woven in broad stripes of black, red, and white.
kahu-whero: a cloak covered with red feathers.
kaitaka: a large, soft, highly esteemed cloak with broad black and white borders.
kārure: a type of *korowai* with loose cords.
korowai: a cloak decorated with black cords.
kotikoti: a cloak of *harakeke* leaves rolled into tubes and dried over the fire, dyed yellow and light brown, which rattled with every movement of the wearer.
kūpara: a cloak like a *kaitaka* without a border, dyed black.
ngore: a cloak decorated with dyed pompoms.
pākē: a rough rain cape of *kiekie* or *harakeke* feathers.
parākiri: a plain rough cloak.
pikerangi: a *korowai* without the black strings, but with a red border.
pukupuku: an armoured cloak or cape of closely woven flax which when wet was impervious to spear thrusts.
pūreke: a rough, undyed, waterproof cape.
taupō: a cloak of flax, every third leaf being dyed yellow, and the other two black.
tōī: a cloak with flax leaves dyed black, but showing some green leaves.
waikawa: a cloak decorated with rolled, dried flax leaves.

The names here might apply to a cape as well as a cloak. It is not an exhaustive list but shows the main types of cloak and their appearance and construction.

Aute, dogs, dyes, feathers, flax, garments, maro, tāniko, warfare, weaving.

CLOUDS *(ao, kapua)*. Hine-kapua was the personified form of clouds. As the cloud girl she guarded her offspring, but frequently the wind children pursued them across the sky. In the Māori creation myths, Tāne was concerned at his father Rangi's nakedness, and he covered the Sky Father with the clouds, which were gathered by Tāwhiri-mātea, the god of the winds, from the warmth and perspiration of Papa, the Earth Mother. The clouds also served to protect her from the fierceness of the sun's rays.

CLUBS *(patu, mere)*. Striking weapons may be divided into two categories – one- and two-handed weapons. The latter are represented by the *taiaha*, a wooden quarter-staff which could be used for striking or thrusting. The most popular of the single-handed clubs was the *mere*. A fighting man usually carried a short striking weapon and a larger one, such as a spear, *tewhatewha*, or *taiaha*.

Clubs were made of wood, bone, stone, and greenstone. The wooden ones, *patu rākau*, were not often used. The *patu ōnewa*, or stone club, was thick and heavy, and was used mainly as a striking weapon. The *patu parāoa* was made of whalebone, flattened, and with a thin edge. Of bone clubs, the *kotiate* is interesting because of the 'sinuses' or 'lobes' on the edges, which give it a fancied resemblance to a violin. These lobes are believed to be purely decorative but it is also said that the design was helpful in breaking the skin of an opponent at the point of impact. The *wahaika* bore some likeness to the blade of a bill-hook, and as a rule was elaborately carved.

But the striking weapon par excellence was the *mere*. It was made of stone and greenstone, the latter being termed *mere pounamu*. For such a prized weapon, greenstone was the most appropriate material. The term *mere* was often synonymous with *mere pounamu*. It was short, about 35–40 centimetres long, and rather less than 5–8 centimetres wide, with a thickened handle bored with a hole so that it could be attached to the wrist with a cord or dogskin thong. The blade was flattened and had a thin edge. Greenstone, not being brittle, was the ideal material to use for these clubs.

Mere pounamu were used both for striking and thrusting, usually the latter. The hard, thin edge could penetrate the bone of a man's temple, and with a quick twist of the hand his skull could be crushed or wrenched open. *Mere pounamu* were usually prized heirlooms, and were held in such esteem that a captive would sometimes beg to be killed with a *mere*, as befitted the death of a chief.

The great advantage of all these small striking weapons was their value in close, hand-to-hand fighting, and the ease with which they could be carried, or concealed under a cloak or cape. When travelling, a warrior thrust his *mere* into his belt, or suspended it from the waistband, or from the wrist. Nearly all clubs were ground to a sharp edge, and were dangerous cutting and smashing weapons, whether a side-stroke was made, or whether the club was thrust forward at a vulnerable part of the body. Most short clubs were tied to the wrist. The thong was wound tightly round the wrist in order to hold the weapon firmly when it was thrust at an opponent.

Implements (agricultural), greenstone, taiaha.

COFFINS. 'Canoe burial' was practised in villages where enemies could not disturb the tombs or coffins. The body of a departed chief was placed in a sitting position on a rack or grill enclosed within two sections of a canoe hull, which had been cut in half and placed upright in the ground. The outer casing was painted red, and sometimes adorned with feathers. The 'sacrifice' of a valuable canoe in this manner helped underline the importance of the dead person.

Once the body tissues had decomposed the bones would then be removed and, after appropriate ceremonials, finally disposed of by being hidden in a secret place.

Rectangular pieces of timber were also used in the same manner as the canoe hulls.

Among some of the northern tribes, carved wooden *waka koiwi* or *waka tūpāpakū*, coffins or bone chests, were used. It has been recorded that amongst the *Arawa* people, closely plaited baskets were sometimes made into which the corpse of a deceased person would be placed.

Burial, canoes.

COLD *(makariri; kōpeke; mātao, tūhauiri)*. The sensation of cold is the subject of a creation myth. Before the separation of Rangi and Papa, Ue-poto, one of their children, ventured out into space, attracted by a feeble glow of light. He called to his brothers to follow, and most of them did so, but they were attacked by Wero-i-te-ninihi, Kunawiri, Maeke, and other personifications of cold, and were forced to cling to the sides of their mother Papa for warmth.

Māori were a hardy people and did little to protect themselves from the cold in winter; on the other hand the intense heat of a crowded *whare puni* was endured with great stoicism. Early missionaries tell of naked Māori crawling out of the narrow doorway of a sleeping house and steaming in the night air.

Greenstone, houses.

COLOURS. Māori had good colour-sense but lacked a comprehensive vocabulary of colour names, relying on the names of objects that were distinguished by their colour, in the same way that modern fashion houses evolve such names as wild rice, apricot, bone, and whisky.

Black (*mangu* and *pango*), white (*mā* and *tea*), red (*whero*, *ura*, and *kura*), are specific names, and there are other terms for the various shades such as pale grey, reddish, dark-coloured, etc.

Of the derived names there are: *kākāriki* for green (from the green parakeet), and also *pounamu* (from greenstone); *kōwhai* for yellow (from the *kōwhai* blossom); *parakaraka* for orange (from the berries of the *karaka* tree); *kororā* for grey (from the plumage of a certain penguin). Blue was a difficult colour, and the word used was *pango* (dark) but sometimes *kahurangi* after the blue-grey colour of a variety of greenstone. There is probably a considerable variation in the use of colour names amongst different tribes.

COMBS *(heru)*. After oiling, a chief's hair was carefully dressed and combs used to hold the hair in place and for ornamental purposes. Most Māori men of rank wore their hair long, pulled up into a topknot. The combs were fashioned from bone and hardwood, and decorated with carved designs and inlaid *pāua* shell. Because the combs had touched the head of a chief they were regarded as being especially *tapu* and were carefully disposed of lest they bring harm to others. Women were rarely permitted to use them.

Hair.

COMETS *(whetū)*. Auahi-tū-roa, a son of the sun, was the personified form of comets. Another personification was Upoko-roa, and both had some connection with fire-making. When the tinder blazed up, the fire-maker exclaimed, 'The child of Upoko-roa appears!' Several other personifications are known.

Tribal gods who were appealed to in time of war sometimes had a physical manifestation in the form of comets, a notable example being the *atua* Tunui-a-te-ika. Comets were often known as *whetū*, and their personifications are regarded as *atua*. The appearance of a comet was considered to be an omen of considerable importance.

COMPASS, POINTS OF. The compass was unknown in Polynesia, but the points of the compass were indicated by wind names, e.g. *raki* (north); *uru* (west); *rāwhiti* (east); *tonga* (south); and intermediate points by joined names, e.g. *tonga-mā-uru* (south-west), *uru-mā-raki* (north-west), etc.

Winds.

CONGER EELS, see EELS.

COOKING. Women, except when they were assisted by male slaves, did all the cooking. The principal method of cooking was by steaming the food in earth ovens. Details of this process will be found under the heading Ovens.

Cooking in a steam oven was called *tao*, roasting was *tunu*, and *kōhua* and *huahua*, boiling by means of hot stones. Although food was usually wrapped in leaves and cooked in a steam oven, rats and birds were sometimes kept in wooden bowls and placed in the oven so that the energy-giving fat draining from the meat would not be lost. Small fish such as *inanga* were kept in baskets while being steamed.

Shellfish were either cooked in the oven, or steamed open by being placed on a bed of embers. *Tuna,* eels, were wrapped in *harakeke*, flax, and steamed, or roasted before the fire. When food was boiled, hot stones were lifted by means of wooden tongs (often a bent stick of *pirita,* supplejack) and dropped into a *hue*, gourd, containing water. The process of boiling water however was usually reserved for dyeing.

The simple cooking utensils used by the Māori were pounders and stone mortars, oven stones, mats to cover the steam ovens, plaited flax bands to place round the rim to prevent the soil falling in, shells for scraping, gourds to contain water, wooden bowls, and flax containers or baskets

The mats have been taken off the steam oven, and the food is being carried in small flax baskets to the people waiting on the *marae*.

to hold the food.

Birds (preserving), eels, fern root, food, houses, ovens, rats.

COUNTING *(tatau)*. Māori employed a decimal system of notation, but also counted in pairs as well as singly. There was an ability to count exactly up to 180 but past that number accuracy fell away, probably because there was little need to count in bigger numbers. *Rau*, for instance, means 100 or many, while *mano* means 1000 or very many. The term *hokowhitu* (literally seven score) which was used for a war party, meant either exactly 140, or about this number. Words such as *kehe, tautahi, tauhara,* etc., indicate a vague additional quantity, e.g. *hokotoru makere* means three score and a surplus, or sixty-odd. Counting, especially of food products, was done by pairs, e.g. *ko tahi pū*, means a pair, brace, or two. Five would even be given as *ka rua pū, tautahi*, i.e. two brace and an odd one. (Note that in counting, *ka* is prefixed to the numeral, e.g. *ka rua, ka toru, ka whā*, two, three, four, while in counting persons the prefix is *toko*, e.g. *kotahi*, a contraction of *tokotahi, tokorua, tokotoru*, one, two, three.) The ordinal numbers first, second, third, etc., were formed by adding the prefix *tua*, e.g. *tuatahi, tuarua, tuatoru*. There were some differences in usage in various parts of the country, but the system was an advanced one, and essentially practical.

Gestures, numbers.

COURTSHIP. Between young men and women of undistinguished birth, courtship was simple and straightforward, but with higher rank the complexities and difficulties multiplied. In the custom known as *kai tamāhine*, a party of young men would visit the village of a young woman renowned for her beauty and accomplishments, and would dance and take part in games in the hope that the young woman would choose one of them as a husband.

Young men would claim a wife at a public meeting, and the assembled people would decide the issue. In the case of young *puhi*, virgins, of high rank, the path of the suitor was particularly difficult. Love messages were conveyed between young people by means of knotted cords that bore a clear meaning to the initiated.

Love charms, marriage, puhi.

CRADLES, see BABIES.

CRAYFISH *(kōura)*. There are two distinct varieties of *kōura* or crayfish, salt-water and fresh-water, and both formed an important food supply. Both men and women hunted the red, salt-water *kōura*, often diving to a considerable depth in order to take them by hand. *Tāruke*, large, baited pots or baskets with stones attached to them as sinkers, were also used. The *tāruke* were made of vines and had a float attached which indicated the location of the pots.

The smaller, black, fresh-water *kōura* was taken in considerable quantities in lakes and streams, either by means of a drag net, or by lowering a large bundle of baited bracken or fern fronds over the side of canoe. After some time the bundle was lifted, and the *kōura* that had entered in search of the bait were shaken out into the bottom of the canoe.

Dredges (fish), swimming.

CREATION. The Māori conception of creation is a majestic one. It is not a single myth, but one of great complexity, with many variants. In the beginning there were the long ages of 'nothingness', succeeded by many ages of night, until the Sky Father and the Earth Mother emerged from the womb of night. They were cradled in each other's arms, and gave birth to many offspring, who were the primal gods. Led by Tāne, the gods separated the primal parents in order to let light into the world that was still in embryo. Amongst the children of Rangi and Papa (heaven and earth) were the departmental gods who controlled natural forces and phenomena, such as land and sea, winds, cultivated food, fish, etc. Tāne was the most active of the departmental gods. He was the deity of forests and birds, and the great principle of fertility in the world. In the developing universe there were 10 or 12 strata of overworlds and several strata of underworlds, the most important of which was the *Rarohenga*, which was the home of the souls of men.

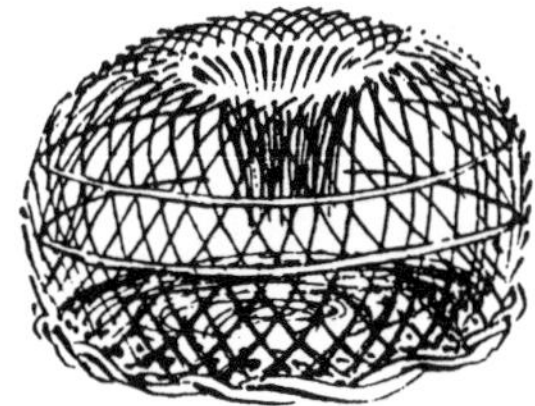

A *tāruke* – crayfish pot.

There were several wars between the gods, some of which are not yet ended. The sea continues to battle with the land, and the wind with the trees and cultivations of mankind.

Tāne's greatest accomplishment was his search for the female element in nature, culminating in the formation of the 'earth-formed woman,' into whom he projected the principle of life. He mated with her, and eventually the goddess of death was the fruit of this union.

Mankind (the mortal element) began when Tū-matauenga formed the first man, Tiki (although some traditions credit Tāne as the father of man). We thus see a gradual evolution of the world and the universe, controlled by the gods, in an ordered economy in which nature and natural phenomena were under the direct guardianship of endless personifications.

Before the creation of the world, a series of slowly developing eras were formulated in genealogies, of which quite a number are preserved. The following is typical of such genealogies:

Te Pū – The Root or Origin
Te More – The Taproot
Te Weu – The Rootlet
Te Aka – The Vine, or the Long Root
Te Rea – The Growth
Te Wao Nui – The Great Forest
Te Kune – The Development
Te Whē – The Sound
Te Kore – Chaos, or Nothingness
Te Pō – Night, or The Unknown

Rangi (Sky) – *Papa* (Earth)

Clouds, cold, dawn, earth, female element, fertility, fire, gods, gods (wars of), Hine-ahuone, Io Kore, light, lightning, man, mist, night, overworlds, Papa, personifications, Rangi, Rarohenga, separation of Rangi and Papa, sky, sun, Tāne, underworlds.

CREMATION. This was not a common practice, and was usually employed only when the body could not be buried, or the bones preserved, through force of circumstance. Where there was no place of concealment, for example, the body would be burned. A raiding party would sometimes burn the body and dry the head of a chief who was killed in battle, and take the sacred head home.

Burial, head.

CROPS, see CULTIVATIONS.

CULTIVATIONS *(māra)*. The four plants that were cultivated by Māori were the *kūmara*, *hue or* gourd, *uwhi* or yam and *taro*. While the *taro* was considered to be a luxury food to serve to visiting guests, in suitable districts the *kūmara* was incomparably the most important food plant. In very fertile areas such as the Tāmaki Isthmus (Auckland) and parts of the Bay of Islands, the suitability of the land for growing *kūmara* resulted in large local populations.

The time to begin work in the cultivations was indicated by the appearance of the constellations, particularly *Matariki* (the Pleiades), and the call of the *pīpīwharauroa,* the shining cuckoo. Similarly *Whānui* (Rigel) was observed as a sign of the time for harvesting.

At work in the *taro* plantation. The women are using wooden grubbers, and one of the men is carrying a *kō* or digging implement.

Conditions for *kūmara* growth varied a great deal from one place to another, and in some parts of the country the ground had to be prepared well in advance. The first task in cultivating was weeding. Any scrub that was removed was burnt and the ashes used as fertiliser. In some cases loads of sand or gravel had to be brought to the clearing for use as a soil conditioner.

Men and women worked together at clearing the ground. Several kinds of wooden implement were used – narrow, wooden spades, pointed digging sticks, grubbing and pounding tools, and others for scraping up the soil and gravel. Long, straight mounds were made for the *kūmara*, and the soil was kept loose. All work was done on an empty stomach, and because of the *tapu* over the workers and their task, no food was cooked until night when the work was done for the day. As men worked in the cultivations they sang songs that helped them to work in unison.

The *tohunga* took many precautions to see that the gods associated with crops and harvest, Rongo and Pani, were appropriately honoured and therefore a special planting of tubers was made for these *atua*.

The cultivations varied greatly in size. Cook mentions seeing areas of 40 or 50 acres in the Bay of Islands. Sometimes they were small and carefully hidden, and scattered in isolated situations in order that they might not be easily discovered and raided by enemies. They were neatly kept, the plants being placed in straight lines. Larger cultivations were divided into smaller plots that were the special care of individual *whānau*, families. Paths divided the plots, and these were always *tapu*, and marked by stones or human hair attached to a tree or post.

There were no native animals to raid the growing crops, but fences were sometimes built to try and keep out swamp-dwelling birds such as *pūkeko* and *weka*. In many localities brush or stone windbreaks were necessary.

As the crops grew, they were kept weeded, caterpillars were removed or driven away with smoky fires, and even by *karakia* chanted by the *tohunga*. At harvest time more ceremonies were

The *kūmara* plantation, which lies in a sheltered position below the fortified *pā*. The diggers keep time to a chant as they turn over the long sods. Two *kō* are at the right, and to the left is a *whata*, or elevated stage, where the tubers are kept ready for planting.

observed, and offerings were made to Rongo and Pani. The tubers were then lifted, inspected, and sorted, and taken away in baskets to be stored in *rua*, pits. A *hākari* (feast) and a season of games, songs, and contests celebrated the completion of the harvesting.

Agriculture, boundaries, caterpillars, feasts, frost, gourds, implements (agricultural), kūmara, Pani, Rongo, taro, women, working bees, yams.

CURSES *(kanga)*. *Kanga*, curses pronounced by *tohunga* who possessed evil powers, had remarkable efficacy and caused illness and death. The most effective were those directed at the head of the victim as this was the most sacred part of the body.

Magic, Rona.

D

DANCES (*haka*). Various kinds of dances were an important feature of Māori life. They provided an outlet and expression for every emotion and were performed on most important occasions. These included going to war, making peace, receiving visitors, divination, birth, at marriage and death ceremonies, greeting the rising of stars which marked a new season of the year, and in joy and sorrow, victory, triumph, derision, and defeat.

The dances were suited to the subject. Some were slow and graceful, others fierce and energetic, but all involved the use of head, body, and limbs, whether they were performed standing, sitting, or kneeling.

Both men and women took part, but the *poi* dance with its graceful movements was restricted to women, while the *peruperu* or war dance was usually though not exclusively performed by men. The *haka* was an outward expression of the strong sense of rhythm possessed by Māori, which was also shown in the songs and chants that accompanied the dance.

The favourite Māori *haka* was the posture dance. In its wilder forms as a *peruperu*, it was an outlet for pent-up emotions and an encouragement to the warriors, making them eager for battle. Eyes and tongues protruded in the defiant *pūkana* gesture, and the dancers brandished their weapons. An early visitor to New Zealand, Augustus Earle, described it as follows:

> It was conducted with so much fury . . . that at length I became quite horrified, and for some time could not divest myself of the feeling that our visitors were playing false, so closely did this mock the screeching of the women, and the menacing gestures . . . were so calculated to inspire terror, that stouter hearts than mine might have felt fear.

The *peruperu* almost always involved a weapons display but other dances were performed without weapons, although the leader might use one to emphasise the leader role.

Those taking part had to ensure a faultless performance because that was an omen of good

The poi dance. This is a *waka poi*, in which the young women are seated like paddlers in a canoe.

fortune. Any mistakes could signify defeat in the forthcoming battle.

There was always a leader for the *haka*. He or she gave time to the music and the motions of the dance, and there were solo and chorus parts – call and response – in the accompanying song.

The following *haka*, which is of some antiquity but is these days associated with the famous Ngāti Toa chief Te Rauparaha, is probably the most well known in the country. The haka is said to describe an incident in Te Rauparaha's life when he hid from his enemies in a *kūmara* pit, unsure whether he would live or die. As he emerges from the *kūmara* pit in which he is hidden, Te Rauparaha compares the shining sun with the darkness of the pit. Loosely translated the words mean: 'It is death, It is death, It is life, It is life, This is the hairy person who caused the sun to shine.'

Ka mate! Ka mate!
Ka ora! Ka ora!
Tēnei te tangata pūhuruhuru
Nāna i tiki mai i whakawhiti te rā,
Upane! Upane!
Upane, kaupane, whiti te rā!

The legendary origin of the *haka* is said to be in the dance of Tāne-rore, the personified form of the dancing, quivering, heated air of summer. Tāne-rore was the child of Te Rā, the sun god, and Hine-raumati, the summer girl.

Action songs, challenges, divination, peace, poi, songs, war dances.

DARKNESS.

Light, night, ponaturi.

DARTS *(niti, teka)*. There were two forms of dart game, the first being used to train boys in the future use of spears. The *teka*, or spears, were usually made from the flower stalk of the *toetoe* or the *harakeke*, flax, or of some other light wood. They were thrown at the boys, who had to avoid them, or parry them with short sticks, or with the hand. They were also thrown direct at a target.

The normal *teka* game was played with straight stalks of fern or bracken, about a metre in length. The stalks were fitted with a knob at one end made from thin strips of flax wound tightly round the stem. The game was played on a level stretch of ground on which a baseline had been marked. Some distance away was a small, rounded mound of earth. The object of the game was to throw the *teka* underarm in such a manner that it struck the mound and glanced off it, the winner being the player who was able to send his *teka* the greatest number of times to the greatest distance.

Magical properties were credited to some *teka*, and there are legends that tell how missing persons were found by casting a *teka* repeatedly until at length it reached its destination.

Darts were sometimes propelled by means of a *kotaha* or throwing stick, to which a cord was tied. The *teka* was stuck lightly into the ground and the free end of the cord tied round it in such a manner that when the cord was taut the knot held fast, but when the tension was released it freed itself. The stick was brought forward quickly and the *teka* was jerked out of the ground and propelled forward, being projected through the air at the end of the stroke. In warfare the purpose of the stick-propelled *teka* was to set fire to the thatch of houses in a besieged *pā*. Combustible materials were tied to the *teka* and ignited before the dart was thrown. A famous example was the destruction of the Te Arawa canoe, when Raumati threw a burning *teka* across the Kaituna River and lit the thatched roof of the shed in which Te Arawa was housed.

Boys, charms, stages (fighting).

DAWN *(haeata, atatū)*. In Māori myth, the dawn girl was Hine-tītama, the daughter of the god Tāne and Hine-ahu-one, the woman he formed of earth and endowed with life. Tāne mated with his daughter and she fled from him in shame to the underworld, where she is known as Hine-

Several forms of dart throwing are shown in this scene. In the foreground men are propelling flax leaves and light rods by means of throwing sticks. Usually the sticks would be over a metre in length. At the left a young man is projecting a dart against a mound, from which it will glance off to fly through the air. He and his friends are engaged in a contest to see who can throw their *niti* the furthest. In the background boys are tossing *toetoe* stalks at each other.

nui-ō-te-pō, the great girl of night, or death. There is a complimentary saying or proverb: *Ko Hine-tītama koe, matawai ana te whatu i te tirohanga* (You are like the dawn girl; the eye glistens when gazing upon you).

Night.

DAY *(rā, rangi)*. An old legend states that day and night followed each other when Tāne took pity on his mother Papatūānuku, the Earth Mother, because she was parched by the heat of the sun. 'Let the red sun take the lead and move in front,' he said. 'Let the waxing moon follow behind him; let the little suns be separated, all following the leading of the sun, even that we may obtain sleep.' The personification of day is Hine-aotea, the day girl.

Sun, Uru-te-ngangana.

DEATH *(mate)*. The path of death was first formed when Hine-tītama fled to the underworld and took the name Hine-nui-te-pō or Hine-nui-ō-te-pō, the goddess of death. Māui the demi-god attempted to drink the waters of life, Te wai ora ā Tāne, by entering the body of the goddess but she awoke and crushed him to death. Had Māui succeeded then mankind would have lived forever.

When anyone neared death, the relatives gathered round. The dying person made his last wishes known, and delivered his *poroporoakī* or *ohākī*, his farewell speech. If he were a chief

Bearers taking the body to a cave, or some secret place, where it would be left until the bones were ready for their final resting place.

he would be addressed with farewell remarks such as, 'Farewell to Hawaiki. Go on towards the Pō. Go your way to Paerau. Descend by the Tāhekeroa,' and then the spirits of those who had departed before would conduct him to the underworld.

Nowadays, most iwi and hapu — even individual marae — will have their own form of farewell Poroporoakī to the departed, and in a modern context those speeches will sometimes incorporate elements of Christianity.

Māori preferred to die out of doors. This was a necessity, for death made a house *tapu* and meant that it could no longer be used. A small *whare* might be burned, but a communal building was a different matter, and it needed to be protected from such *tapu*. The last wishes of the dying chief would be scrupulously observed. As soon as the soul departed from the body, the voices of the mourners rose, and the dirges continued for some days.

After death the body was dressed and trussed in a sitting position for burial. The *tangi*, funeral ceremonials, then commenced. As a sign of mourning men and women (especially women) lacerated their limbs, bodies and occasionally their faces with sharp flakes of obsidian. Close relatives cut their hair and the widow wore a *pōtae tauā* or mourning chaplet of leaves, with pendant strings or seaweed, plants, or feathers. The relatives remained by the side of the body, weeping and abstaining from food, but retiring to a distance when they wished to eat.

The custom of *muru*, ritual plundering of the deceased's home and goods, was sometimes observed at this time. Human sacrifices might

The body of a chief, dressed in ceremonial clothes and seated in the porch of the *whare*, while the mourners give way to grief.

be made at the death of important chiefs as an extreme expression of grief, while it was also expected that because of their grief a chief's wife or wives might commit ritual suicide.

After burial the *tohunga* set up the death wand, the *tira mate*, which sent the *wairua* or soul on its way to the spirit world. Then the *tira ora*, the living wand, was set up to preserve the living, and the gifts that had been brought were distributed among the relatives. Further presents were brought when the bones of the deceased were committed to their final resting place.

Natural death was called *mate ā tara whare* (death by the wall of the house). Māori accepted misfortune, sickness and the decline in physical and mental powers leading to death philosophically.

Burial, dawn, dying speech, evil, Hine-nui-ō-te-pō, Hine-tītama, immortality, laments, lizards, mauri, muru, night, souls, tangi, underworlds.

DECORATION.

Carvings, houses, ornaments, painting, reed patterns, tattooing.

DECOYS.

Birds (hunting).

DEMONS *(tipua, or tupua)*. The word *tipua* is applied not only to demons and goblins, but also to any object, animate or inanimate, which might have weird, supernatural qualities. It can therefore include *taniwha*, and enchanted trees, stones, and other objects. Demons appear in folklore, and most tribes had their own variety of malignant and mischievous goblins. *Tipua* were normally caused by the soul of a dead person endowing various objects with qualities of power and enchantment. Floating logs acquired independent powers of locomotion and the ability to give forth strange, musical sounds; trees and mountains possessed eerie powers; stones moved; and birds appeared whose presence was an omen of coming danger. The *tipua* could be propitiated with charms, and by depositing offerings, a rite which was known as *uruuru whenua*.

DIGGING IMPLEMENTS *(kō* and *kāheru)*.

Agriculture, cultivations, implements, spades.

DISEASE. Maiki-nui, Maiki-roa, and similar personifications were the guardians of sickness and disease. They lived in the underworld and plagued mankind. Other diseases were afflicted on mortals by the *atua*, while illness was often believed to be caused by *kikokiko*, malignant lizards preying on the internal organs.

Leprosy, magic, sickness.

DITCHES.

Pā.

DIVINATION. Divinatory rites were performed by priests for many purposes, such as foretelling the future of the tribe, and of individuals in particular enterprises, discovering whether sickness would be fatal or not, whether the omens for battle would be propitious, etc.

There were many ways in which divination could be practised, e.g. by throwing a leaf in the air and observing its flight, by kite flying, the singing of chants which embodied prophesies imparted by the *atua*, or by observing the performance of the war dance, any mistakes being interpreted as an omen of evil. One way by which it could be decided whether a person had died as the result of witchcraft or not was to recite a spell over a fern stalk and plant it on the grave. If, after a little time had passed, it was found that the stalk had sunk into the ground, it was known that some sorcerer had been responsible for the death, and preparations would be put in hand to find the culprit and kill him, either by magic or by force. Divinatory rites were usually performed at the *tūāhu* of the village.

The *tohunga* at the *tūāhu*, consulting the rods used in divination.

DIVORCE. Although there was no divorce procedure in the normal sense of the word, there was a ceremony that wives adopted to rid themselves of a husband, because of unfaithfulness or other causes. Others could also use it to separate husband and wife. The invocation used by the *tohunga* makes reference to the separation of Rangi and Papa, the primal parents. The *karakia* and ceremony caused feelings of revulsion between man and wife.

Separation of husband and wife was not necessarily accompanied by any ceremony. After a quarrel a wife would sometimes simply return to her own people. Separation also resulted from the *taua wahine*, a war party that made a raid to exact *utu* when a man or woman had committed adultery. The whole *whānau* would be plundered, and afterwards both parties would be free to enter into other contracts. Although a great deal of latitude was allowed in relationships between young people, faithfulness was required after marriage.

Separation of Rangi and Papa, marriage.

DOGS *(kurī)*. Māui the demi-god was jealous of his brother-in-law Irawaru. He went fishing with him, and on his return he pressed the outrigger of the canoe heavily on Irawaru's body, and repeated spells that turned him into a dog. Hina, Māui's sister, and the wife of Irawaru, was dismayed to find that her husband had suffered this transformation. The story is a legendary account of the origin of dogs.

The dog was the only domestic animal Māori possessed. The *kurī* is thought to have suffered from in-breeding and was not a very intelligent animal, nor did it have a well-developed sense of smell. However its flesh was much appreciated in a land where meat was confined to birds, rats, and man. The dog was used for hunting the flightless *kākāpō*, ducks, and the nocturnal *kiwi*. *Kiwi*-hunting dogs were equipped with wooden rattles in order that they could be located in the bush at night. The dogs had long bodies, short legs, long, thick, white tails (which were prized for decorating superior cloaks and capes), pointed heads, and they did not bark.

Birds (hunting), Hina, lizards.

DOORS (*tatau*). The name *Tatau* was applied figuratively to some famous doorkeepers of legend. The *tatau* of a *whare* was made of wood and slid sideways into a recess in the wall. The term *tatau* is also applied to the sliding slab of a window while the expression *Tatau* ō *te pō* (doorway to the night) is a figurative term for death.

Houses, peace.

DRAUGHTS (*tōrere*, or *mū tōrere*). A Māori version of the game of draughts. The base design was an eight-pointed star drawn on sand or on a piece of timber or bark with charcoal. It was played with eight stones, four for each player. The two sets of stones were marked in some way to differentiate them. It seems probable that the game was originally called *tōrere*. When the game of draughts was introduced by the Pākehā, it was called by Māori, *mū* (possibly a form of 'move'), and *tōrere* became *mū tōrere*. The Ngāti Haua chief Tamihana Te Waharoa is famously said to have offered to play Governor Grey with the prize being the whole country. Grey declined to take the wager.

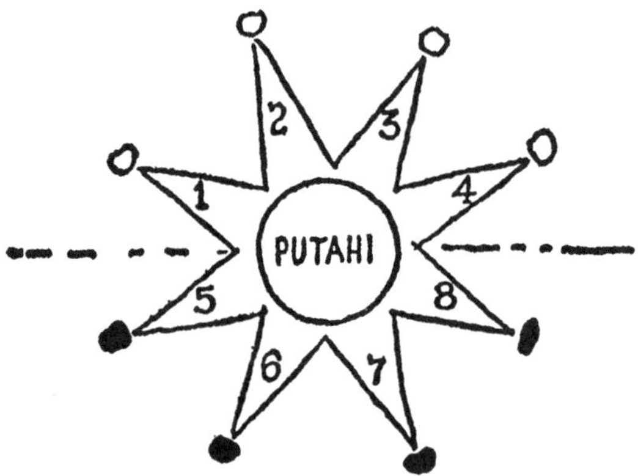

The beginning position in the tōrere game.

DREAMS. It was thought that the soul departed from the body for a while during sleep, a belief that was encouraged by dreams of journeys and expeditions. There were certain dreams that were believed to show what was happening elsewhere at the time, or which foreshadowed the future.

Nets, second sight, sleep.

DREDGES, FISH (paepae). The fish dredge was a long bag net attached to a frame of *mānuka*, tea-tree, rods, and about 3 metres in length. It was weighted with stone sinkers, lowered from a canoe and towed along the bed of a lake to catch freshwater crayfish. The dredge rake (*kapu*, or *mangakino*) was also used in lakes, but was employed in scooping up *kākahi*, a fresh-water mussel. Wooden teeth projected from a frame to which a handle was attached, and the *kākahi* were scooped into the bag.

Crayfish, fishing.

DRIFT VOYAGES. It has always been agreed that there have been countless drift voyages across the Pacific, when canoes were blown out to sea by unexpected changes in wind, or the sudden onset of storms. Some of these accidental voyages have resulted in the settlement of new islands, but in many cases, even when landfall was made, lack of provisions would have resulted in the eventual death of the crew. It was only when women as well as men were in the canoe that uninhabited islands could be peopled.

The drift voyage theory of the arrival of Māori in Aotearoa has been vigorously stated and hotly debated for many years and has its strong advocates. Proponents argue that the difficulties of sailing against prevailing winds and currents, and the absence of stars during storms and cloudy weather, would make it impossible for regular voyages to be made to a distant land, and even more impossible for return

Successive moves which lead to the defeat of an opponent.

voyages. It has also been argued that the arrival of a handful of canoes over the centuries could not account for the full Māori population of the 18th century.

It is difficult to reconcile these cogent arguments with the no less impressive Māori traditions. Briefly, these traditions give clear, detailed accounts of the discovery of Aotearoa by Kupe, of his taking back greenstone and of his description of the land, and sailing directions. These were later used by captains and crews in the wave of migration that is said to have followed and from which the various tribes are proud to claim descent.

The 'traditionalists' claim greater ability in seamanship for the Māori ancestors than the protagonists for the drift voyage theory will admit, and point to the belief that return voyages were made to bring back the *kūmara*, which was not a native plant. Some new theories suggest that these return voyages might in fact have been 'internal' journeys between the islands of Aotearoa itself.

The most likely explanation is that the three types of ocean voyages — the voyages of exploration, the voyages of necessity (caused by food shortages and internecine warfare) and the accidental drift voyages — all occurred in the settlement of the islands of the Pacific, including Aotearoa.

Andrew Sharp, the principal proponent of migration by accidental voyages, claims that most if not all of the Māori accounts of traditional voyages have been imported from earlier Polynesian groups.

Sharp's accidental voyaging theory is challenged in modern times by the achievements of crews in traditional double hulled waka and who have completed both way voyages using traditional navigation techniques.

Kupe, Migration (Great), Moahunters, Mōriori, Toi, voyages, Whātonga.

DRILLS. Māori invented a primitive form of drill. It was manipulated by means of cords wound round the shaft and pulled backwards and forwards to impart rotation. By attaching stones to the shank, pressure was applied. A flywheel made from a disc of wood or a vine lashed in a ring round the shaft was sometimes added. As the invention had not progressed to the point of providing a cap to steady the drill and apply pressure, the holes that were bored in the blades of adzes to attach them to the handles were shallow and bowl-like and often slightly off-centre. They were usually bored from either side, and an abrasive of sand and water was used with a hard stone on the point of the drill.

Adzes.

DRINK. *Wai* or water was the principal drink of Māori before the coming of the Pākehā. It was kept in *hue*, calabashes. For infants, *waiū* was mother's milk, and for adults the juice of the *tutu* berry and the gruel made by sprinkling *kao*, dried *kūmara*, into water were alternative drinks.

Calabashes, water.

DYES. *Tāniko* weaving and reed patterns used on the walls of houses required the use of dyes. To produce black pigment, *hīnau* bark was pounded and mixed with water, and after standing for a few days, a brown mordant was produced. The brown fibre was then placed in dark swamp mud for about a day, when the mud produced a permanent black dye.

A brownish-red dye was made from the bark of the toatoa or *tānekaha*, which was mixed with water and boiled. In order to make the colour fast, the material to be dyed was rolled in hot ashes, and soaked again in the warm water. Yellow and blue-black dyes were obtained from other plants.

Muka, the fine flax fibre used for making cloaks, was often bleached. This was done by taking *raupō*, bullrush, roots which were then washed and pounded in water in a wooden vessel. The *muka* was then placed in the vessel and pounded and squeezed until it was thoroughly impregnated with the *raupō* water, which apart from helping soften the fibre also produced the bleaching effect.

Boiling, tāniko, weaving.

DYING SPEECH *(oha, poroporoakī)*. Before the death of a chief his people assembled to hear his last message. If he made a request for some favourite food or a drink of water from a particular stream or spring, it would be obtained for him at all costs, because it was needed to sustain his soul on the long journey to the Rarohenga. Then came the *oha* or *ōhāki*, the last speech, which was often brief and contained instructions and last wishes for his people.

E

EAR PENDANTS *(mataringa, whakakai)*. Māori wore a variety of articles as ear pendants, the most imposing being the *kuru*. *Kuru* were simple, highly polished, slender, rounded lengths of greenstone, pierced with a hole at one end and suspended by a cord.

Some pendants were curved at the lower end, or flattened, and some were of more artistic design, including circles and fish-hooks. The teeth of sharks, which were highly prized, of dogs and of human beings (relatives, friends and enemies) were also used.

Other items used as ear ornaments included flowers, bunches of downy feathers of the *toroa*, albatross, and *tākapu*, gannet, the lacy tissue of the bark of a coprosma, larger feathers, and complete birds. The most unusual adornment was a living small bird such as a *pīwakawaka*, fantail, its head thrust through a hole in the lobe of the ear, where it struggled to free itself until death overtook it and it remained hanging in position for a considerable time afterwards. Both males and females wore these ornaments.

Greenstone.

EARTH. Papa was the Earth Mother, who loved and nurtured her children. She was the wife of Rangi, the Sky Father, and as they clung together in space, their offspring, the gods, were born. There were 70 male children all told. The story of their struggle for freedom, of how Rangi and Papa were forcibly separated to let in air and light for the convenience of the gods, is told under the heading Separation of Rangi and Papa.

Papa's full name was Papa-tū-ā-nuku (Papa extending afar), but she was given the further name Papa-tirahanga, which has the meaning of Papa facing upwards, or lying open and exposed. For a long time she remained on her back, looking up at Rangi and yearning for him. When her sorrow became obvious to the gods, they arranged the Hurihanga-a-Mataaho, the turning over by Mataaho, when she was turned face downwards so that she might no longer see her husband.

Tāne covered her nakedness with vegetation, and from her perspiration rose the mist and clouds which sometimes cover the body of Rangi. As the gods were male, it was in the Earth Mother that they sought for the female element that was necessary for the creation of mortals. Tāne finally discovered it. He formed the body of the first woman from the earth, and thus the first mortal appeared.

Papa remains the eternal friend of mankind, giving life and health to their bodies with her fruits, and receiving them again at their death.

When Rangi proposed that their offspring should be punished for what they had done, Papa replied, 'Not so. I brought them forth to the world of life; in death they shall find rest with me; though they have erred and rebelled against us, yet they are still my children. Mine be the care of the dead.'

Creation, earthquakes, female element, gods, one, Rangi, Tāne.

EARTHQUAKES. Earthquakes were personified in Rūaumoko, the youngest of the gods, who was not born at the time of the separation of Rangi and Papa, and remains in her womb, where his movements cause volcanic eruptions and earthquakes. In spring he turns over in the earth to bring the warmth to the top, and in autumn he turns again to bring cold to the surface, thus causing summer and winter, and the tremors which shake the body of his mother.

Evil, fire, Rūaumoko.

EARTHWORMS *(toke)*. Worms were esteemed as a great delicacy. There were several kinds that were craved as a last meal before death. *Toke* were soaked in water, steamed, and eaten with various greens.

Eels.

ECHOES. In the Te Waka a Māui, South Island, legend Rona was the man (not woman) in the moon, and the father of the Echo children.

EELS *(tuna)*. In ancient legend Tuna, or Tunaroa seduced Hina, the wife of Māui, and made an enemy of the demi-god. Māui dug a long trench and placed nine skids over which the unsuspecting Tuna advanced. Māui broke through a stop-bank when Tuna entered the trench and the giant eel was engulfed in the flood of water. Māui then chopped off his head and tail and cut the rest of Tuna's body into small pieces. Each fragment became some creature either in the water or on land. The most important fragments were the head, which became the conger eel, and the tail, which became the fresh-water eel.

The same legend is also related of Tiki and the woman he created.

Originally both salt- and fresh-water eels were supposed to have come to the earth from the heavens and were the grandchildren of Te Ihorangi, the personification of rain.

Eels were an important source of food. They were obtained in large numbers from most lakes and streams, and were noted for their huge size. Eels were speared, caught in nets, and taken with bob and by hand. The most popular method was the use of the *hīnaki,* eel pot, which was set in open water or at the mouth of eel weirs.

Much labour was devoted to the making of eel weirs, which were strongly constructed by driving posts deep into the bed of a river, and interlacing them with brushwood and the branches of trees. Matting or brushwood was also pegged down between the fences to prevent the bed of the river from scouring. There were several different ways in which the fences were arranged, either in zigzag form, or in one or more Vs, with the point of the V set downstream. In rivers that were noted for their eel populations, a number of weirs, each with several fences, would be erected in suitable locations.

A substantial *pā* or eel weir in a river. Two eel pots are being conveyed in the canoe.

The *hīnaki* were sited at the outlets of the weirs where the current would carry the eels into them. *Hīnaki* were woven carefully and closely from roots, branches, stems, and leaves of a number of different plants, elongated and circular in shape, with a narrow entrance. They were fastened to a guiding net that in turn was attached to the posts of the weir or, when set in an open stream, to some convenient support. The trapped eels were removed through a door in the side of the pot.

In quieter rivers and lakes, the eel pots were made with an opening at each end and a constriction at the mouth that prevented the eels from escaping once they had entered. Bait, consisting of earthworms placed in bags, was placed in the pot. In some cases the eels were so large that whole birds were used for bait. When travelling, temporary pots were made of flax leaves, strengthened and distended with supplejack vine. Talismanic stones, or *mauri*, were placed near important eel weirs.

Of other methods of taking eels, bobbing was the most popular. Baits made from worms, spiders or *huhu* grubs were attached by a cord to a short rod. When the eel was landed it was killed with a club.

Eel spears had several sharp, hardwood tines.

Hand nets were used in several different ways, and small eels were caught in clumps of baited bracken or brushwood that were lifted from the water and the eels shaken out on to the ground.

Eels were usually taken at night when they could be attracted by torchlight. Men and boys enjoyed taking them by hand.

Eels are slimy, slippery creatures and the most effective way of holding them until they were landed was between the teeth.

A favourite method of cooking was to wrap the eels in green leaves and roast them by the fire. When cooked in the steam oven, flax leaves were wound round them spirally. Large quantities were dried for future use on a platform over an open fire or split and dried in the sun.

Cooking, fishing, mauri, spears.

EGGS *(hua)*. During Tāne's search for the female element, Peketua formed the first egg that he took to Tāne, who advised him to give it life. Peketua did so and the egg produced the *tuatara*, which is thus related to birds.

During the same quest, Punaweko also formed an egg from which came the land birds, and Hurumanu an egg that produced the sea birds.

Eggs of many birds were an important item of diet for Māori. In the earliest days of settlement the gigantic eggs of the moa were blown, enclosed in a protective bag and used as water containers.

Birds, reptiles.

EVENING. The personification of evening is Hine-ahiahi, the evening girl.

EVIL. One theory of the origin of evil is that it came into being when the gods separated the primal parents. But that was an action from which good emerged so the usual belief was that it emanated from Whiro during his long struggle with Tāne. This battle raged through the heavens and ended in the defeat of Whiro and his expulsion to Rarohenga, the underworld. There he is recognised as the god of evil, inflicting harm on men and women in Te Ao Mārama, the world of light.

He entered into partnership with Rūaumoko and the Maiki brothers, who are responsible for sickness and disease. Whiro is also the god of thieves. All evil comes from him, and an evil person is termed a *whiro*. Māori were conscious of evil, but did not have a strong conception of goodness as the antithesis of evil, other than the belief that Tāne fought against it. It is said that the supreme deity Io designed nothing but good for his children, but it is difficult to set aside the possibility of missionary influence from this belief.

Evil is linked with death, and as the lizard is the physical form of Whiro on earth, it is not surprising that placatory offerings were made to Whiro. It is one of the paradoxes of Māori belief that evil is supposed to be confined to the world of man and is unknown in Rarohenga, even though it is Whiro's home. There are many forms of evil spirits, and part of the work of a *tohunga* was the exorcism of such spirits from the body.

Disease, earthquakes, fire, gods (wars of), Io, magic, sickness.

EXPERTS *(tohunga māori)*. The title of *tohunga* was given to a priest, wizard, or an expert in some aspect of Māori life. Suitable persons sometimes possessed all three of these qualifications. The functions of expert and priest cannot be completely separated because the border between magic and the practical world could easily be crossed and the supernatural world at all times invaded the world of natural and daily life.

The *tohunga* who diagnosed the cause of sickness and exorcised it was a priestly expert, while the specialist in carving was no less an expert in the recitation of *karakia* and the performance of ceremonies connected with his craft.

Young men were trained in the *whare wānanga* (the school of learning), and when the course was completed, they too became *tohunga*. Those who devoted themselves to practical and mundane matters, working to possess the knowledge and skill of their teachers and their predecessors, were known as *tohunga māori*.

Typical of such specialists were the *tohunga kokorangi*, experts in the observations of stars and weather, the *tohunga whaihanga*, experts in woodwork, the *tohunga whakairo*, experts in carving and tattooing, the *tohunga tārai waka*, experts in the making of canoes, and the *tohunga whaiwhare*, experts in house building. The one thing they had in common was the *tapu* that applied to the exercise of their skills.

Priests, whare wānanga.

A *tohunga whakairo moko* carrying two tattooing chisels suspended from his ear.

F

FABLES *(kōrero tara, pakiwaitara). Pakiwaitara* were pleasant and amusing stories with a moral or teaching theme that featured creatures as the central characters. Typical of such stories is the fable of the ant and the cricket, which bears a remarkable likeness to Aesop's fable of the ant and the grasshopper and might be indicative of missionary influence. Others include the story of the attack made on man by the *namu*, sandfly, and the *waeroa*, mosquito, the conversation between the *kauri* tree and the *tohorā*, whale, and the fight between whales and shellfish.

The fable of Pōpokorua and Kikihi, the ant and the cicada.

FAIRIES (*patupaiarehe, tūrehu*, and many other terms). There was a firm belief in the existence of *patupaiarehe*, a term which is usually translated as fairies. The use of the title fairy can lead to a wrong impression of these beings. They were not the lovable 'little people' of popular Western belief. *Patupaiarehe* were supernatural beings or spirits, supposed to assume a human form either male or female, and to meddle for good or ill in the affairs of mankind. The *patupaiarehe* were fair or white-skinned, usually feared and dangerous to mortals. They were found in several parts of Te Ika a Māui, the North Island, but were confined to the dense forests or the tops of high hills like Ngongotaha near Rotorua, Pirongia in the Waikato and Moehau on the Coromandel Peninsula.

When they ventured out of their *pā*, they chose wet or misty days because they had no liking for strong sunlight. The plaintive notes of their flutes were said to exercise a fatal fascination for young women whom they lured away into the forest. There were two defences against them – cooked food and *kōkōwai*, red ochre.

In Te Waka a Māui, the South Island, the role of the *patupaiarehe* was filled by the fierce *maero*, hairy creatures with long fingernails that they used to spear fish. The lights by which they fished could sometimes be seen at night in estuaries and harbours.

The fairies closest to the Western conception are the *Tini-ō-te-hakuturi*, the mysterious, midget forest creatures who, together with insects and birds, helped raise up and restore the tree which Rātā had felled because he had failed to propitiate the forest god Tāne.

The *ponaturi*, sea fairies, were an especially malignant race. They came ashore only at night. This was because sunlight was fatal to them and they were forced to retreat before the sun rose.

Fireplaces, maero, mist, nets, ochre (red), ponaturi, Rātā.

Representatives of three generations of a typical *whānau*.

FAMILIES (*whānau*). The term *whānau* means offspring as well as family, but it is usually the term for an extended family group rather than the Pākehā concept of the nuclear family of just parents and children.

The *whānau* was a closely knit unit deriving from a common ancestor, which was more important as a group than the individuals that comprised it. They lived and worked together in their own gardens and, as a rule, made collective decisions on all matters that affected them; but in turn they could be subordinate to the wishes and welfare of the *hapū*, sub-tribe, and the *iwi*, tribe. In their own domestic affairs it was always the family that counted and acted in concert.

There would often be a considerable number of people and several generations in a single-family group. A term such as *mātua* was used to describe uncles and aunts and all other relatives of the same generation as the parents. As *whānau* grew they evolved into *hapū* and, eventually, *iwi*.

Betrothal, hapū, iwi, tribes.

FASTING. Many *tapu* ceremonies were accompanied by abstention from food. When *tohunga* presided at important ceremonies, no food could be cooked until the ceremonies were completed. Even the ordinary people of the tribe had to abstain from eating when engaged in important work, such as planting *kūmara* tubers, because of the *tapu* that surrounded the work. At such times the evening meal was not cooked until the day's work was done. *Taua*, war parties, were especially banned from eating while they travelled along.

FAT. Roasted birds were preserved by placing them in suitable containers and then covering them with their own fat, reserved at cooking time.

Birds (preserving), cooking.

FEASTS (*hākari*). Feasting was an important part of Māori life, symbolic of the generous nature of the people on festive occasions. As in other parts of the Pacific, Māori sometimes experienced long periods of semi-starvation (often resulting from the abandon with which they had entertained visitors), where meals were reduced to one a day or less. But when food was plentiful, every opportunity was seized to celebrate with feasts, and prodigies of consumption were performed.

There were two kinds of *hākari*; those asso-

A huge stage erected to hold provisions for a feast.

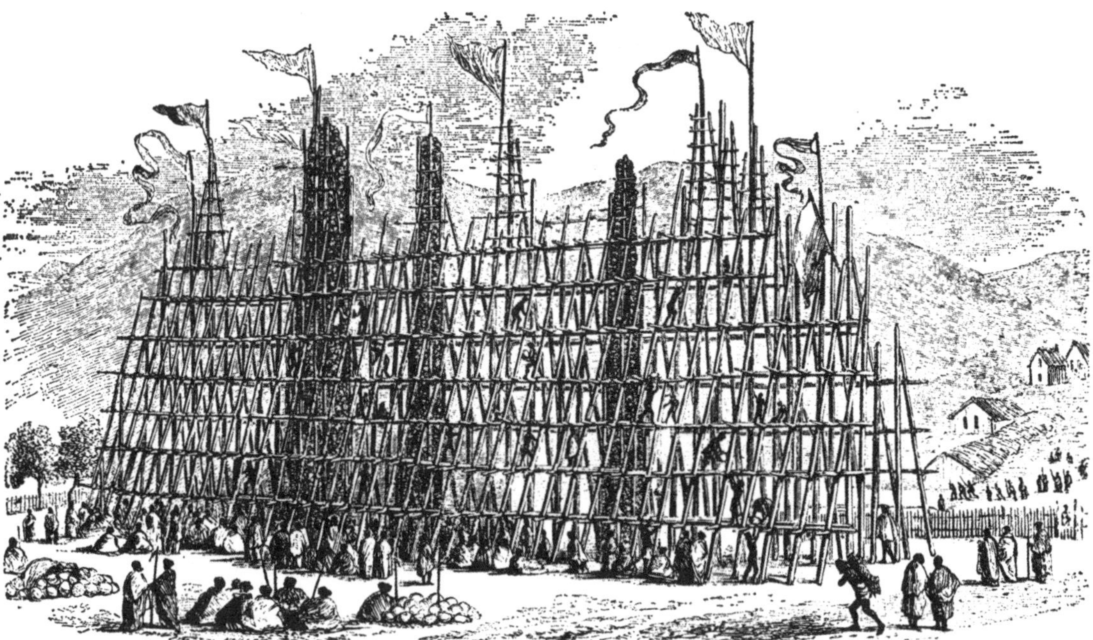

A food stage prepared for a feast. This stage was erected in the Bay of Islands in 1849 to celebrate peace between Māori and Pākehā.

ciated with religious rites and ceremonies, and those arranged for the entertainment of guests. The religious or semi-religious *hākari* were occasions of rejoicing and of games, contests and dancing; they marked the festivals of the year: harvest time, new year and the celebration of peace. On many occasions the hosts of these *hākari* would invite distant relatives and other *hapū*. *Hākari* were the time for political and important tribal matters to be discussed, as well as playing games, sports and general celebration. Almost all of the important stages of life were marked by *hākari*– baptism, betrothal, marriage and death ceremonies.

Much labour was expended in preparations for the *hākari*, often started as much as a year in advance. Additional ground was broken in for *kūmara* cultivation, and huge quantities of fish, birds, eels, and other delicacies were gathered together and stored or preserved. When the time for the *hākari* grew near, messengers were sent out to deliver the invitations with appropriate ceremony. The food, prepared by women and slaves, was then piled up in long stacks, more than a metre in height and often hundreds of metres in length, while precious gifts such as cloaks and weapons were added to the heaps. In the northern parts of the country the food was placed on many- tiered, tall stages. When the guests arrived they were greeted in the traditional manner with the waving of garments and branches, and cries and songs of welcome. There were many speeches and gifts were exchanged.

A *noa* (*tapu*-lifting) ceremony was usually performed by the *tohunga* accompanying the visitors. He repeated *karakia* over the food to remove any dangerous *tapu* that might be lingering there.

An important part of the ceremony was the distribution of the food and other gifts to the guests, *whānau* and *hapū*. A senior person would oversee the distribution, solemnly calling out the name of each group in turn to come forward and collect their share. The generosity of the hosts in this way was a public display of the *mana* of their own *whānau* or *hapū* and put an obligation on the guests to return the display of generosity, or better it, at some time in the future.

Meetings, peace, presents, stages, visitors.

FEATHERS (*rau manu*). A number of different kinds of feathers were prized as ornaments and personal decorations. Long, floating plumes of feathers were attached to the stern carvings of large canoes and the stands made for storage *hue*, calabashes, were often ornamented with feathers; but they were employed principally for personal ornaments. They were used to adorn the hair, the most prized variety being the tail feathers of the *huia*, which were black with a band of pure white at the tip. Albatross, long-tailed cuckoo and *kōtuku*, white heron, feathers were also prized.

Bunches of *toroa*, albatross, down were used to decorate canoe lashings. For personal adornment, down was often placed in the ears, while on Rēkohu, the Chatham Islands, men entwined the down with their beards. Young women sometimes wore necklaces of downy feathers. Men were known to thread long feathers through the septum of the nose or wore them – pointing forward – in the hair.

Feather cloaks were valued heirlooms, for much labour was expended on them, each feather being attached separately to the foundation of woven flax fibre. *Waka huia*, richly carved wooden boxes, were used for holding feathers – an indication of the degree to which the feathers were prized.

Birds (hunting), boxes, burial, cloaks, fishhooks, hair, huia, ornaments, tewhatewha.

FEMALE ELEMENT (*uha*). In the beginning of time the children of Rangi and Papa were all immortal and of the male sex. It was their desire to populate the world with human beings, but before the *ira tangata* (human life) could come into being it was necessary to find the female element as a prelude to propagation. The gods began their long search and, led by Tāne, they mated with various beings or personifications without success, giving rise to the defeatist saying: 'Unseen, unsuitable, unacquired.' As a result of these experiments, many personifications were created, all of whom had an important part to play in the ordering of natural phenomena, but the *uha* constantly eluded them.

Finally Tāne went to the *puke* (mons veneris) of his mother Papa, and taking some of the earth, he moulded it to the shape of the human form and endowed it with human life. The woman so formed, who was the mother of mankind, was named Hine-ahu-one.

The *uha* of the *ira tangata* was of enormous importance to the preservation of the human race. It was destructive of *tapu* (which of course was a property of the *ira atua*), and explains why women were employed to lift the *tapu* from new houses and canoes, and on other important occasions. Similarly, the presence of a woman at many sacred tasks would destroy *tapu* with disastrous results.

At times a form of listlessness or nervousness would overtake warriors. If a woman was available, the warrior would lie down and the woman would step over him, so that he 'passed below her thighs', and was cured of his complaint, which was driven away by the malign force that emanated from woman. The effect of the female element on *tapu* no doubt explains the parallel belief in its destructive power.

Earth, eggs, Hine-ahu-one, ira tangata.

FENCES. In the absence of wild animals, fences round cultivations were needed only as windbreaks, and in some places to keep out *pūkeko*, swamp hens. The substantial stockades erected round fighting *pā* are described under Palisades.

Cultivations, pā, palisades.

FERN ROOT (*aruhe*). Fern root, as the rhizome of the bracken fern is popularly called, was the staple article of diet – 'the staple which can never fail.' It was tasteless, and required much preparation, but it had the outstanding advantage of being found everywhere, and available at all times of the year. It was so important as a vegetable food that it had its own god, Haumia, who was supposed to be its origin and personification. Haumia-tiketike was the *atua* who presided over all uncultivated or wild food plants.

Some varieties of fern root were more suitable

A toki poutangata or large greenstone adze used as a weapon (see page 7), from the Ngāti Maru tribe. Auckland War Memorial Museum

A tatā or canoe bailer with a carved, decorative handle (see page 15). Te Papa, Wellington, New Zealand [B.018422]

The handle of a *toki poutangata* or adze (see page 7). The phallic-like protrusion is the handle, and the blade would have been lashed at a right angle to the handle, with the carved figure sitting at the back of the blade. *Te Papa, Wellington, New Zealand [F.003150/41]*

A calabash made from a hue or gourd was an essential storage vessel for everyday life (see page 27). Te Papa, Wellington, New Zealand [B.018129]

The *kākāpō*, the largest ground parrot in the world. Now extremely rare, it once had an enormous range and provided food for travellers in what was sometimes inhospitable country (see page 22). *Te Papa, Wellington, New Zealand [B.019734]*

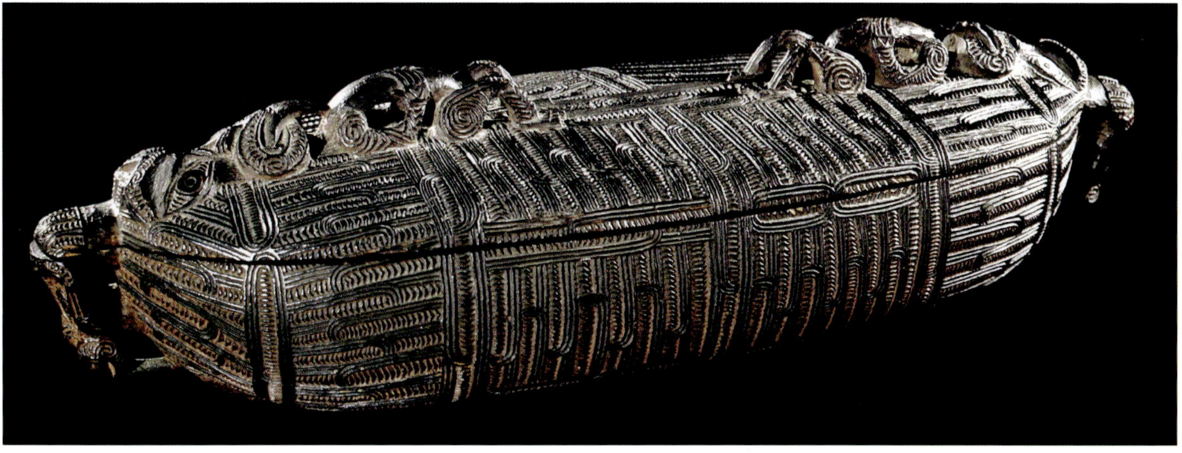

A *waka huia* or carved storage box which often contained the valuable tail feathers of the *huia* bird. They were an important decorative item for chiefs and others of high rank (see page 24). *Te Papa, Wellington, New Zealand [F.002929/10]*

A *mutu kākā* or carved perch for snaring *kākā* (parrots). The calls of a decoy *kākā* would attract other birds (see page 21). *Auckland War Memorial Museum*

A *pātua* or basket made of bark (see page 17), from Wanganui. *Auckland War Memorial Museum*

A *tauihu* or figurehead of a canoe (see page 29) in the south Taranaki style of carving. *Auckland War Memorial Museum*

A *kumete* or wooden food bowl (see page 24) from Ohura. *Auckland War Memorial Museum*

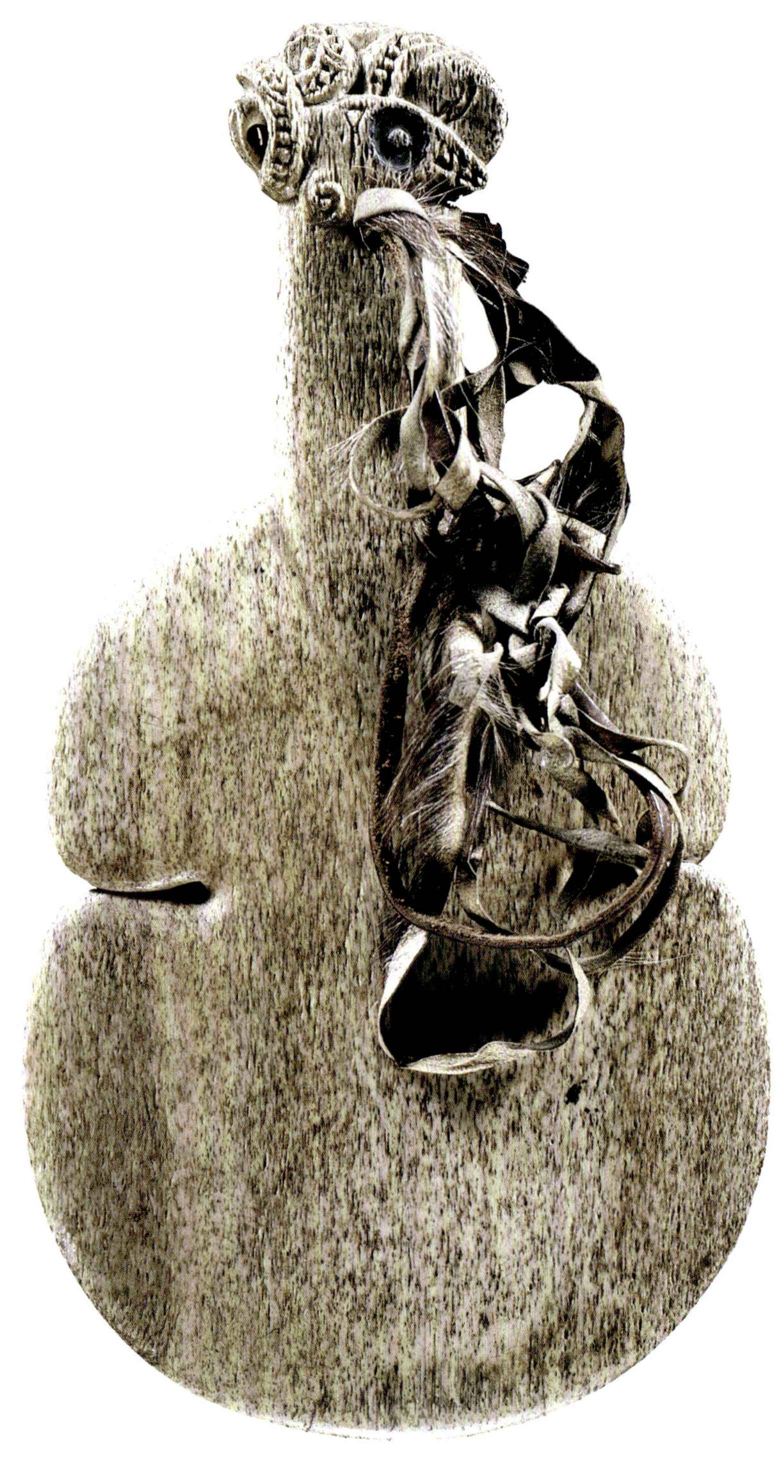

A *kotiate parāoa* or whalebone club. The notches on the sides were intended to break the skin of a victim when striking him (see page 42). *Te Papa, Wellington, New Zealand [B.024913]*

A *tahā* or calabash (see page 27) for holding preserved birds, from Lake Rotorua. *Auckland War Memorial Museum*

A model *waka taua* or war canoe. The equivalent of a Maori war machine, a *waka taua* could be as long as 25 metres and carry over 100 men (see page 28). *Auckland War Memorial Museum*

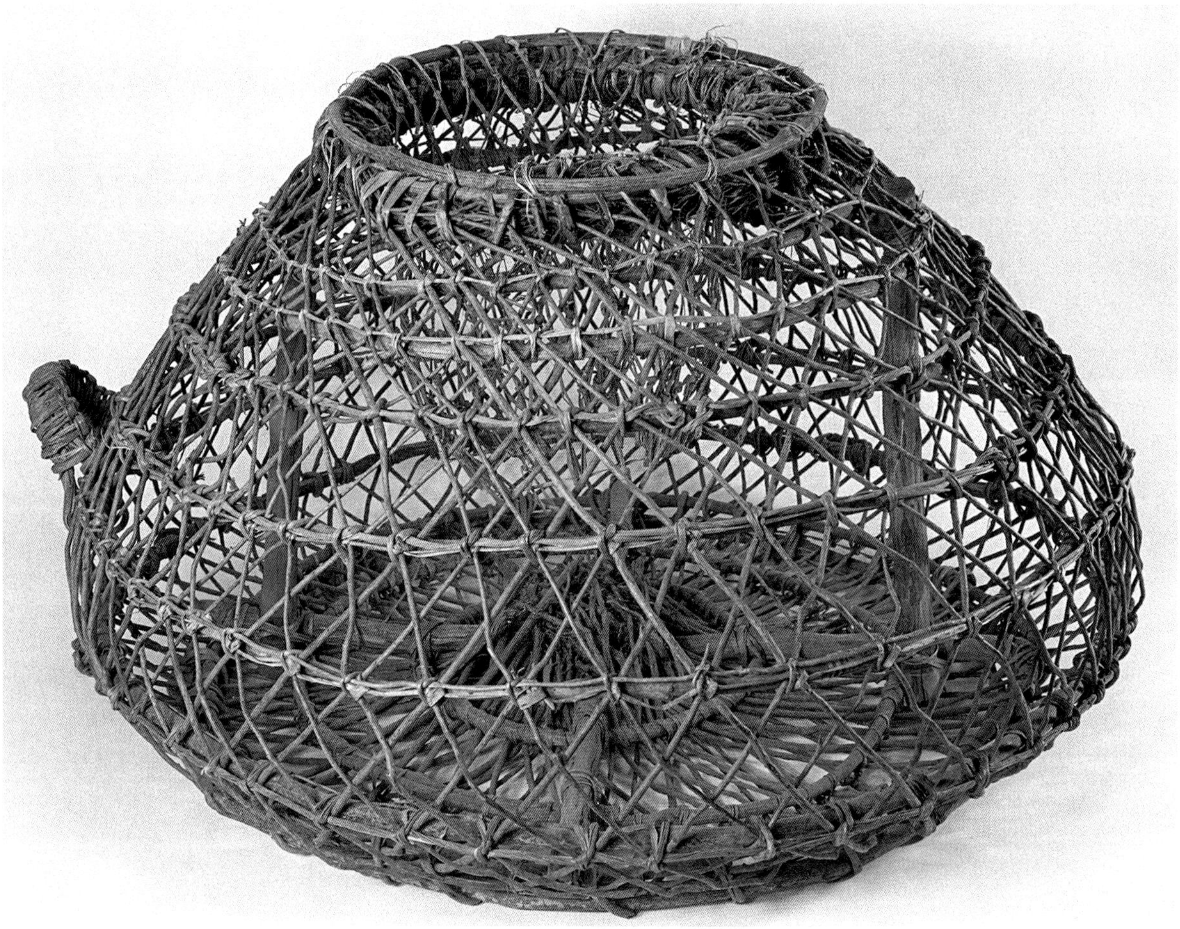

A *täruke köura* or crayfish pot (see page 45), made of *mānuka* and supplejack, from the Thames area. *Auckland War Memorial Museum*

A *patu whakairo*, or carver's mallet (see page 38), made of whalebone from Ōhinemutu, Rotorua. *Auckland War Memorial Museum*

A *heru* or comb, made from whalebone. Combs were used by men to hold their hair in place after it had been oiled and dressed (see page 43). *Te Papa, Wellington, New Zealand [I.002517]*

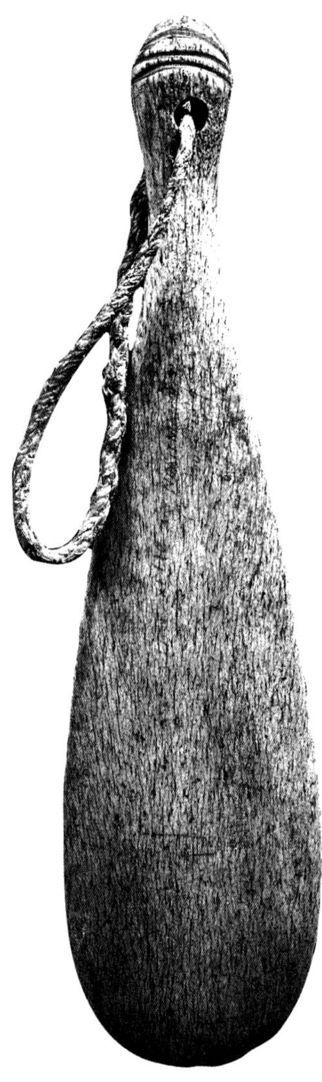

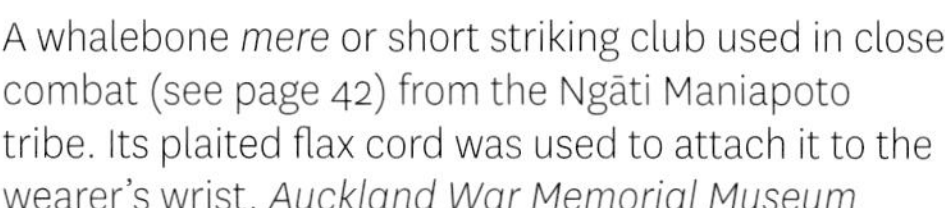

A whalebone *mere* or short striking club used in close combat (see page 42) from the Ngāti Maniapoto tribe. Its plaited flax cord was used to attach it to the wearer's wrist. *Auckland War Memorial Museum*

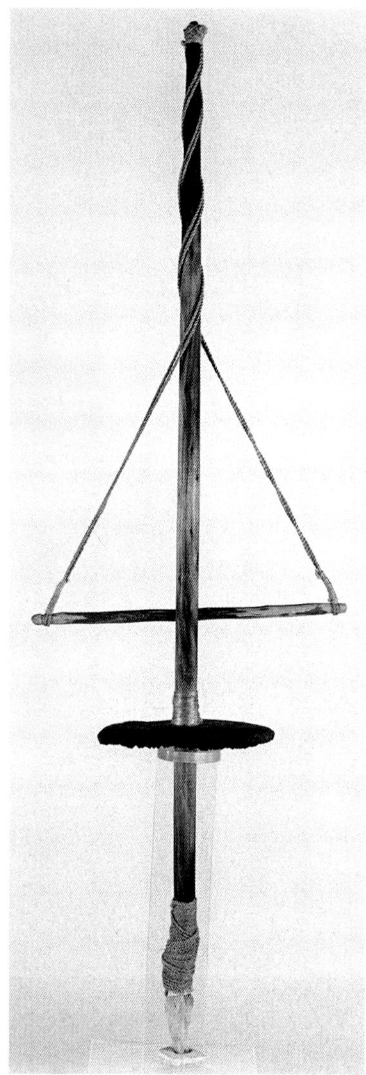

A *porotiti* or reproduction pump drill (see page 55): the stone flake at the bottom end is used for drilling, with a wheel made of whale vertebrae. *Auckland War Memorial Museum*

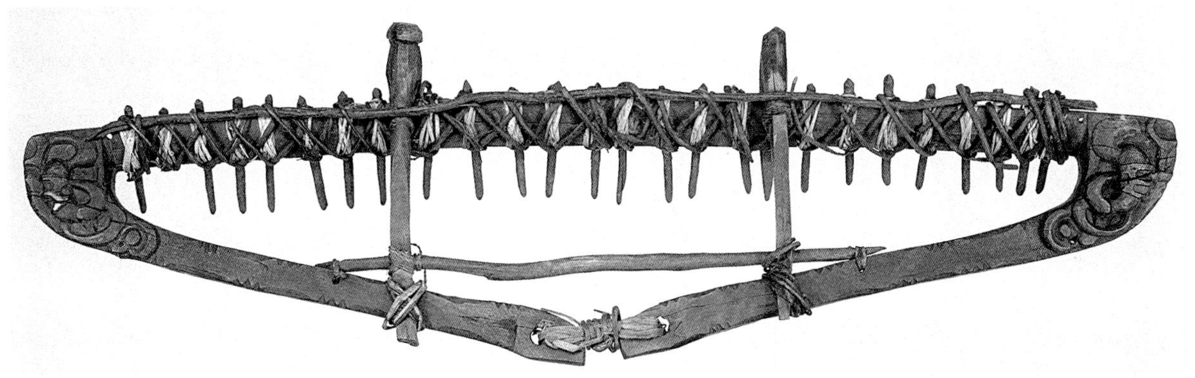

A *rou kākahi* or dredge for obtaining shellfish (see page 54), from Lake Rotoiti. *Auckland War Memorial Museum*

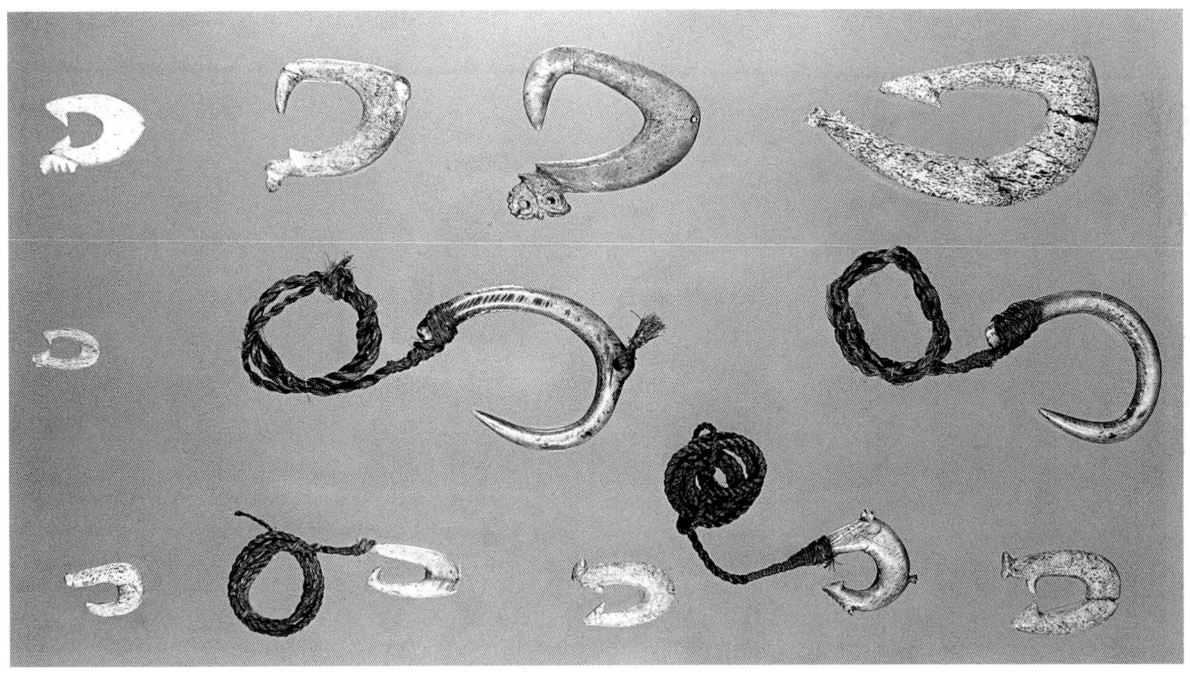

Matau, or fish-hooks made of bone, wood, shell or stone, were used with fish or shellfish as bait, and with feathers or slivers of *pāua* shell as lures. Most were barbed (see page 68). *Auckland War Memorial Museum*

The *nguru* or nose flute was an instrument peculiar to Māori. It was played by being held to a nostril and blowing gently into one of the holes (see page 70). *Te Papa, Wellington, New Zealand [B.017937]*

Kōauau or flutes (see page 70): those on the outside are made of wood, the two in the middle from bone, the left one being from an albatross. *Auckland War Memorial Museum*

A greenstone *heitiki* (see page 83). This one is said to have been taken to England by one of the officers on board Captain Cook's Endeavour. *Auckland War Memorial Museum*

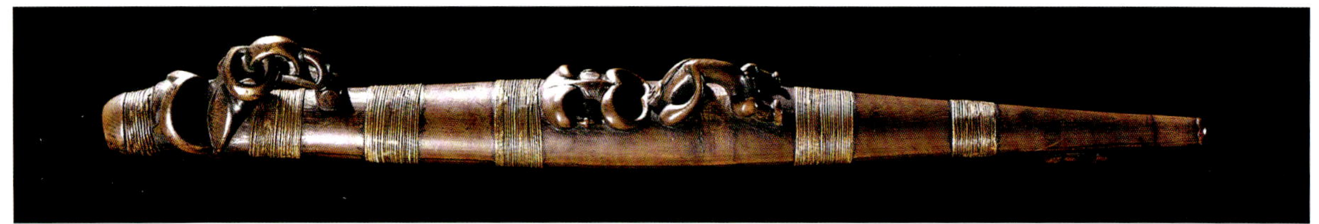

The *pūtōrino* flute was played like a piccolo (see page 70). This fine example is carved and carefully lashed. *Te Papa, Wellington, New Zealand [B.024928]*

The *huia* was caught by hunters who imitated its cry and snared it when it came close by means of a running noose on the end of a stick. Its distinctive tail feathers were much prized as head ornaments for chiefs (see page 90). It is now extinct. *Te Papa, Wellington, New Zealand [B.036764]*

A *tima mangaiti* or wooden instrument used for grubbing the soil (see page 91). *Auckland War Memorial Museum*

A *karetao* or jumping jack with a finely carved face. Strings were used to activate the arms of the toy (see page 95). *Te Papa, Wellington, New Zealand [I.004321]*

than others for human consumption. The roots were dug with pointed sticks and dried on an elevated stage, after which they were stored for future use, suspended in bundles from the roof of the storehouse. The cooking process was a lengthy one. The roots were roasted, the hard exterior scraped off, and the inner part pounded with a stone *patu aruhe*. If the root was eaten at this stage, the stringy fibres had to be spat out as the root was chewed. Alternatively, the fibres were picked out, a tedious process, and the roots pounded and roasted again. Before the second roasting they were sometimes rolled into cakes and soaked in tutu juice, and thus became a delicacy. Alternatively, the roots were squeezed with the hands in a wooden bowl of water to extract the starch, which was made into cakes and cooked. The coarse nature of *aruhe* was a heavy contributor to the rapid decay in Māori teeth.

Haumia-tiketike.

FERTILITY. All the operations of nature were dependent on the principle of fertility. The essence of procreation and fertility in the universe was represented by the god Tāne with many legends being woven round this important conception.

Creation, Tāne, Tiki.

FIGHTING, see WARFARE.

FIRE (*ahi*). When Papa was overturned the gods were sorry for their youngest brother, Rūaumoko, who was still unborn. For his comfort they gifted him with *ahi tipua* (sacred or volcanic fire – it was also the name for lightning) and this was the origin of fire.

It was the demi-god Māui who sought the source of fire and tamed it so that man could acquire it whenever he wished. He put out the village fires and asked his mother where he could obtain more. She directed him to his grandmother Mahuika in the underworld. She was the goddess of fire, and the sister of the goddess of volcanic fire. One by one she gave Māui her fingernails

In legend, Mahuika gave fire, which was stored in her fingernails, to her grandson Māui.

and toenails, each containing the seed of fire, but Māui extinguished them one by one, and returned for more. When she was reduced to her last nail, Mahuika was exasperated and threw it at him. It fell to the ground and burst into a raging fire, before which Māui was forced to fly for his life.

He underwent several transformations during his desperate flight, first into a bird and then a fish, but the fire was overtaking him and threatened to engulf the whole world. Māui called for help from the personifications of rain and hail. In the deluge that ensued the fire was practically extinguished, and Mahuika feared for her life. As a last effort she threw the remaining seeds of fire into several trees, the most important being the *kaikōmako*, the wood of which became the most suitable for fire-making by friction.

There are many myths of early, strange people who ate their food raw, indicating that at one time the art of fire-making and its use in cooking was not known. For Māori, fire was an essential element of life. Fires gave light and heat, cooked food and played an important role in the ceremonial life of the people.

Sacred fires were used in religious rites and ceremonies, and there were names for different types connected with warfare, tree felling, houses, hunting, food gathering, and funeral ceremonies. The *ahi manawa,* for instance, was the fire in which the heart of the first enemy killed in battle was roasted. Travellers who carried food cooked by means of an *ahi tapu* were protected from evil influences, and this is probably the only occasion on which sacred fires were in any way associated with cooked food. Another use of sacred fire was to ward off evils such as sickness, frost, and malignant spirits. In fact the *ahi taitai* was a ceremonial fire that could preserve the welfare and life principle of a whole tribe.

It is said that there were occasional cases of fire walking, which were probably linked to ceremonies to ward off evil.

Ahi kā, long-burning fires, was a term used to denote continuous occupation of land by a particular *whānau* or *hapū,* while a *whānau* that had died out was termed *ahi mate* (fire that has died).

Darts, earthquakes, fire-making, fireplaces, land, magic, Papa, thermal regions, travellers, trees.

FIRE-MAKING. The act of generating fire was known as *hika ahi.* A suitable stick was rubbed vigorously in a groove on a flat piece of wood, the pointed rubbing stick was called the *hika* or *kaurimarima*, while the flat board was known as the *kaunoti.*

The flat piece was usually held steady by one person, often by simply placing their foot on the board, while another – most often a man – operated the *hika.* It was a strenuous task that continued until wood dust had accumulated at the end of the groove. After a short break the work was resumed until the wood dust began to smoke and smoulder, and finally came alive. The burning dust was emptied on to a small heap of combustible material such as dried leaves, which were waved in the air or blown upon until a flame appeared and the fire could be lit.

A *wāhine* holds the flat board firmly with her foot while the man rubs a stick in the groove to kindle a fire.

Comets, fire.

FIREPLACES. In a large house one or more fireplaces, consisting of small pits lined with stones, were sunk in the central passage, and wood or charcoal was burned in them for warmth. While the smoke sometimes escaped through a vent in the roof, the air soon became smoke-laden and foul. Asphyxiation by charcoal fumes occurred often and these people were thought to have been victims of malignant *patupaiarehe.*

Small fireplaces were sometimes built on platforms in canoes.

Fire, houses, smoke.

FISH (*ika*). The god and personification of fish was Tangaroa, one of the departmental *atua.*

In the Māori creation stories fish varied in size but not in shape, until a woman asked Tangaroa to help her to find her missing husband. The quest ended in a battle with mankind. It was fought on land and the tide of war was running against the fish until the whales came ashore

In the legend of the battle of the fishes, these were sent by Tangaroa to attack a fortified village but failed until the palisades were broken down by the whales.

to help by destroying the palisades of the *pā* in which men were sheltering. As a reward for their bravery Tangaroa bestowed gifts on his followers, and an entertaining legend tells how these gifts were used to change their colours and shapes.

The sea, lakes and rivers teemed with fish, which were a most valuable part of the Māori diet. A list of the more common names, Māori and Pākehā, follows. Where no corresponding English name is given, the fish is known to the Pākehā by its Māori name.

āhuruhuru:	red mullet
araara:	trevally
aua:	yellow eye mullet, or sprat
haku:	yellowtail, or northern kingfish
hāpuku:	groper
hiku:	frostfish
hiwihiwi:	kelpfish
hoka, or *hokarari*:	ling
hui:	blue *maomao*
īnanga:	whitebait
kahawai:	kahawai
kanae:	mullet
kehe:	marblefish
koarea:	red snapper
kōheru:	horse mackerel
kohikohi:	trumpeter
koinga:	southern dogfish
kōiro:	conger eel
kōkiri:	rough leatherjacket
kōkopu:	*kōkopu*
kōpūtōtara:	porcupine fish
korokoropounamu:	bluefish
korowhāwhā:	anchovy
kōura:	crayfish
kumukumu:	red gurnard
kupae:	sprat
kuparu:	John dory
makō:	shark
manaia:	seahorse
mangā:	barracouta
mangō:	shark
maomao:	blue *maomao*
mararī:	butterfish
maroro:	flying fish
mata:	pink *maomao*, or longfin
matiri:	griffin's silverfish
matua-whāpuku:	red scorpion fish
moeone:	bass
mohimohi:	pilchard
moki:	*moki*
nanua:	red *moki*
napia:	hagfish
ngākoikoi:	kelpfish
ngōiro:	conger eel
oia:	butterfly perch
okeoke:	northern dogfish
oru:	stingray
paea:	broadbill swordfish
pahuiakaroa:	sea perch
pākaurua:	stingray
paketi:	spotty
pākirikiri:	spotty, or blue cod
pākurakura:	red pigfish

pāra:	frostfish
parāoa:	whale
parore:	*parore*
pātiki:	flounder
pātutuki:	blue cod
pau:	soldier or scarlet parrotfish
piharau:	lamprey
pioke:	northern dogfish
pōrae:	*pōrae*
pūharakeke:	yellow eel
puramorua:	pigfish
pūwaiwhakarua:	soldier or scarlet parrotfish
rarī:	butterfish
rāwaru:	blue cod
reperepe:	elephant fish
roha:	stingray
taharangi:	frostfish
taiwharu:	gudgeon
takeke:	garfish
tāmure:	snapper
tarakihi:	*tarakihi*
taumaka:	rockfish
tawatawa:	mackerel
tīkati:	southern kingfish
tohorā:	whale
tōiki:	tiger shark
toti:	bass
upokororo:	grayling
warehou:	*warehou* or trevally
whai:	stingray
whāpuku:	*hāpuku* or groper
wheke:	octopus

Cooking, fishing, mauri, reptiles, shellfish, Tinirau, Tutunui.

FISH-HOOKS (*matau*). A great deal of skill was shown in the manufacture of fish-hooks, which were made of bone, wood, shell, and stone. They were used with fish or shellfish for bait, and with feathers or slivers of *pāua* shell as lures.

Some were made without barbs, but the majority were barbed. The barbs were an integral part of the hook, or were lashed in position, frequently with the barb on the inside. The invention of the barb was ascribed to Māui, whose notable fish-hook, made from the jawbone of his grandfather, was used to bring Te Ika a Māui, (The fish of Māui) the North Island of Aotearoa, to the surface of the ocean.

Large wooden hooks, at times inset with dogs' teeth, were used to catch sharks. Wooden lures were also used to catch fish such as barracouta, kingfish, and *kahawai*. The shanks were lined with *pāua* shell and towed behind the canoe, or were tied to the end of a cord and thrashed to and fro in the water. The fishing line was called an *aho*.

The point of the hook was set close to the shank, making it harder for fish to escape once they were caught. In this way several hooks could be tied to the line, or to a wooden spreader, without the need to take the line in when a single fish was caught.

Hooks were made in one piece, or with two pieces lashed together. Gum or resin was spread over the lashing of the hook to hold the separate pieces firmly in place. Stone, greenstone and bone points were often used, the latter frequently being made of human bone. Wooden hooks were sometimes made by bending growing twigs to the required shape. Bone and stone hooks were first shaped by boring holes through the material, outlining the hook shape. The hook was then finished by rasping and scraping it smooth.

A variety of fish-hooks of shell, bone, and wood.

In addition to hooks, gouges were also used. These slivers of bone, pointed at both ends and attached to a cord at the centre, were buried in the bait and swallowed whole. When the line was pulled the gouge swung sideways and prevented the fish from escaping.

Fishing.

FISHING. Fish were caught by all the conventional methods – by nets, fish-hooks and lines, spears, dredges and rakes, and baskets or pots. Fishing was an important industry that could be carried out in all parts of the country. It was a *tapu* occupation, and food could not be eaten while fishing was in progress, nor during the manufacture of nets, hooks, and other apparatus.

Mauri were used to ensure that the supplies of fish were adequate, and sometimes even appear to have been substituted for bait in attracting fish. Fishing was a skilled occupation where certain days and nights – often related to phases of the moon and tide conditions – were regarded as more propitious than others. The boundaries of fishing grounds in lakes and rivers and at sea were carefully defined by reference to prominent features of the landscape, and by rows of stakes and posts. Infringement of fishing rights was often a prime cause of war.

Māui and his brothers draw up the huge fish of the North Island from the bed of the sea.

Taking fish by net was a co-operative undertaking, often conducted on a large scale. According to legend the use of nets for fishing was a comparatively late discovery and a brief account of the legend is found under the heading Nets.

Fish traps included eel pots, and others for taking whitebait, lampreys, grayling, and a few other fish, which entered the mouth of the trap and were unable to escape. The traps were beautiful examples of native craftsmanship. Their efficiency was increased by the repetition of appropriate charms over them.

Flounders and eels were taken by spears consisting of a number of hardwood prongs lashed to a short handle.

Hooks and lines were used freely, with the three main methods of fishing being by line, line and pole, and trolling. The first fish caught with a new hook or line was dedicated to the male and female ancestors of the fisherman. Sea fishing was carried on from the shore, or from canoes. The best fishing grounds were well known and the canoes that fished them were often equipped with wells to hold the catch. Canoe fishing crews were composed solely of men, but women had the task of carrying the fish from the canoes to the ovens or drying stages.

Crayfish, eels, fish, fish-hooks, mauri, nets, spears, whitebait, women.

FISHING NETS, see NETS.

FLAX (*harakeke*). The so-called New Zealand flax (*Phormium tenax*) was a plant with a thousand uses. It provided fibre for cordage, which was used for making garments, mats, fishing lines, and ropes, and used extensively in plaiting and weaving.

The green leaves were used for weaving flax baskets, and such varied articles as temporary eel pots, trumpets, and nets.

Flax fibre was made by firstly soaking the leaves in water. The leaves were then treated by scraping and drying. If a soft fibre, muka, was required, it was made by pounding the leaves with wooden beaters.

The *kōrari* or flax stalk is very light, and was used for making darts for children to play with or tied together in bundles to make mōkihi or rafts or miniature canoes.

Baskets, cloaks, darts, dyes, mats, plaiting, rafts, sails, weaving.

FLEET, THE. This is the name often given to the now discounted theory of a Great Migration of ancestral canoes that travelled together, bringing Māori to Aotearoa in about the 14th century a.d.

Migration (Great).

FLOWERS.

Ornaments.

FLUTES (*pūtōrino, kōauau, nguru, etc.*). Many fine examples of these instruments have been preserved. The *pūtōrino* has been described as an instrument like a piccolo, or an alto bugle flute. It was a slender, cylindrical, wooden instrument up to about 50 centimetres in length, with a single hole. The body was usually swelled at the centre, but some *pūtōrino* were double, separated in the middle, and joined at the ends, bound neatly together, and usually elaborately carved. The tune was sung or breathed into the instrument. It was also believed to be a medium of communication between men and atua, gods.

The *kōauau*, described as a flute, had several holes, but was a shorter instrument usually made of wood or bone. The thighbones of relatives and enemies were sometimes used in the making of *kōauau*. They were usually richly carved and were played by blowing with the mouth or nostril.

The small end of the rather dumpy instrument termed nguru (which can only be described as a nose piece) was played by placing it to one nostril, the other being closed by the player's thumb, and blowing. The *nguru* was made of wood, stone, or bone.

Early Pākehā visitors to Aotearoa were divided in their opinion as to whether these instruments were melodious or not.

Fairies, musical instruments.

FOLKLORE. The fertile field of Polynesian myth and legend was enriched by the imagination of the people. The stories — referred to as pakiwaitara — might have been told by the fireside in the meetinghouse, or on the marae, were also told on islands all around the Pacific but were changed and added to so that they had a local flavour. Many of these tales evolved in the new land.

The stories of creation portrayed a pantheon of gods while the overworlds and underworlds were peopled with spirits, personifications, guardians, gods and the souls of men and women.

Māui, the mischievous demi-god of Polynesia, was present in Aotearoa, while the Tawhaki cycle provided hero stories of men and gods; every tribe had its own *atua*; the forests were peopled with fairies and ogres; enchanted logs and trees were to be found in bush and lake; there were giants, giant birds, and flying men; stories of monstrous creatures called taniwha were told in every part of the land; there were homely but supernatural tales of birds, beasts, fish, insects, of sun, moon, stars, winds, and clouds, strange, eerie stories of magic and enchantment, tender love tales, and stirring accounts of battle, exploration, and discovery.

The deeds of men were also remembered and the legends surrounding the discovery and settlement of Aotearoa and the explorers Kupe, Toi and Whatonga and a host of others were told and retold.

Creation, fables, fairies, giants, gods, kōrero, magic, Māui, personifications, spirits, taniwha, Tawhaki, tipua.

FOOD (*kai*). Maintaining food supplies was the biggest problem for traditional Māori communities and this ceaseless task took up most of their time. The difficulties started from the very beginning of their arrival in Aotearoa, because the new land had a climate that was entirely different from the island homelands. There, food culti vation and growing had been relatively easy but this was not the case in Aotearoa. Much time and energy was spent in cultivating, hunting and fishing, and in the subsequent preparation of food.

Of the imported foods, only the *kūmara* had a wide area of cultivation, and even with this important vegetable there were many areas where it could not be grown. The yam and *taro* were even more restricted. Favoured crop-growing districts such as Tāmaki Makaurau (the Auckland isthmus) supported a large population, and areas where fish and bird life were plentiful were widely renowned and much sought after.

But in many districts food supplies were limited and lacking in variety. The majority of un-cultivated vegetable foods, for example, were probably tolerated only through necessity. As a result, the occasional feasts were memorable functions in which the participants displayed an enormous capacity to eat.

Most forest birds were eaten and seabirds such as *tītī*, muttonbirds, *toroa*, albatross and *kūaka*, godwits. Moa and their eggs were also taken.

All of the mammals, *kekeno*, seals, *kurī*, domesticated dog, *kiore*, rats and *pekapeka*, bats, were eaten but were seldom available in quantity. Human flesh was also esteemed, but was not a regular article of diet. The flesh of stranded whales was eaten and in the southern districts even the *tuatara* lizard was eaten.

Fish, both salt and freshwater, were taken along with huge quantities of shellfish of all kinds.

In addition to the cultivated *kūmara*, yam, and *taro*, young *hue* or gourds were also eaten. Plant foods gathered from the wild included the aruhe or fern root, the roots, pith, and shoots of *tī kouka*, cabbage trees, young fern fronds known as pikopiko and the roots of some other tree ferns, *shoots* of the *nīkau* palm, several kinds of leaves and the roots of the *raupō* or bullrush were all gathered and eaten. *Karengo*, a seaweed, also served as a 'vegetable'.

Berries of the *hīnau*, *karaka*, supplejack, *matai*, *kahikatea*, *tutu*, *kōtukutuku*, *poroporo*, *tītoki*, and the pollen of the *raupō* were all gathered and eaten. An especial favourite were the flower bracts and fruit of the *kiekie*. Several kinds of fungi were eaten raw.

Some grubs and insects were added to the Māori diet, including worms and the fat grubs of the *huhu* beetle.

Baskets, bats, birds, cannibalism, cooking, crayfish, dogs, drink, dying speeches, earthworms, eels, fairies, feasts, fire, fish, forest, gods (wars of), hīnau, huhu, karaka, kümara, magic, meals, ovens, pā, presents, preservation (food), rats, storehouses, tapu, taro, travellers, tutu, underworlds, whales, yams.

Typical foods: *taro*, birds, gourds, *kūmara*, and berries.

FOREST (*ngahere*). Te Wao Tapu Nui a Tāne (The great sacred forest of Tāne). The forest and its resources were central to Māori life in the physical and spiritual sense. Māori regarded the forest as protector and the source of food. They knew every stone, creek, hill and tree intimately for those reasons.

The forest also had a spiritual role because its creator, Tāne, also had a hand in the creation of mankind. Therefore, Tāne was the mystical link between the forest and mankind. It was Tāne himself who had provided the trees to clothe Papa, the Earth Mother. It was believed that the forest was peopled with personifications of trees, rocks, and streams, and that it was also the home of the *patupaiarehe*, fairies, usually hostile to man.

As well, it was filled by the multitudes of Hakuturi – birds, insects, and supernatural creatures. When a tree was felled and taken, Tāne and all the forest creatures had to be placated by appropriate rituals.

The forest was protected by *tapu* before the bird-hunting season began, and no cooked foods could be taken into it. This was so that the *hau*, or life essence, of the forest would not be polluted.

Fairies, hau, mauri, Rātā, Tāne, trees.

FORT, see PĀ.

FROST. Frost could damage growing crops. In some districts a ceremony that attempted to dispel frost involved the use of a burning log that was taken to the *turuma*, communal latrine, where it was waved in the air and appropriate *karakia* recited.

FRUIT.

Food.

FUNGUS.

Food, poisons.

G

GAMES. Any large meeting house used for playing games or other forms of entertainment was known figuratively as the whare tapere. Adults as well as children played games, and participation in sport had a special place in festivals and community gatherings. The games of skill by which young Māori youths developed strength and good hand and eye co-ordination were valuable because they gave the young men an early introduction to the fighting skills they would need in later life. Young women gained grace, and their limbs became supple through practising the dances and games particular to them.

Equipment used by Māori children demonstrates the universal nature of stilts, kites, spinning tops and other toys. Much of the enjoyment came from the pride in the craftsmanship used in the making of these toys. The games that were played with them were an important feature of Māori life and custom.

The outdoor games included playing on the *moari*, the giant-stride or roundabout, riding sledges, running, walking on stilts, canoe racing, swimming, kite flying, darts, wrestling, tree climbing, and water games of all kinds.

Amongst the games of skill that encouraged mental and manual dexterity were stick games, string games, top-spinning, hand games of many kinds, breath-holding games, and a primitive form of draughts or checkers called *mu*.

Boys, breath, canoe racing, cat's cradle, climbing, darts, draughts, hand games, hoops, jumping jack, kites, puzzles, riddles, running, sledges, spears, stilts, swimming, swings, tops, toys, water games, wrestling.

GARMENTS. There is no general term for clothing, though the word kākahu is sometimes used with this meaning. Coming from a warmer climate

Women wearing a variety of cloaks, capes and aprons.

where the light *aute*, paper-mulberry bark cloth, was sufficient for all their needs, Māori required more substantial garments and were fortunate to find the *harakeke*, flax, growing so freely in Aotearoa. *Harakeke* was the source of fibre from which almost all Māori clothes were made.

Garments were used for warmth, and protection against wind and rain. There were only two principal garments, the *korowai*, cloak, that covered the shoulders and the *maro*, kilt, worn around the waist. Ordinary *korowai* were roughly and strongly made while ceremonial cloaks were elaborate, with woven borders and richly decorated with feathers and tufts of dogs' hair. They varied in size from small capes to large mantles that covered the whole body. Often the *korowai* was discarded and merely the *maro* worn. Women always wore some covering around the waist but men often went naked except for a waist belt used as a carrying pouch.

Belts, cloaks, kilts, sandals, weaving.

GATEWAYS (*kūwaha, waha ngutu, waharoa*). The entrance to a *pā* was usually narrow, sometimes being so small that anyone entering it had to stoop. The requirement to stoop made anyone entering vulnerable to attack and was but one of the many defensive measures used to help guard the *pā*. The entranceway was also an opportunity for the people of the *pā* to make a statement about their prestige, with the structure frequently towering high above the stockade, the upper part being ornamented by a flat slab of elaborately carved timber.

GENEALOGIES (*whakapapa*). Māori attached much importance to heredity and lines of descent and had a remarkable memory for them. *Whakapapa* tables could be divided into three main types. Firstly there was the immediate line of descent from the eponymous ancestor of a tribe. That line of descent might cover 30 generations. Secondly, Māori preserved a legendary descent from gods though heroes; and lastly a mythical line from the beginning of creation through the personified ages of darkness, to Rangi and Papa and their offspring, the primal gods. It was considered essential to be able to trace descent from those ancestors who came in the migration canoes.

Creation, gestures, marriage, memory, sticks (genealogical).

GESTURES. Māori were fluent speakers who made their words even more descriptive and arresting by natural gestures.

Raising the right arm and closing the fingers, as though the question or statement was being grasped firmly, was a gesture of assent, as was an upward nod of the head. An arm outstretched with the hand open indicated dissent. If the chin were sunk on the breast it was a sign of being defeated in argument or a plea for further time to consider the question.

Friendship and desire to protect were shown by doubling the forefinger of the right hand and placing the second joint on the nose, for this was symbolic of the *hongi*. Shutting the eyes and nodding downwards was a significant gesture with several meanings, most often showing agreement but in some instances, disagreement or concession of a well-made point.

In counting, the fingers were opened out one by one, but in reciting genealogies they were closed successively. Holding the palm of the hand horizontally was an indication of height while holding the palm vertically showed the height of a child.

Signals.

GHOSTS (*kēhua*). Ghosts were never seen in the daytime, but they wandered abroad at night and were very much dreaded. It was fear of *kēhua* that kept Māori indoors at night. Travellers and war parties forced to remain outside during the hours of darkness were terrified lest *kēhua* should appear. They lit large fires and talked loudly to keep that possibility of bay.

A warm current of air was thought to be a certain sign of their presence and they could actually be seen in the darkness.

The *wairua* is the soul that takes possession of man at birth. After death it takes its departure for the spirit world, but there were some that never reached their final destination and remained to plague mankind.

Among some tribes a ceremony called *takahi* or *whaiwhai kēhua* (literally 'ghost-chasing') was held after the funeral, first at the deceased's residence and later at other places closely connected with him, the purpose being to discourage the ghost of the dead person from returning to its earthly abodes. At times there is little distinction to be made between *kēhua* and *tūrehu*.

Kikokiko were malevolent spirits, often of stillborn children, and which took possession of men and women, causing them to become insane or extremely ill. There were certain rituals to 'lay' *kēhua*, but they were always lying in wait for careless or unsuspecting human beings once night fell.

Souls.

Matau, the giant whose body was burnt and sank deep into the ground to form Lake Wakatipu.

GIANTS. There are only a few examples of giants in legends, and even when they appear in some tribal accounts, in others they are reduced to more normal stature. There were certainly a number of men who were said to be nearly 4 metres in height, one being the gigantic Ruaeo who fought with Tama-te-kapua of the Arawa canoe.

In one version of the legend of Rongokako, this powerful man strode across Cook Strait with a whale under his arm, and took giant strides up the east coast of Te Ika a Māui, until he disappeared in the Bay of Plenty.

The principal legends relating to giants seem to have mostly originated in Te Waka a Māui, the South Island.

GIFTS, see PRESENTS.

GIRLS (*hine*). The training of girls was not as extensive as that of boys, reflecting the values of a warrior society. Boys needed to become expert in war and hunting, while girls were prepared for a hard life of domestic drudgery. They lived a comparatively carefree existence when young except that they were required to carry and care for younger brothers and sisters. In fact the short years of childhood and young womanhood were their only time of extended pleasure and enjoyment. After marriage they were destined to have their time fully occupied in rearing babies, cooking and other domestic tasks and in working in the cultivations and food-gathering. They had little leisure time. A list of the skills that a girl was required to learn appears in a *karakia* under the heading Baptism.

Baptism, children, dances, games, tama.

GODS (*atua*). The term *atua* is one that applied to supernatural and immortal beings, but covers a wide variety of conceptions. There were four main types of *atua*:

Io, said to be the supreme God, omnipotent and omniscient, known only to the *tohunga*.

Rangi and Papa, the Sky Father and the Earth Mother, and their offspring:

- Departmental gods who controlled and were responsible for the principal forces of nature.
- The remainder of the 70 children of earth and sky, some of whom were also personifications (see below).
- Personifications: There were thousands of personifications and in this conception the imaginative Māori mind reached its zenith.
- Tribal and war gods.

In addition, demons, evil spirits and even ancestors were frequently known as *atua*. It is questionable whether these beings, which inhabited both living and inanimate objects and caused much suffering and annoyance, should really be termed *atua*, but the term is a flexible one. Examples of their work and activities will be found amongst the many references that follow.

Canoes, creation, female element, genealogies, gods (tribal and war), gods (wars of), Haumia-tiketike, Hina, houses, insects, Io, ira atua, kūmara, mana, mauri, nature, offerings, overworlds, Papa, personifications, poutiriao, primal offspring, Rangi, Rongo, Rūaumoko, spirits, stones (sacred), Tāne, Tangaroa, Tāwhiri-mātea, travellers, Tū-matauenga, Whiro.

GOD STICKS (*niu*). These carved, wooden divining sticks served as dwelling places for the *atua*, who would take infrequent possession of them. They were usually invoked in time of war when they were deposited in the *tūāhu*, or taken with the war party and used to divine the outcome of forthcoming battles.

When used in ritual, they were often bound with flax fibre cord, smeared with *kōkōwai*, and dressed with feathers, after which the *atua* entered into the images. The *niu* were driven like pegs into the soil of the *tūāhu*.

GODS, TRIBAL AND WAR. Tribal *atua* were primarily war gods, although some had more peaceful characteristics being guardians of domestic life and gardening. A few were regarded as more powerful than others and were shared by a number of tribes. Predominant among them were those who had already won a reputation in Hawaiki, and were 'imported' to Aotearoa. Maru, Uenuku, Rongomai, Kahukura, and Aitupawa are examples. Each such *atua* had an *ariā* or manifestation, for example Uenuku was made manifest as the rainbow. Other manifestations of the presence of a particular *atua* were thunder, lightning, meteors, comets, stars and sometimes particular human beings.

Comets, Kahukura, mediums, night, rainbows, warfare.

GODS, WARS OF. The wars fought between the offspring of Rangi and Papa were necessary in order to establish order in the universe. There were three main conflicts:

The first war was when Tāwhiri-mātea, god of the winds, vanquished Tāne and Tangaroa, who represented land and sea, but could not overcome the fierce Tū-matauenga, god of warfare and man. Rongo-maraeroa and Haumia-tiketike, representing wild and cultivated foods, were also involved. They were hidden by Papa, but discovered and eaten by Tū-matauenga. The conflict is a parable of the ceaseless warfare between wind, wave, and shore, and the superiority of man, together with his discovery of wild and cultivated food.

The second war was waged over attempts to secure the baskets of knowledge. Tāne and Whiro were the antagonists. Tāne was devoted to the welfare of mankind while Whiro and his followers embodied evil. The war started after Tāne separated Rangi and Papa and was fuelled by the conflicting loyalties and jealousies amongst their sons. There was a shifting of allegiances because in this campaign Tāwhiri-mātea assisted Tāne in dispelling the evil spirits and insects helping Whiro. The god of evil was eventually driven down to the underworld from where he sends sickness and trouble to mankind.

The third war was waged between Tāne and Rongo-maraeroa, Tū-matauenga, and others. The war is the mythical origin of quarrels, disobedience and strife in the heavens, or 'overworlds'. As a result men are now mostly unable to communicate with the overworlds.

Baskets of knowledge, creation, gods, Tāne, Tangaroa, Tāwhiri-mātea, Whiro.

GONGS (*pahū*). Sentries on duty on watchtowers sounded an alarm by beating a wooden *pahū* with a stick. The *pahū* was usually a slab of wood suspended from two posts, but was sometimes in the form of a *waka*, canoe, or was made with a hole or slot in which the striking stick was rattled. Occasionally hollow trees were used for the same purpose. A *pahū* in the Maungakiekie *pā* on the Tāmaki Isthmus (Auckland) was supposed to have been made of *pounamu*, greenstone.

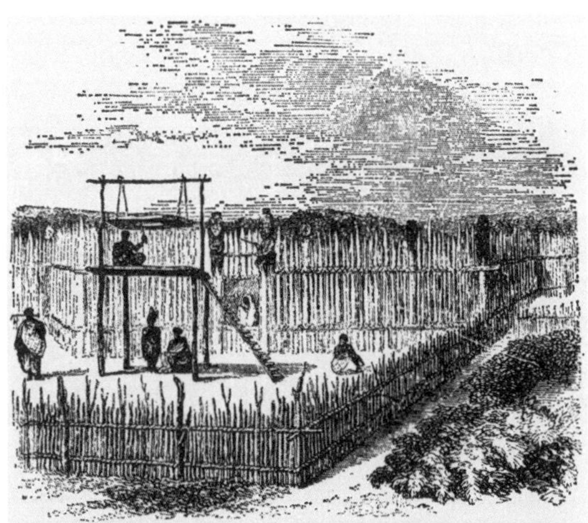

The alarm being sounded by striking the wooden gong in the *pā*.

GOURDS (*hue*). The *hue* plant was introduced from Hawaiki. Although the young plant was occasionally steamed and eaten, it was grown principally for making calabashes, drinking vessels or storage containers from the dried husks of the *hue* fruit. To make a bowl the top of the fruit was cut off and the outer, dried skin then served the purpose. Drinking vessels were made by boring a hole in the top of the gourd and the inside pith removed by shaking stones and gravel inside. Such vessels were frequently fitted with wooden mouthpieces or spouts, and the skin ornamented with carved or painted patterns. There have been reports of gourds pierced with several holes and provided with a mouthpiece which were used as musical instruments, but no specimens have been preserved.

Bowls, calabashes, cooking, cultivations, Hinemoa, tops, water.

GRAVEL (*kiri*), see SANDSTONE.

Hine-moana.

GREENSTONE (*pounamu*). Jade, which varied in colour from black to milky white, was prized on account of its hardness, enduring quality, and beautiful appearance, and was therefore the subject of many legends. It is said that Tangaroa, the god of the sea, mated with Anu-matao, the personification of cold. Their children were Pounamu and Poutini.

In many respects the legend is confusing. Poutini was the guardian of Pounamu, who was sometimes known as the fish of Poutini. One story says that it was the priest Ngāhue who brought Poutini to Aotearoa. Poutini eventually took refuge at Arahura on the west coast of Te Waka a Māui, the South Island, and that is why his fish, Pounamu or greenstone, is found there.

But when we come to the border of legend and history, we find that the early explorers Kupe and Ngāhue discovered *pounamu* at Arahura and took a large piece back to their homeland. From the same place come several further legends designed to explain the origin of the several varieties of *pounamu*. One of these, *tangiwai*, weeping water, a flecked variety, is said to be the body of the lost wife of a famous explorer. When he found her, his tears fell on her, imparting the

Tamatea searches Piopiotahi (Milford Sound), and finds his wife turned into *tangiwai*, a form of greenstone.

characteristic 'tear drops' found on this kind of greenstone.

As *pounamu* was found principally on the remote west coast of Te Waka a Māui, it had a rarity value linked to the dangers and difficulties in securing the raw material. *Pounamu* was an important barter and gift item between tribes. Browning Pass across the southern mountains was the recognised route for travelling parties who came from the eastern side to procure the precious stone.

Such a rare stone could be used only for the most prized possessions, the principal forms being ear and neck pendants, including *tiki*, war clubs (*mere pounamu*) and *toki*, adzes. The making of *pounamu* items was a laboriously tedious task. Slabs of the stone were cut to the approximate size and shape by rubbing with water and sandstone in a groove on both sides until the slab could be broken off the larger block. The subsequent shaping and grinding occupied months of work, and even after this was completed, the polishing still had to be done. The best method of putting on the final finish was by rubbing against the bare skin – a favourite occupation of old age, which might continue for many months, and even for years.

Clubs, ear pendants, Kupe, obsidian, peace, tiki, Tutunui.

GREETINGS. There are various forms of greeting, depending upon the number of persons addressed:

Tēnā koe: Greetings to you – one person.
Tēnā kōrua: Greetings to you – two persons.
Tēnā koutou: Greetings to you – more than two persons.

In addition, *Haere mai* means welcome and *Haere rā*, farewell. *Kia ora* has the meaning of good health, greetings, and is the informal, everyday greeting. A little speech of welcome to a group of people might be: *Kia ora koutou katoa* (Greetings to all of you).

Nose pressing.

H

HAIR. Although the hair of the Māori was almost invariably black, there were notable exceptions. People who were fair-skinned and red-haired were known as *urukehu*. They were believed to be descendants of Tama-te-uira and Hine-te-uira, who were the personifications of lightning.

Characteristic hairstyles of men and women. The woman is wearing a *hei- tiki*, and the man a *mataringa*. Note the contrast between the *moko* of the male, and the tattooing confined to the lips and chin of the female.

As a rule women wore their hair short, but if it was allowed to grow long, it was tied behind the head. Men usually wore their hair long, and had it attended to by their wives. It was drawn up on top in the characteristic topknot by being tied close to the scalp, or through a wooden ring, the ends tucked inside, and tied again. Feathers and combs could then be inserted in the topknot. Sometimes a number of knots were tied, and after the dressing was finished, the hair would be combed and oiled. There were many occasions, however, when it was more convenient to wear the hair short, but feathers could still be worn by inserting them in a plaited headband.

As the human head was exceedingly *tapu*, *tohunga* and high-born chiefs were often notable for their dishevelled, filthy locks, for none but a *tohunga* of great *mana* was permitted to cut them, and prolonged *tapu*-lifting ceremonies had to be observed. Because of the sacred nature of the head, a number of beliefs centred round human hair. It represented the *mana* of noble men and women. It was used as a medium in black magic, and was also the *ariā* of certain *atua*. Its *tapu* nature accounted for its use on *rāhui* posts. After a battle, a lock of hair from the head of a dead enemy was a token of victory, and the taking of the lock was supposed to weaken the desire of the defeated tribe for vengeance.

Hair was cut with sharp flakes of obsidian. The cutting was sometimes the concluding item of a religious rite. It was burned, or deposited on the *tūāhu*, and offered to the gods. The cutting of hair was a sign of mourning, and the ceremonial haircut of the chief mourner formed part of the *tapu*-lifting rite.

Combs, cultivations, death, heads, magic, rāhui, widows.

HAKA, see DANCES. The main types of *haka* are *haka waiata* (dance to a chanted tune), *haka poi* (*poi* dance), and *haka taparahi* (posture dance without weapons).

HĀKARI, see FEASTS.

HAND GAMES. A considerable degree of skill and dexterity were needed in the many hand games that were played by older people as well as by children. Specimens of these games are:

Punipuni, in which one player held out his hand with the fingers spread wide apart. The second player closed his eyes and also spread his fingers, and tried to interlock them with his opponent's. The saying of the right charm had an important effect on the end result.

Tīringa began by calling out '*Tī*'. *Ringa* means hand, which accounts for the name of the game. One player had to copy the movement of the other's hands. The first player placed his two hands with the fingers interlocked, and with thumbs together so that the backs of the hands were showing. He quickly opened several fingers

A scene on the verandah of a house on a wet day. Children are playing several forms of hand games, which were equally popular with older people. The carved frame of the doorway and the painted rafters are clearly seen in the illustration.

and the second player had to copy him without a pause. If he made a false move he lost a point. This was a vigorous game, and players often stripped to the waist to give themselves freedom of movement. Similar games in which various gestures and positions of the hands were used were *whakaropiropi* (or *hōmai*) and *hei tama tū tama*, a speeded-up version of Simon Says.

In *tutukai* a stone was passed from one player to another, while a charm was repeated. The first player held up the stone, saying, 'Here it is!' It was then passed on, and when the players came to the last words of the charm and were repeating '*Kei ā wai*?' (Who has it?), one of the players had to guess who was holding the stone. A simpler form of the game was played by small children, who hid the stone and asked, 'Is it in my mouth? Is it in my left hand? Is it in my right hand?'

These games inculcated skill and adroitness, both useful to girls in *poi* dances and weaving, and to boys in warfare, particularly when it came to anticipating the moves of an opponent.

HĀNGI, see OVEN.

HAPŪ. A *hapū* was a section of a large tribe (*iwi*) in the same sense as a clan, sub-tribe or amalgamation of several closely related *whānau*, extended families.

Families, tribes.

HARAKEKE, se FLAX.

HAU. There is no English equivalent for this word. The ethnographer Elsdon Best wrote that 'The *hau* of a person seems to be his vital personality, or vital principle, or vital mana, certainly it represents his vital welfare.' *A Dictionary of the Māori Language* gives a further definition as 'the vitality of man, the vital essence of land, etc., which was particularly susceptible to the attacks of witchcraft.'

Hau can therefore be expressed as the essential vitality contained within all living things and which ceases to exist at death. The *hau* is protected by a *mauri*, an object such as a stone, in which the *hau* is ritually placed for its protection. The *hau* is further protected by the ritual location of an *atua* inside the *mauri*. It is the *mana* of the *atua* that provides the *mauri* (and therefore the *hau*) with its spiritual protection. The physical manifestation of the *hau* was in the breath of a person so that when a person sneezed it was said to be the *hau* expressing itself. Hence many orations begin with the words *Tihe mauri ora!* (I sneeze, it is life!).

Loss of a *mauri* containing, for example, the vital essence of a *kūmara* cultivation, might lead to the failure of that crop. If an evil *tohunga* gained the *hau* of a person, he could kill him. The *hau* might in such cases be represented by part of the body, such as a hair, fingernail or even by a footprint or shadow.

Mauri.

HAUMIA-TIKETIKE. One of the departmental gods who personified *aruhe*, the root, or more correctly, the edible rhizome of the bracken fern. As this was the staple Māori food, Haumia gained *atua* status, becoming the god of uncultivated food.

Fern root, gods (wars of).

HAWAIKI. The name of the ancestral homeland of the Māori people. There has been a great deal of conjecture about the location of Hawaiki and there are a number of theories placing the homeland in Western, Northern and Eastern Polynesia. However, most scholars, including Māori, tend to agree that there are many Hawaiki and that the name may in fact be of a symbolic nature, i.e. the name of the last departure point.

Modern research, based on linguistic and archaeological evidence, traces a Polynesian journey over thousands of years from west to east before one branch of the great Polynesian family, the Māori, found and settled Aotearoa. This proposition is based on the fact that there are languages related to Polynesian as far to the

A romanticised depiction of *waka* leaving Hawaiki for Aotearoa.

west as India and the island of Madagascar off the East African coast.

But it is generally agreed that the Polynesians had a South-east Asia origin, probably from India or southern China. The ancestors of the Polynesian peoples were thought to have been driven out of the South-east Asian mainland by invaders from the north, starting a journey down through Micronesia and settlement first in Samoa and Tonga, and then in Tahiti. From these centres they spread out over the rest of the Pacific island groups, as far east as Easter Island and to the south, Aotearoa.

Kupe, kūmara, Rangiātea.

HAWAIKI-NUI. Hawaiki-nui or Hawaiki-rangi was sometimes said to be a huge *whare* or temple on a mountain in the Hawaiki homeland. It was a way station along the journey for the spirits of the dead. They first set out for the far north of Te Ika a Māui, to Te Reinga, the leaping place, where they plunged beneath the waves, and journeyed to the place of the setting sun, eventually reaching Hawaiki-nui. There were four doors in the temple, giving access to spirits who came from every direction, but only two paths led from it, one to the underworld and the other to the heavens. There was no suggestion of heaven or hell in these destinations and the reason for the difference in the final destinations of the *wairua* is now lost and cannot be determined.

Souls.

HEADS (*upoko*). To Māori the *upoko*, head, was the most sacred part of the body and most subject to *tapu*. Those who were heavily *tapu*, such as high-class *tohunga*, dared not let hands or food touch the head, and had to eat their food impaled on sticks, and drink from a stream of water poured from a calabash.

At times of great emotion, when mourning or at the meeting of old friends, one might sit with the head covered with a cloak.

The sacredness of the head led to the development of the practice of drying and preserving them. In the case of enemies, heads taken as battle trophies were treated in this manner so that they might be further mocked and reviled beyond death. They were set on stakes and, in the event of attack, the line of preserved heads of slain enemies along the palisades of the *pā* were a demonstration of defiance and a reminder of the power of the defenders.

In the case of friends, the heads of chiefs were kept and brought out on important occasions, when they were greeted as old friends, and wept over. So important was the head that when chiefs were killed in battle, their bodies were sometimes burnt to prevent desecration and the heads brought home by their comrades.

The usual method of preserving heads was to build a special oven in the normal fashion. A hole was left in the top of the oven over which the head was placed and the escaping steam started the process. After steaming, the soft flesh was carefully removed from under the skin, the eyes taken out and the eyelids sewn up. The covering skin was then well oiled and the head smoke dried. In the early days of contact between Māori and Pākehā, a distressing trade in dried heads, *mōkai*, developed, for they were much in demand by Western collectors.

Burdens, hair, mourning.

HEAVENS, see OVERWORLDS.

HEI TAMA TŪ TAMA, see HAND GAMES.

HEITIKI. The name given to a neck ornament made from *pounamu*, greenstone, in the form of a human figure. Some rare early specimens were made of bone.
Tiki.

HIDE AND SEEK (*taupunipuni*). The usual form of game known to the Pākehā was played by Māori children.

HIKA AHI, see FIRE-MAKING.

HINA. The personification of the moon, or the moon goddess, her name appeared in several forms. She was the wife of Tinirau, and as Hine-te-iwaiwa is the personification of the domestic arts of women. She was also regarded as the daughter of Tangaroa, as the wife of Māui, and again as the sister of Māui and the wife of Irawaru.
Dogs, moon.

HĪNAKI. Wicker eel pot or trap.
Eels.

HĪNAU. The berries of the *hīnau* were used for food. They were pounded until the stones inside the fruit were separated. The remaining meal was mixed with water and cooked by means of hot stones. These were then made into large 'cakes' which were steamed in the *hāngi* or *umu*. The cakes were very oily and after this treatment would keep well for future use.
Berries.

HINE. Girl, daughter.
Girls.

HINE-AHU-ONE. After a fruitless search for the female element, Tāne took some of the earth from his mother Papa and formed the body of a woman. He endowed it with life, thus ending his quest. Certain ceremonies were performed to rid her of *tapu* and she became the first mortal woman and was given the name Hine-ahu-one (earth-formed woman). Tāne mated with her (or as some legends say, Tiki-āhu mated with her and was the first male parent), and she gave birth to several daughters, of whom the best known was Hine-tītama.
Female element, Hine-tītama, Tāne, Tiki.

HINEMOA. The most famous woman of Māori history or legend, Hinemoa was a virgin, a *puhi*, who lived at Ōwhata on the shore of Lake Rotorua. She fell in love with the chief Tūtānekai who lived on Mokoia Island in the middle of the lake. She could hear him at night playing

Tāne creates the earth-formed woman.

his flute to guide her to him. Hinemoa's people suspected her intentions and beached all the canoes. Undeterred, the young woman obtained some gourds to buoy her up and swam across the lake to Mokoia in the darkness, guided by Tūtānekai's music. After her swim she bathed in the warm pool Waikimihia (now known as Hinemoa's Pool) where she was found by Tūtānekai. They married and their descendants still live at Rotorua.

HINE-MOANA. The personification of the ocean, whose name means the ocean girl. She is always at war with the Earth Mother, lashing her sides and eating away the land, so that bays and inlets are known as Te Ngaunga-a-Hine-moana (the gnawing of Hine-moana). To protect Papa, the personifications of rock, gravel, and sand come to the rescue of the Earth Mother, and they repulse the wave children of Hine-moana. Her offspring are seaweed and shellfish. In mid-ocean there is said to be a ridge called Te Tua-hiwi-nui-a-Hine-moana (the great ridge or shoal of Hine-moana), which helps in the regulating of the tides.

Kiwa, ocean, tides.

HINE-NUI-Ō-TE-PŌ (or Hine-nui-te-pō). In the ao-mārama (world of light) this goddess was called Hine-tītama. She fled from her father-husband Tāne to the underworld and there took the name of Hine-nui-ō-te-pō (literally, the great girl of night, but usually rendered as the goddess of death). Naturally she was feared but it should be noted that she provides balance to the role of her father-husband Tāne. He cares for his children in the world of light while she guards and protects her human offspring after death.

She appears in a more unfavourable light in her contest with Māui. The demi-god attempted to kill the goddess by crawling through her body while she was asleep. It was thought that by reversing the birthing process, Māui could bring immortality to humankind. But one of his attendant birds, the *pīwakawaka*, fantail, laughed as he saw Māui's legs dangling outside Hine's body. Woken by the fantail's mirth, the goddess crushed Māui between her legs, killing him and thwarting his bold attempt to free mankind from death.

Death, Hine-tītama, night, underworlds.

HINE-TE-APARANGI. The wife of Kupe.

Aotearoa.

HINE-TE-IWAIWA. Patroness of the art of weaving and of childbirth, as well as of other domestic arts. Under her other name Hina-uri, she was the personification of the moon.

Hina, moon, Rupe, tiki, Tinirau, weaving.

HINE-TĪTAMA. The dawn girl, the eldest daughter of Hine-ahu-one and Tāne. Tāne had an incestuous relationship with his daughter, and several children were born, the most notable being Hine-rau-whārangi, the personification of plant growth. Subsequently Hine-tītama discovered that Tāne was her father as well as her husband. In her shame she took refuge in the underworld, and the path of death was opened to mankind. She remains there and is now known as Hine-nui-ō-te-pō.

Hine-ahu-one, Hine-nui-ō-te-pō, Tāne.

HINU. Fat or oil. Game such as pigeons and rats were cooked and preserved in their own fat.

HŌANGA, see SANDSTONE.

HOE, see PADDLES.

HOEROA. A weapon made of whalebone about 1.5 metres in length, and some 4 centimetres wide,

The artist W. Dittmer's 'art-deco' conception of Hine-nui-ō-te-pō. Death and dawn, the two attributes of Hine, are depicted in this work.

and rounded at the ends. It was made from the lower jawbone of the sperm whale and had a graceful double curve. Exactly how the weapon was used has now been lost.

One story is that it was employed in an unusual manner, being thrown at a fleeing enemy to connect with the spine, and then retrieved by pulling it back with the cord to which it was attached. But the lack of weight of the weapon makes this seem unlikely.

HOKIOI. A mythical bird that is sometimes heard screaming in the night.

HOKOWHITU, see WAR PARTIES.
Counting.

HONGI, see NOSE PRESSING.

HOOPS (pīrori). These were made by binding vines such as supplejack in a circle. Children threw them to one another, fending them off with sticks, or catching and returning them, but they were not bowled along the ground. Adults often played children's games too and in hoop-throwing there was a grim adaptation of the pīrori game. The skin of a slain enemy was stretched over the pīrori, and the tossing back wards and forwards of this memento was a way of satisfying feelings of revenge. Supplejack hoops were made for other purposes, such as supports for the openings of hand nets, etc.

HOROUTA. A migration canoe commanded by Pawa. The descendants of the canoe occupied the east coast districts of Te Ika a Māui, the North Island. The Horouta was supposed to have returned to Hawaiki for a cargo of fern root before finally drifting ashore at Whakatāne.

HOSPITALITY. The Māori are a generous, open-hearted people. They were always ready to welcome relations and friends without any thought of their own future welfare. Guests were fed and entertained with whole-hearted generosity that frequently depleted the food stores of the hosts, and reduced them to semi-starvation until the next harvest and hunting seasons.

HŌTEO, see CALABASHES.

HOTUROA. Captain of the Tainui canoe.

HOUSES (*whare*). There were three principal types of house — superior *whare* (large, elaborately carved and decorated *whare*), large, unornamented ones, and smaller, inferior houses.

The superior type, built with squared timbers, and with carved designs and much interior deco-ration, was termed a *whare whakairo*. Houses of this kind might be 20 metres or more in length. The alternative name for a modern *whare whakairo* is simply *whare nui* or big house. A simpler type, robustly constructed but without decoration, was the whare puni, which varied from 6 to 10 metres in length.

The inferior houses might be termed huts. They included small living houses and perhaps kāuta, or cooking sheds, which were very primitive and were used for storing wood, and for cooking when the weather was too severe for the open-air ovens to be used; and wharau, or temporary shelters which were constructed by travelling parties and hunters. The word whare was also used in a figurative sense, e.g. the whare *pōtae* was 'the house of mourning'.

The building of a *whare whakairo* proceeded along the following lines: the ground was cleared and pegs were driven in to fix the position of the ends of the back wall. Cords were used to measure the diagonals, and pegs placed at the front corners, the area being squared off carefully. The next stage was the erection of the large centre poles of the front and back walls, and all measurements were made with great care. The massive

The house on the left is a *whare* with carvings on the upright posts and on the bargeboards, with a *tekoteko* on the gable, while the building on the right is the simplest form of *whare*. The *whare whakairo* in the centre is richly adorned with carvings, painted rafters, and decorative reed panels.

ridgepole, which locked the whole construction together, was adzed to shape and raised on to the end posts. In the case of the largest houses there might be one or two middle posts as well, to support the great weight of the ridgepole. The method of raising was to erect two tall, temporary poles with cross-pieces at each end of the house. The ridgepole was raised with ropes which passed over the cross-pieces and lowered on to the main posts of the house. It projected beyond the front wall, and provided a cantilever support for the roof of the verandah. The walls were made of spaced slabs or wide planks of timber planted firmly in the ground with the top

A more detailed view of a *whare whakairo*.

A food store (*pātaka*) under construction. The ridgepole is in position on the centre and end post. The *tohunga* is controlling the building operations.

sloping slightly inwards, the intervening spaces being filled with decorative panels. Substantial baulks of timber were used as rafters. They were notched into the ridgepole and rested on the side slabs, and were tightened by a rope passed from ground level over the rafters and the main beam, the ridgepole thus bearing the whole weight of the house. The rope was strained taut, left in position, and covered with thatch.

Battens were laid on the rafters to support the thatch, which was composed of bundles of reeds and an outer covering of more durable materials. The walls were also thatched with reeds, grass, and *toetoe*, and the decorative reed panels were made by women, although sometimes patterned, woven mats were used instead. The inside of the roof was also lined with bark or *toetoe* culms. A single sliding door and window were built into the front wall under the verandah.

The interior of the *whare* was quite bare. There was no covering on the earth floor, no furniture of any kind, and no partitions. Two beams were laid on the ground, providing a central passage. Sleeping mats were laid so that heads were to the outside wall and feet towards the beam. A sunken, stone-lined pit provided a fireplace in the middle of the central passage.

In the case of *whare whakairo*, a great deal of labour was devoted to the carving and other decorations of the house. There were few fully decorated examples of this kind, and the amount of carving, painting, and *tukutuku* work varied with the importance of the house. Outstanding examples of superior houses had carved designs and figures on all the posts, slabs, bargeboards, and their supporting posts, the outer end of the ridgepole, door and window, door posts and lintel, and the beam which enclosed the porch at ground level, while the front gable was crowned by the *tekoteko*. Painting was confined mainly

Parts of the Maori Meeting House

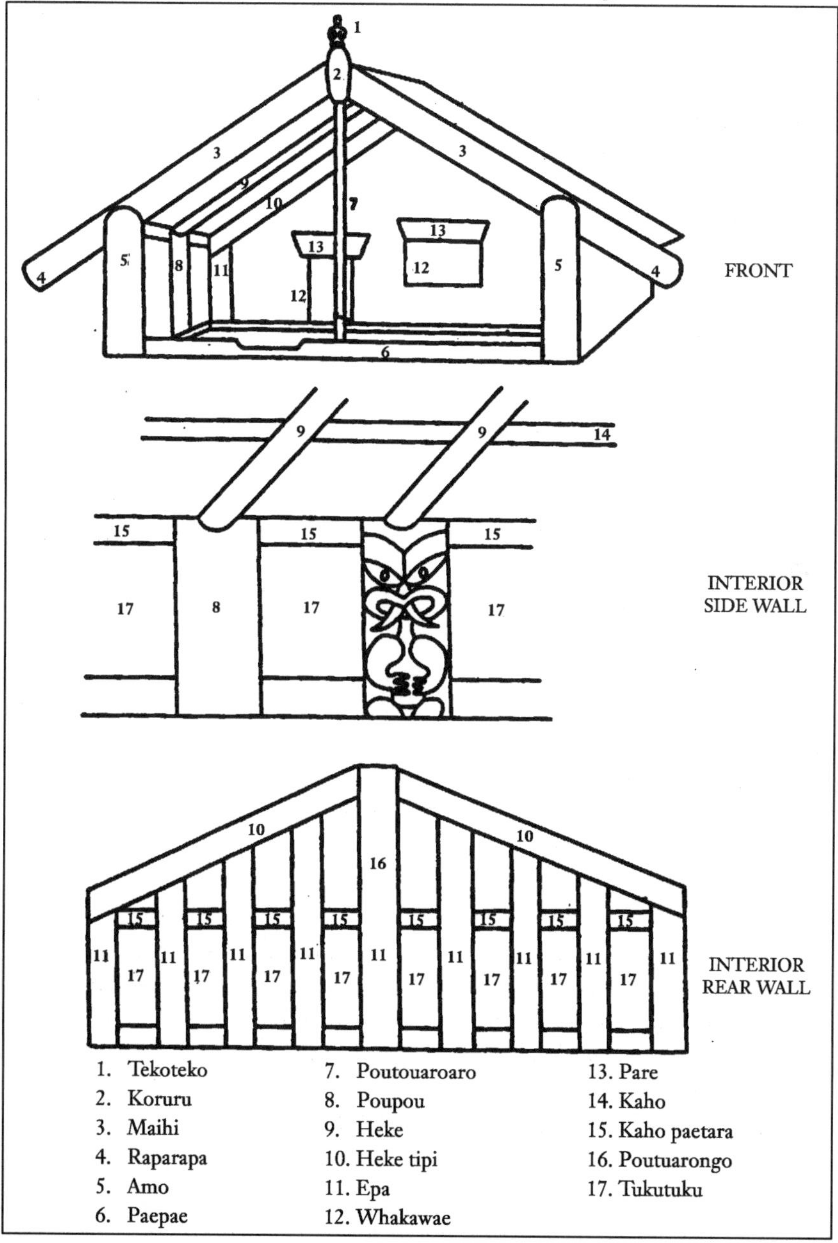

Reproduced with permission from *Carved Histories*, Roger Neich, published by Auckland University Press.

to the rafters.

Small living huts were a great contrast to the *whare whakairo*. They had small doors, less than a metre in height, and the door frame was the only part of the building which was richly carved. The occupants had to crawl through the opening, and the greatest height inside was about 2 metres, while at the side-walls there was only about 60 centimetres clearance. These huts were weather-proof and almost airtight. Although Māori were hardy and could face the elements with little clothing, they could withstand heat and fumes that might have finished off a Pākehā. The same conditions occurred in the *whare puni*, which sometimes had a sunken floor, with earth piled against the walls to keep out the draughts.

The most sacred parts of the house were the roof, the right side where the families of highest rank slept, and the rear post. Buried in the earth at the rear post of the *whare whakairo* was the *mauri*, which enshrined the *mana* of the tribe. Rain which fell on the roof could not be used for drinking on account of the *tapu*. During construction the superior house was under the protection of the gods, and elaborate rites were performed to remove the *tapu*. The *tapu* was lifted by a young woman, who would cross the threshold and proceed to the rear post. She would kneel there above the buried *mauri*, facing the door, while the *tohunga* recited the incantations that permitted the house to be opened and used.

Carving, cold, doors, fireplaces, Hawaiki-nui, pō, painting, porches, reed patterns, sacrifices (human), schools of learning, sleep, smoke, store houses, tekoteko, thatch, whare, whare wānanga, windows.

HUA, see EGGS. The word also means fruit.

HUAHUA. Birds captured and preserved for food were known as *huahua*. It was also the name given to a vessel in which water could be boiled.

Cooking.

HUATA. A long spear.

HUE, see GOURD.

HUHU. The large, white grub of the longicorn beetle, which is found in decayed *rimu*, *matai*, and *kahikatea* timber, and which was greatly prized as a food.

HUI. Meeting, assembly or gathering of people from far and near.

HUIA. The *huia* bird was caught by hunters who imitated its cry and, when it came close, caught it by means of a running noose on the end of a stick. The distinctive, black, white-tipped feathers were prized as head ornaments for chiefs.

Though now extinct, the *huia* was once plentiful in some parts of the country. The Huiarau Range, for example, was so named because of the large number of the birds that were once found there.

Feathers.

HUI-TE-RANGIORA. A great sea rover who was said to have sailed southwards and discovered the great southern land of Antarctica.

HUNTING, see BIRDS (HUNTING).

I

IHO, see UMBILICAL CORD.

IKA, see FISH.

IKA A MĀUI, TE. Literally, the fish of Māui, the name given to the North Island of Aotearoa. It was also known as Te Ika-nui-a-Māui, Māui's big fish, and Te Ika-roa-a-Māui, Māui's long fish.

Legend says that it was hauled up from the ocean bed by Māui, whose fish-hook caught in the house of Tonganui, the son of Tangaroa, the sea god. When it came to the surface, there were houses, men and women, and fires on the surface of the fish. Māui left for Hawaiki to propitiate the gods and warned his brothers not to disturb the fish until he returned. They ignored his words and trampled over the land, dividing it amongst themselves by slashing at it with their knives and disturbing the smooth surface. As the fish writhed under their blades, mountains and valleys appeared. If they had not disturbed it, the land would have remained smooth and flat.

According to one legend, Māui's canoe was preserved on Mount Hikurangi: in another the South Island was the canoe from which the fish was caught, hence the name Te Waka a Māui (the canoe of Māui), and Stewart Island was Te Punga-o-te-waka-a-Māui (the anchor of Māui's canoe). Kaikoura was the thwart of the canoe.

The eyes of Māui's fish were Wellington Harbour and Lake Wairarapa, Taupō-moana was the heart, Cape Egmont and East Cape the fins, and the long Northland peninsula the tail. Māui's fish-hook (Te Matau-a-Māui) is seen in the curving coastline of Hawke's Bay.

South Island.

IKAROA, TE, see MILKY WAY.

IMMORTALITY. Because the gods themselves were immortal, they had great difficulty in discovering the *ira tangata* (mortal life) with which to endow mortal man. The demi-god Māui attempted to overcome death in order that man might become immortal, but failed. Nevertheless, after death the *wairua* of man makes its last journey to Rarohenga, the underworld, where it may be presumed it lives on forever. Other traditions say that the *wairua* descended lower and lower until eventually meeting a second death, or being reincarnated in the form of a moth.

Death, gods, Māui, mauri, souls, spirits, underworlds.

IMPLEMENTS, AGRICULTURAL. Four main tools were used when cultivating the *kūmara* and other plants. Large implements, termed *kō* and *kāheru*, were used to loosen the soil and turn it over. For ease of reference further particulars can be found under the heading Spades, though neither of these tools was a true spade. Clods of earth were broken up with paddle-shaped tools termed *wauwau*, and by the *tima*, which was a curved, grubbing instrument. Clubs were also used to pulverise the soil, and in some places a small scraper was used to heap the earth into rows or mounds. The smaller tools, such as the *timo*, club, and *wauwau* were used in a sitting position. All agricultural implements were fashioned from wood.

Cultivations, spades.

ĪNANGA, see WHITEBAIT.

As Māui hauls on his line, the *tekoteko* on the gable of Tonganui's house appears above the water.

INCANTATIONS (*karakia*). The subject of *karakia* is also dealt with under the heading Charms. *Karakia* formed an important part of religious observances, but while the words of ancient *karakia* have been carefully preserved in many cases the allusions are so arcane that the meaning has been lost. *Tohunga* of experience and *mana* who were familiar with the most powerful *karakia* were said to be able to command unseen powers and to win the support of the *atua*, gods.

Charms, choking, frost, houses, mana, peace, songs.

INFANTICIDE. Though this custom was practised in Polynesia, it was seldom observed in Aotearoa. Māori were indulgent parents when their children were young.

INSANITY. An insane person (*keka*) was supposed to be under the control of a malevolent ghost or spirit (often that of a still-born child) known as a *kikokiko*, or to be the victim of *mākutu*, black magic spells cast on him by an enemy.

INSECTS. There were many personifications of insects, all of whom were descended from the primal gods Tāne, Tangaroa, Peketua, and Haumia. The *hakuturi*, which were forest guardians and spirits, and were descended from Tāne, included all insect inhabitants of trees. A legendary canoe, the Mangarara, was supposed to have brought many insects to Aotearoa.

Māori had names for nearly 300 insects; butterflies and moths with the larvae and pupae, beetles, worms, lice, spiders, flies, grasshoppers, locusts, cicadas, ants, fleas, *wētā*, sandflies and mosquitoes.

Caterpillars, huhu, spiders, vegetable caterpillars, Whiro.

IO. The supreme god. The traditions concerning Io were collected very late (in the 20th century) and must be considered in that light. The name

In the legend of Rātā, the tree which he felled was raised again by insects, birds, and Te Tini o te Hakuturi, because he had not propitiated the forest god.

of Io was said to be *tapu* and so sacred that it was probably unknown to most Māori people.

A creation chant describes Io, the high-god, as living in space where there was neither sun, moon, nor stars. Darkness brooded over the all-pervading water. Io commanded the light to come. He looked on the endless waters and divided them with the earth and sky, creating Rangi and Papa.

The priestly cult of Io and the revelation of the names and attributes of Io were first made in *The Lore of the Whare-wānanga*, by the Wairarapa *tohunga* Te Matorohanga and published in 1913.

This conception of God the Almighty lay so far outside the stream of Polynesian belief that the ethnographer Elsdon Best thought it must surely have been 'the creation of leisured minds, or a priestly class of people dwelling as a cohesive, self-contained nation in some far land... Amid the hampering maze of gross superstition and shamanistic ritual they took the first steps on the long road that leads to monotheism.'

Without doubt the cult of Io is lofty and inspired, and comes very close to duplicating the Hebrew concept of Yahweh.

It is said that Io was known by *tohunga*. But the influence of Christianity on the teachings of Te Matorohanga has been a subject of scholarly debate.

Charms, evil, mana, mareikura, overworlds, peace, Rangiatea, Rehua, religion, schools of learning, souls, stones (sacred), Tāne.

IPU, see GOURD. The *ipu* had a narrow mouth. The generic name for the gourd was *hue*.

IRA ATUA and **IRA TANGATA**. *Ira atua* was supernatural and described immortal life as enjoyed by the gods; *ira tangata* was the essence of mortal life. The gods wanted to establish mankind on earth, but were unable to do so until they discovered the *ira tangata*. It was for this reason that they searched for the female element that would contain the *ira tangata* (the gods all being of the male sex), and after many experiments Tāne succeeded.

Female element, man.

IRIIRI, see BAPTISM.

ISLANDS, ARTIFICIAL. Artificial islands were occasionally constructed in lakes, notably in the Waikato and Horowhenua districts. They were built up in shallow water to form refuges and fortresses against enemies. When such lakes were situated on a plain the defensive positions on the islands provided the protection that was needed, and enabled the people to guard against surprise attack.

IWI, see TRIBES.

Families, hapū.

J

'JAW HARP' (*rōria*). The rōria was a simple musical instrument. It consisted of a very thin, flat piece of wood placed against the teeth and struck with the hand or a stick. A primitive form of rōria was made from a short length of supplejack split lengthways.

Two forms of *rōria*.

JUMPING JACK (*karetao*). A wooden toy loved by small children but probably used also by adolescents and adults. It was a carved human figure with its arms tied loosely to its body. When a cord was pulled the arms swung backwards and forwards, and at the same time the toy was shaken in the hand so that it looked as though it were dancing. Special songs were composed to be sung to the gesticulations of the *karetao*.

K

KĀHERU, see SPADES.

Implements (agricultural).

KAHU, also KĀKAHU, see CLOAKS.

KAHUKURA. The personification of the rainbow and the name of a tribal war god who was also sought after in cases of illness. Kahukura came to Aotearoa by crossing a bridge from Hawaiki, which he made from the body of his mother, Hine-te-wai (rain girl), in the form of a gigantic bow.

Kahukura was also the name of the chief who tricked the *patupaiarehe* into showing him the secret of net-making.

Nets, rain, rainbow, gods (tribal and war).

KAI, see FOOD. The word also means to eat, while other alternative meanings are puzzles and riddles.

KĀINGA. An unfortified village. The word is derived from *kā*, meaning to take fire, to burn, or to be lit. Literally, therefore it means a place where the fire has burnt, and so applies not only to the village, but also to 'country' and to an encampment. In the special sense it means home.

The *kāinga* was the home of the tribe, *hapū* or *whānau* in times of peace. It was chosen for its situation, nearness to cultivations, a reliable water supply, firewood, etc., and usually housed all its important buildings, *tūāhu*, store houses, and the like. The fortified village, or *pā*, was the place where the residents retreated to when an attack was threatened.

An illustration of a *kāinga* from Polack's *New Zealand. Whare, whata,* and *pātaka* are depicted. Although there is a stockade, the village is not heavily fortified.

Pā.

KĀKĀ, see BIRDS, HUNTING.

KAO. *Kūmara* that has been grated, cooked, and dried in the sun. When needed, the *kao* was crumbled into water to make a gruel.

Drink, kūmara.

KAPUA, see CLOUDS.

KARAKA. The large, orange berries of the *karaka* tree were esteemed as a food, but care had to be taken not to eat the poisonous kernels until after the fruit was cooked. The usual remedy for poisoning was to bury the patient up to the neck until a cure had been effected. It was thought that the pressure of 'burial' squeezed the internal organs and helped expel the poison.

The ripe berries were gathered in baskets and pounded with the feet in water until the flesh came off. The *karaka* kernels or 'nuts' were cooked in ovens for about a day, and then stored in water-filled pits until required.

Berries, food, poisons.

KARAKIA. Charms, incantations, invocations, spells, or prayers. Further details are found under the entry Charms, but *karakia* is a difficult word to define. *Karakia* are probably best described as a formula of words that were chanted to obtain benefit or avert trouble. Different levels of *karakia* were used by children, laymen, and *tohunga*, in increasing order of importance, and were further divided into subdivisions relating to their functions. With few exceptions *karakia* were not addressed directly to the gods.

ātahu: love charms
hoa: to split stones, wither leaves, and kill birds.
hoa tapuae: to give speed to a pursuer and to impede the pursued.
hono: to cause broken bones to knit together.
kaha: to give success in hunting birds.
kawa: to remove the *tapu* from a newly-built house.
ki tao: to endow spears with power.
ki rākau: to endow weapons with power.
ngau paepae: to protect a war party against spells (this is the beam-biting ceremony in the *turuma,* latrine).
pou: to cause the mind to retain chants and other knowledge.
rāoa: to cure a choking fit to expel a foreign body from the throat.
rotu: to put people to sleep.
tohi: the invocations and ceremonies used in the baptismal rite. Similarly, the *tohi taua* rites were performed over a war party.
tūā: the dedication of children to the gods after the cutting of the *iho*.
tūāpā: to ward off ill luck.
whai: to cure burns and wounds, also efficacious in choking fits.
whakanoa: to remove *tapu*, or make common, a most important type of *karakia*, without which normal life would have been impossible.

Charms, choking, love charms, schools of learning, songs, whakanoa.

KAREAO, see SUPPLEJACK.

KARETAO, see JUMPING JACK.

KATIPŌ. The only poisonous native spider found in Aotearoa.

Poisons, spiders.

KAU, see SWIMMING.

KĀUTA, see KITCHENS.

KAUWAE RARO and KAUWAE RUNGA. Historical traditions and celestial lore were taught in the *whare wānanga* in two streams. The *kauwae raro* (lower jaw) was the knowledge of tribal history and other matters of a terrestrial nature while the *kauwae runga* (upper jaw) was esoteric knowledge pertaining to the gods, creation myths, and sacred lore and ritual.

Baskets of knowledge, schools of learning, whare wānanga.

KĒHUA, see GHOSTS.

KELP, BULL (*rimurapa*). Containers called *pōhā* were made of bull kelp and were used to preserve food supplies in the southern parts of New Zealand. The interior partitions of the kelp 'leaf' were separated by hand and then inflated, thus making large containers in which food such as *tītī*, muttonbirds, could be placed. When the hot fat – retained from the cooking of the birds – was poured in and allowed to set, the flesh inside could then be kept for a long time. The *pōhā* were protected with bark covers and the whole enclosed within a wooden frame.

Baskets, birds (preserving).

KERERŪ, see PIGEONS.

KETE, see BASKETS.

KIEKIE. The tough leaves of the *kiekie* were frequently used instead of flax in plaiting and weaving. The aerial roots supplied material for making traps and for other purposes.

KIKOKIKO, see GHOSTS.

KILTS (*rāpaki, maro*). The kilt or *maro* was made of dressed flax and generally only used by men in war. It was worn either singly in front and drawn back through the crutch by a string at the base of the triangle, or as a pair with one each at front and rear joined at their apices and tied at their sides around the waist.

Ordinary kilts or *rāpaki* took the form of skirts, reaching to above the knee for single women and men and below the knee for married women. They were mostly made of woven flax and varied in quality and ornamentation according to the status of the wearer. The finely woven kilts with a broad ornamental border were called *weruweru*.

KINSHIP, see RELATIONSHIP.

KIORE, see RATS.

KIRI (gravel), see Sandstone. Another meaning is skin.

KITCHENS (*kāuta*). Because cooked food was a pollutant of the *tapu* state, to avoid such a risk, all cooking was usually done in the open. In bad weather the oven might be prepared in an open-sided shelter normally used for drying wood. The 'walls' of these shelters were formed from the stacked firewood that would later be used for the oven.

Cooking, houses.

KITES (*manu*). Kite flying was called *manu tukutuku, tukutuku* meaning to pay out the cord. Kites were made of *raupō* or *toetoe* stalks and tied with strips of flax, and often decorated with feathers. They were made in a number of different designs, some shaped like crosses, some like human faces, and some like birds. *Manu* means both kite and bird. Kites were also called *kāhu* (hawk) and *manu pākau* (bird's wing). Children recited charms to assist the flight. *Karere* or 'messengers,' flat wooden discs with feathers round the edge, could be sent up the string by

Sending a *karere* or messenger up to a kite, which is in the shape of a bird.

the wind.

Adults were as interested in kite flying as children and the largest kites, with a wingspan of 3.6 metres or more required two strong men to handle them. The average wingspan was about 1.5 metres. Cockle shells were attached to the largest kites so that they would make a rattling sound.

There are many traditional tales of kites being used in time of war. In one story some Māori, besieged in their *pā*, made their escape by flying over the heads of the enemy on kites, while in another tale kites were used by ambushers to imitate birds diving on fish, thereby luring people out of their *pā* and to their doom. Priests used kites for divination, and by the power of magic, kites could be used to find lost people. Small *manu aute* were made of the light bark of the paper mulberry.

Divination, magic.

KIWA. The guardian of the ocean, which was known a Te Moana-nui-a-Kiwa (the great ocean of Kiwa). Kiwa's first wife was Parawhenuamea, the mother of water, and his second Hine-moana, the goddess of the sea.

Hine-moana.

KIWI. The flightless, nocturnal bird was valued for its flesh, and for its feathers, which were used for decorating superior cloaks. It was hunted with dogs.

Dogs.

KNIVES (*māripi*). The cutting implement known as the *māripi* was the closest approach to a knife possessed by Māori. The handle was usually carved in an intricate design, frequently of an open-work pattern, and the edge set with sharks' teeth. The teeth were set in a narrow groove on the edge of the instrument and lashed to the blade. The tool could thus be described as a saw with detachable teeth. The *māripi* was used mainly for cutting flesh.

KNOWLEDGE, see WĀNANGA. An abstract conception of considerable importance.

Baskets of knowledge, schools of learning, stones (sacred), Tāne.

KNUCKLE STONES (*kōruru*). This game closely resembles the Pākehā children's game of knucklebones, and is played in a similar manner with five stones. In the Māori game, however, a rough square is traced in the ground and the stones are placed in the corners. The player tosses the remaining stone in the air, picks up one of the corner stones and catches the first before it touches the ground. As the game continues it becomes more difficult as two, three, or four stones must be picked up before the first stone is caught.

Children playing at *kōruru*, or knuckle stones. A bullroarer lies on the ground in front of them.

There are also variations in which more than one stone at a time is thrown in the air.

KŌ, see SPADES.
Implements (agricultural).

KŌAUAU, see FLUTE.

KŌHUA. A Māori oven, a vessel for boiling water by means of hot stones, or the process of boiling.
Boiling, bowls, cooking, ovens.

KŌKŌWAI, see OCHRE, RED.

KONO. Plaited plates or platters for holding food.
Baskets, plaiting.

KOPA. A pouch or basket for carrying objects when travelling.
Baskets.

KŌRARI. Flax flower stalk. It had several uses, such as for light darts or spears used in play, making small canoes or rafts, etc.
Darts, canoes, rafts.

KORE. This word indicates the negative, no, and not, with a further meaning of want or absence, annihilation, destruction, or 'nothingness', cessation of being, and the act of destruction or annihilation.

The Kore was one of the ages or eras that preceded the creation. It represented chaos, the absence of light, form, matter, and life.
Creation.

KŌRERO. As a verb *kōrero* means to speak or to address; as a noun it is conversation, speech, discussion, news, or a story. To a people without a written language, the preservation of tradition, history, and lore could only be transmitted by speech. Tribal discussions were important in making decisions. The *whaikōrero* was an integral part of community life. *Kōrero pōrākau* and *kōrero tara* were legendary tales and fables, and stories of monsters and supernatural beings were a never-failing source of entertainment.
Folklore, speeches.

KOROTANGI. A famous carved stone *kura* or heirloom in the form of a bird. It is probably of Asiatic origin. One conjectural view is that it may have come from a Tamil vessel wrecked between Kawhia and Raglan in the forgotten past.

It was held in great veneration and the Tainui people believe that it was brought from Hawaiki in their ancestral canoe.

KŌRURU, see KNUCKLE STONES.

KOTIATE. A stone weapon or club with a thin, flat blade and a short handle, remarkable for deep indentations on either edge which gave it a faint resemblance to a violin. The thin, tapered edge made it effective both for thrusting and striking, with the indentations ensuring that at the very least the skin of the opponent was broken.

Clubs.

KOTIRI, see METEORS.

KŌURA, see CRAYFISH.

KŌWHATU, see STONES, ROCKS.

KŪMARA (sweet potato). The *kūmara* was without question the most important cultivated Māori food. It was not native to Aotearoa, and there are a number of traditions, some of a fabulous nature, relating to its importation. It was brought from Hawaiki, and in some traditions may even have been the cause of a special return voyage to collect it.

It is apparent however that *kūmara* tubers were brought to the new land in more than one canoe. It could not be cultivated in all parts of the country, but grew well in most parts of Te Ika a Māui, the North Island, and in Te Waka a Māui, the South Island, reputedly as far south as Banks Peninsula and, according to some traditions, even further.

It was natural that such a highly prized, staple article of diet should be surrounded by ritual observance and religious ceremonies. Not one, but two gods presided over the welfare of the crop – Pani, god or personification, who was regarded as the 'mother' of the *kūmara* and Rongo in his alternative male personification of the moon. The moon was intimately connected with fertility and favourable 'nights of the moon' were chosen to ensure the success of plantings.

There were several varieties of *kūmara*, the tubers all being smaller than those grown in modern times. The planting began with religious ceremonies, and when the crop was harvested, the first fruits were offered to the gods. All operations associated with growing *kūmara* were highly *tapu*.

A great deal of labour was expended on the cultivation of *kūmara*, beginning with the building of brushwood fences for windbreaks. In some places they were built to keep out *pūkeko*, swamp hens. Sand and gravel were spread on the ground to help raise soil temperature, while wood ash was added for fertility. Each individual plant was grown in a heaped-up mound. These were kept weed-free and maintained in neat rows. Caterpillars, the only pest that attacked the plants, were smoked out with fires, collected by hand and burnt. They might also be driven away by the charms of the *tohunga*.

The tubers needed no preparation for eating other than cleaning and cooking in the earth ovens, and thus compared favourably with the majority of other foods. Young *kūmara* were frequently scraped and dried in the sun. The resulting product was known as *kao*. *Kao* could be kept indefinitely and was often carried in this dehydrated form when travelling.

When *kūmara* were steamed they were considered a delicacy. A gruel made by mixing the steamed *kūmara* with water was relished by sick people who needed a light diet.

Caterpillars, cultivations, Horouta, implements (agricultural), kao, kūmara gods, mauri, Pani, Rongo, underworlds.

KŪMARA GODS (*taumata atua*). A 'kūmara god' was a stone image set up in the cultivations to encourage the fertility of the crop. These images were *taumata*, or resting places of the *atua* who in most cases was Rongo (god of the moon and responsible for the fertility and growth of the crop). The popular term 'kūmara god' is Pākehā in derivation and does not completely capture

The *kūmara* god, Matuatonga, of Mokoia Island.

the function of the stone images. The images might also contain the *hau*, the vital essence of the *mauri* or life force that resided in all things associated with human endeavour or activities. The 'kūmara gods' were alternatively known as *mauri* for this reason.

Mauri, Rongo.

KUMETE, see BOWLS.

KUPE. Although there are several legendary accounts of the arrival of early explorers, modern research seems to indicate that Aotearoa was first settled at a much earlier time than had previously been thought. The first arrivals are generally accepted as being Kupe and Ngāhue.

It is estimated that these explorers came from the Hawaiki homeland somewhere about the 10th century A.D. in the canoes Matahorua and Tawirirangi. Other traditions place them in canoes of different names.

The dating of the arrival of canoes, either legendary or historical, is calculated by counting the number of generations revealed by the *whakapapa* of their descendants. However it is not a precise method in that *whakapapa* can sometimes be notoriously inaccurate.

Their landfall was made in the north, and the canoes sailed down the East Coast, entering what Māori now call Te Whanganui a Tara (Wellington Harbour). Subsequently *Raukawa*, Cook Strait and the Porirua inlet, were explored, and the canoes continued down the West Coast of Te Waka a Māui, the South Island, where greenstone was discovered and a *moa* was killed.

A block of greenstone and the preserved flesh of the *moa* were taken back to Hawaiki.

In the traditional account of Kupe's explorations he sent his pet *kawau*, to test the currents of the tidal estuaries. At French Pass the *kawau* was overcome by the tide rip.

The account of the expedition encouraged later generations to make the long voyage to Aotearoa, when conditions became impossible in the homeland because of food shortages caused by over-population.

One tradition states that Kupe found no inhabitants in the new land, but the same tradition says nothing about any inland exploration. From other traditions some inferences may be drawn that early settlers, *tāngata whenua*, were in fact in occupation at that time.

Because all knowledge of Kupe is derived from legendary accounts, some scholars speculate that the accounts relate to excursions to other island groups and were brought to Aotearoa as part of a general body of traditions, and applied to the new land.

Aotearoa, drift voyages, greenstone, octopus, tāngata whenua.

KUPENGA, see NETS.

KURA. This word has several meanings, including the knowledge of *karakia* and other lore. But it was also the colour red, and described red feathers and other treasured possessions. *Kura* – red feathers – were kept in *pātaka* or storehouses.

Schools of learning.

KURAHAUPO. Two famous *waka*, canoes, carried this name. Whatonga commanded the first. The original name of his *waka* was Te Hāwai, but it was renamed when Whatonga set out on his famous search for his grandfather, Toi.

The second Kurahaupo was the migratory canoe that was badly damaged at Rangitahua (Sunday Island) on the journey to Aotearoa. Most of the crew joined the Aotea *waka* but the Kurahaupo was later repaired and is said to have sailed to Aotearoa with a skeleton crew.

The Kurahaupo descendants lived at Tāmaki, Taranaki, Whanganui, and in the Manawatu.

Canoes, Toi, Whatonga.

KURĪ, see DOGS.

KŪWAHA, see GATEWAYS.

L

LADDERS. Poles were tied to a tree trunk and used as ladders by bird hunters who climbed up by gripping the lashings that held them in place. Steps, providing access to *whata*, elevated store houses, were made by adzing recesses in an inclined log.

Pā.

LAMENTS (*waiata tangi*). These dirges and laments, often specially composed, were sung or chanted at funeral ceremonies. The oldest known lament is *Te Tangi a Apakura*, which gave rise to the saying, 'Lacerating, mourning women and ocean waves know no rest.'

Death.

LAMPREYS (*piharau*). Lampreys were taken in much the same way as eels, but there were some modifications in the shape of the *hīnaki*, traps or pots, so that the lamprey would enter them as they swam upstream.

Eels.

An early explorer claiming new territory for his tribe.

LAND (*whenua*). Māori had a close affinity with the land that was claimed and occupied by themselves. The boundaries of that land, which was communally owned, were clearly defined and carefully taught to young people. In most cases a large area, with its forests, streams, lakes, hills, valleys, and fishing grounds, was 'owned' by an *iwi*, tribe. It was subdivided into areas owned by *hapū*, and the cultivated portions were again subdivided and owned by individual *whānau*, families. *Hapū* and *whānau* could have ownership of a particular resource such as a bird-snaring tree or particular fishing spots. Nevertheless, the whole area was usually regarded as being the possession of the *iwi*.

The rights of the tribe to the land it possessed were vigorously defended. 'By land and women are men taken,' is a well-known proverb. Possession was established and maintained by occupation while the rights to land that had been abandoned by a tribe were said to have become 'cold'.

Notable explorers such as Ngatoro-i-rangi, Hei, Tia, Turi, etc., claimed formal possession of the country by viewing it from advantageous points, but their claims had to be subsequently established by occupation. It then remained in the possession of the tribe from generation to generation by ancestral right. But land could also be claimed by conquest with the affirmation of that conquest being subsequent occupation of the territory.

The expression *ahi kā* (lit fire – sometimes long-burning fire) indicated that occupation continued so long as the fires of the people burned. If the land remained unoccupied, the successful invaders could claim it, but it automatically reverted to the original owners if they returned and lived there again.

Ancestral rights of ownership were termed *take tūpuna* while rights by means of conquest were termed *take raupata*. The Māori attitude to land was captured in the proverb: 'People die, are killed, migrate or disappear; not so the land, which remains for ever.'

Boundaries, cultivation, mana.

LANGUAGE. The Māori language is a variant of the far-spread Polynesian tongue, but has changed during centuries of isolation and has become adapted to the needs of a new country. There were dialectical differences in various regions, an example being in the use of '*k*' in the Te Waka a Māui (the South Island) in place of the Te Ika a Māui (the North Island) '*ng*'; hence Waitaki in the south becomes Waitangi in the north.

The 15 sounds of the language are represented by the five vowels and the 10 consonants *h*, *k*, *m*, *n*, *p*, *r*, *t*, *w*, plus the two diphthongs *ng* and *wh*. Each syllable ends in a vowel and no two consonants come together.

Though there were few abstract nouns in the language (but the few were of great importance), Māori had a great capacity for abstract thought, principally through belief in personifications and the material forms or vessels of abstract conceptions such as *ariā*, *mauri*, etc.

Pronunciation.

LATRINES (*turuma*). The importance of sanitation in the safe disposal of human waste was fully realised by Māori and for that reason the *turuma* of a *pā* or *kāinga* was surrounded by *tapu* to ensure the safety of the people.

The *turuma* was usually situated on the edge of a cliff or bluff, and consisted of a horizontal beam, *paepae*, and vertical poles that were grasped while squatting on the *paepae*. The *turuma* was dedicated to the rites used in warding off evil spirits, while a peculiar custom known as *ngau paepae* (biting the beam), accompanied by appropriate *karakia*, was resorted to by those who were sick, and by warriors before they set out to war. The gods then protected them from ill fortune.

Magic, mana.

LAWS. Although there was no code of laws in the traditional Māori world, daily life and social controls were managed by a number of conceptual institutions and customs that served in their place. Prominent among these were the institutions of *tapu, mana, mākutu, muru,* and *utu*, all of which exerted a restraining influence.

Mākutu, mana, muru, tapu, utu.

LEPROSY (*ngerengere*). This disease was supposed to have come from the Hawaiki homeland in 'the leprosy canoe', *Te waka tuwhenua*, or *Moekakara*. The only known cure known to Māori was the recitation of *karakia*.

LIFE PRINCIPLE (*mauri*). The life principle of people and their activities in connection with animals, vegetation, forests, rivers and lakes had to be carefully preserved. In men and women it could be readily identified and sometimes confused with the soul (*wairua*). The subject is dealt with more fully under the heading *Mauri*.

Mauri.

LIGHT. According to the Māori creation myths, the Pō or eras of darkness were succeeded by the Ao (light), or Te Ao-nui (the great light). The Pō were feminine and the Ao masculine. In the beginning the primal gods lived in darkness before the separation of their parents Rangi and Papa.

It was Ue-poto who first observed the glimmerings of light beyond the confines of his parents' bodies. It was a feeble light or phosphorescence, as of a glow-worm, and Tāne and most of the brothers were eager to live in that light, while Whiro and his followers wanted the darkness.

But light entered the world after the separation and grew in intensity from the tiny, glow-worm-like gleam to the sunshine that flooded all when the heavenly bodies were placed on Rangi, the sky. In the legend of the warfare between Tāne and Whiro we see the eternal conflict between light and darkness.

Ponaturi, primal gods, separation, stars, sun, Tāne, Uru-te-ngangana.

An *amo* or litter for carrying the wounded. The pipe being smoked by one of the bearers is an indication that the incident comes from the period of the land wars.

LIGHTNING. Personified by Tama-te-uira (forked lightning) and Hine-te-uira (sheet lightning), lightning was believed to be a form of supernatural fire. The two personifications and a number of others were appointed guardians and controllers of the lightning children, who were numerous and troublesome. Tawhaki the demi-god was also connected with lightning that was said to spring from his armpits.

Lightning storms were regarded as omens. If the flash was vertical it was an evil omen, usually announcing a death in the *iwi*, but if it seemed to be aimed at the *pā* of another *iwi*, it signalled disaster for those people.

Fire, hair, Tawhaki.

LITTERS (*amo*). Severely wounded warriors were carried on litters made of carrying poles, vines and leaves.

LIZARDS (*mokomoko*). Even to set eyes on a lizard was a dreadful experience, for it was an evil omen and often a harbinger of death. The lizard was the *ariā* or physical manifestation of Whiro, the god of evil.

Death was sometimes thought to be the result of a *kikokiko*, a malign spirit in the form of a lizard, entering the body and eating the vitals. If a lizard was seen, there were apparently only two ways of rendering its influence harmless: by getting a woman to step over it, thereby destroying its inherent *tapu*; or to kill it quickly, cut it in pieces, and burn the pieces (which on several occasions proved to be the only effective way of killing a *taniwha*). There is a connection between *taniwha* and lizards, which they are supposed to resemble, and both were descended from the mating of Tāne and Hine-maunga.

There is an amusing fable of a battle between dogs and lizards. The former won and feasted on the lizards, but the meal affected their fertility and ever since the number of dogs has always been small.

Most depictions of animals and plants in traditional Māori art have become so conventionalised they have lost resemblance to the originals. The lizard is the one exception, for it is depicted either in a naturalistic way, or in various degrees of stylisation. The lizard is frequently found in Māori woodcarving, occurring rarely in bone and stone, or as painted motifs.

Because it was a representative of Whiro, the personified form of death and evil, the lizard is often found as a decorative motif on bone chests or in association with other forms of death symbolism.

Carving, death, disease, evil, reptiles.

'LOST TRIBE'. This was a Pākehā epithet for the Ngāti Mamoe *iwi* who were formerly in possession of most of Te Waka a Māui or the South Island, but were driven to the end of the island by the invading Ngāi Tahu *iwi* and into the almost impenetrable mountains, fiords and rain forests of the far south. However the two tribes remain linked through the shared bloodlines of intermarriage.

One or two members of the tribe were discovered by Captain Cook in Dusky Sound in 1773, and in the years that followed a number of Pākehā-inspired legends of these people sprang up. These mainly centred on the existence of a wild and untameable race of 'savages', living and roaming amidst the West Coast sounds. The story was believed so implicitly that in 1863–4, the Provincial Government of Otago issued a manifesto cautioning Wakatipu gold-diggers and others from attempting to penetrate these territories, unless well armed and in numbers sufficient to repel native aggression.

The last known contact with full-blooded members of Ngāti Mamoe was thought to have been made by Sir James (then Dr) Hector in 1862, at Martins Bay, when he met the old chief Tu-toko and his two daughters. Mount Tutoko is named for the chief.

LOVE CHARMS (*ātahu*). White magic, known as *ātahu* or *iri*, was used to cause feelings of love to rise in the heart and mind of a member of the opposite sex. It was also used to restore affection to a deserted husband or wife.

One method employed by a suitor was to obtain part of the hair or of a garment of a loved one, take it to the *tohunga*, and hang it on the *amo*, bargeboard, of his house. The suitor then spat into a *kūtai*, mussel, or pipi shell, and the tohunga took it in his hands and chanted a karakia over it. He set it afloat on the water, and it would then bear a message to the loved one. Feathers, living shellfish, and birds have all been used for this purpose. The ātahu was the karakia or charm that was recited over 'the messenger of love'.

Courtship, magic.

LULLABIES (*oriori, pōpō, ara*). Māori mothers sang their babies to sleep with lullabies. The word oriori comes from ori meaning to sway, or move to and fro. An oriori pūtaka is a song that was sung while spinning tops.

MAERO or **MAEROERO**. Often described as wild men of the forest, these fearsome creatures seem to be a Te Waka a Māui, South Island, version of the northern *patupaiarehe*, or fairies. They were malignant and fearsome, lying in wait for travellers and unsuspecting hunters. They often fished at night, using their long fingernails as spears, and the lights they fished by could sometimes be seen shining across the water.

Fairies.

MAGIC (*ātahu* and *mākutu*). In the traditional Māori world there was only a thin line separating magic and sorcery, with both having religious overtones. For the sake of convenience we might think of magic as being 'white magic' and sorcery as 'black magic' or *mākutu*.

Mākutu was contained in the *kete tuatahi*, the basket of knowledge of evil, and was taught out of doors in the *whare maire* (a figurative expression). The young men who trained to become a *tohunga mākutu* were forced to undertake many unpleasant ordeals. Lessons were graphically remembered by the forced eating of repulsive foods and, as proficiency increased, the trainee *tohunga* was required to demonstrate their knowledge and skill by destroying plants, trees, birds, and, the ultimate test: human beings.

To test the resolve of the trainee, the victim might be a relative or sometimes the instructor himself. This test required the *tohunga* to be able to kill at a distance by weakening the life force of the victim and even to destroy the target's *wairua*, soul.

Mākutu or 'black magic' was usually practised at the *tūāhu*, at the *wāhi tapu* or at the village *turuma,* communal latrine. Media such as lizards, stones, and other objects were used, and a form of sympathetic magic employed in which the *tohunga* required a hair, fingernail or portion of the spittle of the victim.

Tohunga well versed in *mākutu* could conjure up storms or weaken the morale or resistance of the enemy, rendering their fighting skills useless by blasting their *wairua*, souls.

There are tales of *tohunga* who defeated the enemy by releasing kites over which spells had been cast, so that if the trailing kite cord touched an enemy his courage would fail.

By way of contrast, white magic was almost wholly beneficial but it too required appropriate media. An *ahi tapu*, sacred fire, might be used to protect against evil influences. The fire would be used to cook food that could be carried by travellers to safeguard them against the sorcery of hidden enemies and evil spirits. Single hairs over which *karakia*, charms, had been recited were used to repel the attacks of *taniwha*. Hairs could also be used to cause springs of water to well up through the ground. Magic darts were used to find the location of missing people and hidden or unknown places, while charms were used to win brides, or to keep wives faithful to their absent husbands.

One method of causing a woman to conceive was to cut a leaf in the shape of the human figure. By performing the correct ritual over the leaf it was possible to remove harmful influences and bring the woman to the pure condition of Hine-ahu-one, thus embuing her with the power and fertility of the first woman.

These rites and others used to restore the sick to health, and to counter the arts of *mākutu*, were also frequently performed at the *tūāhu* and formed a part of everyday life.

Baskets of knowledge, darts, mana, natural phenomena, religion, souls, tohunga.

MĀHANGA, see SNARES.

MAHAU, see PORCHES.

MAHUHU. A migration canoe from which some of the tribes living in the northern part of Te Ika a Māui are descended. It was said to have brought *kūmara*, *taro*, and possibly coconut and *aute*, the paper mulberry tree. The latter two plants did not prove to be successful in the new land. The captain of Mahuhu was Rongomai.

MAHUIKA. The goddess of fire and grandmother of the demi-god Māui.

Fire.

MAIKI. Personifications, brothers, who were allied to Whiro and were responsible for sickness and disease.

Disease, evil, sickness, Whiro.

MAKŌ. The *makō* shark, but also a generic name for sharks or sharks' teeth.

MĀKUTU. Black magic, sorcery, seer, or spell.

Magic, schools of learning.

MAMARI. A migratory canoe commanded by the ancestor Nukutawhiti. It was wrecked on its arrival. The descendants of its crew settled in the far north of Te Ika a Māui.

MAN. Tū-matauenga was the god of mankind. Having decided that men rather than gods should inhabit the earth, Tū-matauenga produced the *ira tangata* by forming man in his likeness and giving him life. The first man created was Tiki and he became the father of the human race.

In one legend he mates with Hine-ahu-one, the earth-formed woman created by Tāne, but this tradition was not normally taught. The name of Tiki's first wife has been lost.

Tū-matauenga, being the god of war as well as of man, was the guardian of mankind and especially of men, thus representing the male element that is symbolised in Tiki.

Gods (wars of), Hine-ahu-one, ira tangata, Tiki, Tū-matauenga.

MANA. It is impossible to provide a single English word to correspond with this significant concept. Williams's *Dictionary of the Māori Language* gives the following definitions: authority, control, influence, power, prestige, psychic force; and, as an adjective, effectual, binding, authoritative; vested with effective authority.

Mana came with birth but could be increased or decreased by an individual's actions. Skill in warfare, wealth, bravery, and powerful allies increased *mana*. The higher the *mana*, the greater the degree of personal *tapu* of that person. Persons of high *mana* were sensitive to infringements of that state and protected it jealously, often seeking *utu*, revenge or satisfaction, for the most minor of real or imagined infractions.

A *tohunga* who was able to control the forces of nature, such as the production of a peal of thunder, was said to be exercising *mana tangata* (human powers) and *mana atua* (supernatural powers).

Mana tangata was inherent in a person, usually by reason of birth, while the *mana atua* were the supernatural powers that a person might gain when trained as a *tohunga*. *Mana* was sometimes transmitted from a teacher to a pupil, and from father to son, usually by biting some part of the body, as the *wairua*, soul, departed at the moment of death.

It was the *mana* of the *atua*, gods, that gave power to *karakia* and religious ceremonies invoking their assistance; and it was that *mana* which made *mākutu* effective.

The quality that endowed a *tipua*, a ghost, was *mana*.

In its meaning of authority, there is *mana marae*, the right of a woman to exercise hospitality to visitors.

Mana also conferred certain rights over land. The *mana* that accrued to a high-born person through birth, personal merit and brave deeds greatly increased the influence and authority of that person.

As a highly *tapu* place the *turuma,* latrine, had considerable *mana*, giving power to the rites performed at it. When the laws of *tapu* were violated, *mana* was endangered.

Houses, offerings, tapu, tohunga, stones (sacred).

MANAIA. According to legend, Manaia was an early arrival in Aotearoa in the first Tokomaru or Tahatuna canoe. He was pursued here by Nuku in the Waimate, Te Houama, and Tangiapakura canoes. Manaia made peace with his pursuers at Paekākāriki, after which he went to the east coast of Te Ika a Māui before finally settling on the opposite west coast where the Āti Awa tribe claim descent from him.

Manaia was also a *whakairo*, carving, design in which the head comes to a point like a beak, giving rise to the description 'bird-headed man' and to the belief that it represents a relic of an ancient bird cult. Another Polynesian example of bird-figure designs is found on Easter Island.

Other theories say that it represents the malignant spirit of a bird that attacked man in ancient times, or that it represents the *mana* or spiritual power of the human figure it usually accompanies.

Further analysis shows that the *manaia* is in effect a single half of a conventionalised head, and that therefore it represents the head in profile, the 'beak' being a portion of the upper lip rather than the nose or beak.

The *manaia* was a popular motif. It occurs in many different forms and was integrated into most *whakairo* design work.

Carving.

MANGŌ, see MAKŌ.

MANU, see BIRDS, and KITES.

MĀORI. In the traditional world, *māori* meant normal, usual, or ordinary; *tangata māori*, a human being, not a supernatural creature; *wai māori*, ordinary fresh water, compared with *wai tai*, salt water; *kurī māori*, native dog; *rākau māori*, ordinary, inferior trees, not good timber trees.

Māori has subsequently come to serve as the name for the indigenous people of Aotearoa. For Māori themselves there was no need for a word to define the people until the arrival of the Pākehā.

Moa-hunters.

MĀORITANGA. The ancient meaning of this word was to explain, to make clear, or to reduce to ordinary understanding. The modern meaning is Māori ideology, 'Māori-ness'.

The revival of interest in traditional Māori culture has brought an added importance and stature to this word. It embraces those elements of traditional Māori thought and action that are considered to express the essential nature of Māori culture.

The Ngāti Porou leader Sir Apirana Ngata gave eight components of *māoritanga*:

- *Te reo,* the Māori language.
- *Whakataukī* or sayings of ancestors.
- *Waiata*, traditional chant-songs.
- *Haka,* posture dances.
- *Whakairo, d*ecorative art.
- Traditional Māori houses and *marae.*
- *Tikanga,* the body of *marae* custom, particularly that pertaining to *tangi* and *powhiri.*
- Retention of *mana,* prestige, and the nobility of Māori people.

MĀRA, see CULTIVATIONS.

MARAE. The enclosed space in front of a ceremonial house, a courtyard, or a *kāinga*, village, 'common' where public meetings were held and visitors were greeted and entertained. These days it has come to be a term that describes the whole complex consisting of the *wharenui* and *wharekai* plus any ancillary buildings such as ablutions. The open space itself is often referred to as the *marae atea*.

Mana, meals, houses, whare.

Activity on the marae.

MARAKI-HAU. Taniwha or sea-monsters with a human head, and with long, tubular tongues that were used for sucking up men and canoes. The monster was equipped with a fish's tail. The marakihau was a *whakairo* motif used in house carvings in the Bay of Plenty district in particular.

Carvings.

MĀRAMA, see MOON and MONTHS.

Ao mārama.

MĀREIKURA. According to a late collected tra dition, *māreikura* were female beings who lived in the twelfth overworld, attending the supreme being, Io. They acted as messengers and visited the other overworlds and the earth, reporting to Io on events within his universe. They shared these duties with the *whatukura*.

Overworld, whatukura.

MĀRIPI. A shark-toothed cutting implement.

Knives.

MARO. Aprons or loin-cloths.

Kilts.

MARRIAGE. There were three types of marriage:

- Of *taurekareka*, slaves and commoners, in which man and wife slept and lived together without any marriage ceremony.
- Of ordinary *rangatira*, in which there might be celebrations, giving of presents, and feasting, but no religious ceremonies.
- Of high-born *rangatira* and the children of the *ariki*, in which the social customs were observed, and the marriage consecrated with religious ritual. There were few marriages of this type, but when they occurred they were important occasions which attracted a great deal of attention.

Most marriages occurred within the *iwi*, tribe, and *hapū*, sub-tribe or clan, but degrees of consanguinity were noted. Marriage was not permitted between cousins. Marriage within three generations of a common ancestor was permitted, and al though there were a few occasions when a union took place within these limits, they were frowned upon.

One of the reasons given for the frequency of marriages within the *hapū* was that if any friction arose between husband and wife, it was simply a family quarrel, but if they belonged to different iwi, it might lead to conflict.

Amongst the family of *ariki*, marriages were mostly political in nature, with the bridal couple coming from different tribes in order to cement ties of peace and friendship.

The betrothal might occur in several ways — by mutual declaration and consent of the couple; by a formal betrothal arranged by elders, sometimes during the infancy of the couple; by the nomination of a woman for a certain man by a prominent *rangatira*; by forcible capture or abduction; and by competition and contest. In nearly every case the choice had to be ratified by the *iwi*, for cogent objections might well occur to the elders. When a young man sought a wife for himself, it was usual for him to ask formal permission of the girl's parents.

Mutual affection was common, and there were many instances of young persons who braved the anger of their people by eloping. After some lapse of time they could usually return without being taken to task too severely. Sometimes a girl who maintained her right to marry the man of her choice against the wishes of her people was confined to the narrow limits of a *pātaka*, storehouse, in an attempt to bring her to reason.

Puhi, who were aristocratic virgins, were closely guarded and highly *tapu* until the *iwi* approved a suitor of sufficient *mana* to wed her. Visiting parties of young men would attempt to win the favour of the young women of the *iwi* in the hope that one of them might be fortunate enough to win the *puhi* as his bride.

Amongst young people a degree of sexual freedom was permitted, but after marriage young women were expected to remain faithful to their husbands. Polygamy was practised only among important *rangatira*, and was a sign of rank and *mana*. The limit was usually two wives, but a chief might well have a number of slave wives in addition. Their lot was not enviable, for they were forced to perform all the menial tasks.

Girls usually married young, for they reached puberty at an early age, but young men had to prove their prowess and come to full manhood before marriage. There is some evidence of polyandry amongst high-born female *rangatira*.

In the case of the few important marriages, the bridegroom's *whakapapa*, genealogy, was recited, the bride and bridegroom were adorned with the best cloaks, a new oven was made in which their food was cooked, and occasionally a new *whare*, house, was built for their use.

Some scholars are sceptical of the elaborate marriage rituals described by early ethnographers such as Elsdon Best, although it is clear that there was a distinction between the liaisons of young lovers and the acceptance of a couple as man and wife. Children born on the *takapau whara-nui*, the 'wide-wefted sleeping mat' of lawful marriage, were clearly distinguished from those born out of wedlock. These distinctions imply some social observance marking marriage.

It is generally accepted that important marriages were times of rejoicing and of feasting, games, and the making of gifts.

The Te Arawa scholar, Wiremu Maihi Te Rangi-kaheke, left an amusing manuscript account (1850) of the 'courtship' activities of men and women and their attempts to attract attention:

> Now the women also desire the men. In the evening the women gather at their house. They light the fire and begin to sing and dance. The voices reach the men. They arise and go to watch. The women see the men. Lo, they roll their bellies in the dance, and make sport, and pull faces. The men come as far as the porch of the house, on the courtyard of the village, and they sit there. They remained outside in order to tempt the women to come outside and dance.
>
> It remained for the men's party to dance. They stood up singing. The son of So-and-so performed the action known as 'weaving an apron'. Behold, he was as graceful as running water. The women started to come out, like parrots lured by a decoy. They came out singing together. They danced and sang together.
>
> Then the men danced as they rose up from the ground. It was as if their arms and the upper parts of their bodies had been massaged to suppleness. They gazed at the women as if they were startled by them. As soon as the men had finished the women were on their feet. Looking at them their eyes seemed like the full moon.

Betrothal, courtship, polygamy, presents, puhi, sex, tribes.

MASSAGE (mirimiri). Babies were massaged frequently to make their limbs supple and shapely. But older people suffered more drastic treatment. A cure for pains in the back and physical exhaustion was to trample on the patient's back as they lay on the ground — a cure still practised in parts of the Pacific. Squeezing and massaging the flesh was used to treat minor aches and pains.

Babies.

MATAATUA. A migration *waka* commanded by Toroa or, in some traditions, Ruaura. When the *waka* arrived in the Bay of Plenty it was left unsecured as the people went ashore. The canoe was in danger of being lost but was saved by Toroa's daughter, who 'whakatāne' (acted as a man), thus giving the name to that place and the river which discharges there. The Whakatōhea, Ngāti Awa, Tūhoe, Ngāiterangi and Ngāti Pukenga tribes all trace their descent from the crew of this waka.

Some accounts say that after an argument amongst the crew, the Mataatua was taken to the far north by Toroa's younger brother, Puhi, who founded the Ngā Puhi iwi. The final resting place of the *waka* is said to be in the bed of the Takou River on the Northland east coast.

MATAHORUA. One of the waka, canoes, said to have brought the explorers Kupe and Ngāhue to Aotearoa.

Kupe.

MATAKITE, see SECOND SIGHT.

MATAU, see FISH-HOOKS.

MATE, see DEATH, SICKNESS.

MATIMATI, see HAND GAMES.

Sleeping mats.

MATS (whāriki, takapau). Beds in a Māori whare were made very simply. Brushwood, bracken, lycopodium, and similar resilient shrubs or plants were laid on the floor and covered with coarse mats. On top of these were laid the more finely woven mats. Those made from flax leaves were often woven in patterns, but the more highly prized mats woven from *kiekie* were usually left plain. The upper mats of flax had the leaves lightly scraped and passed over a fire to remove the green colouring.

Mats were also made for placing on top of earth ovens to trap the steam and keep out the soil, as well as many other purposes.

Houses, plaiting, sleep, weaving.

MĀUI. Māui-pātiki or Māui-tikitiki-a-Taranga, to employ the usual names that distinguished him from his brothers, all or most of whom were also called Māui, is usually depicted as a whimsical and irresponsible demi-god whose exploits were known throughout Polynesia. After a miraculous birth and upbringing, he won the affection of his parents and taught useful arts to the people. In his many adventures he snared the sun, tamed fire, and found new lands by pulling them up from the bottom of the sea, but eventually he met his death while attempting to kill Hine-nui-ō-te-pō, the goddess of death. Had he succeeded, mankind would have become immortal.

While his greatest deeds were of great benefit his malicious humour made his relatives suspi-

Tama-nui-ki-te-rangi discovers Māui-tikitiki-a-Taranga (Maui in the topknot of Taranga).

cious of his motives. S. Percy Smith wrote that he:

> ...might appropriately be called a hero because he embodies the Polynesian idea of a hero – a gifted, clever, daring, impudent, rollicking fellow, endowed moreover with that kind of *mana* – which in this connection may be termed supernatural power – that enabled him to outdo the feats of ordinary mankind.

Aotearoa, cat's cradle, death, dogs, eels, fire, fish-hooks, Hina, Hine-nui-ō-te-pō, Ika a Māui (Te), North Island, pigeons, plaiting, Rupe, South Island, Stewart Island, sun.

MAU KAKĪ, see NECKLACES.

MAUNGA, see MOUNTAINS.

MAURI. *Mauri* was a vital concept in Māori thought. All things, animate or inanimate, either possessed or had the potential to possess, *mauri*, the life principle. The essence or vitality of that life principle was known as the *hau*. In individuals the *hau* was identified with the breath and activities such as sneezing were said to be an act of the person's *mauri*. For people, the *hau* and the *mauri* were both located within the body.

For every other case, the *hau* – the vitality of that entity, understood as being equivalent to a person's breath – was strengthened and protected from enemies by being ritually located within an object such as a stone, also known as a *mauri*.

At the same time an *atua*, god, sometimes more than one, was located in the *mauri* as well. In this way the *mauri* brought together the vitality of the entity and a guardian spirit. If the *mauri* were protected and kept safe, all would be well with the people, the land or the resource with which it was identified. For this reason *mauri* were often hidden with accompanying *karakia* and ceremonial. The main protection however came from the *atua* that had been located in the *mauri*. The *mana* of the *atua* protected the *mana* of the entity the *mauri* represented.

The *mauri* of inanimate things such as land always related to their use by humans. The best example is that of land being used for a *kūmara* garden. It was the human use of the land, the gardening, to which the *mauri* became attached. The *mauri* of a garden was usually represented physically by a small rock or stone figure. In some cases the rock would be roughly shaped to represent the god of cultivated food, Rongo. Equally, a branch of *māpou* or *karamū* might serve as the *mauri* of a *kūmara* plantation. It was a way of ensuring success and good fortune in the use of the resource, i.e. the very important task of growing and harvesting *kūmara*.

Similarly with the *mauri* of a forest, which again could be represented materially by a hidden object. Should the *mauri* of the forest be lost or offended – for example, by plucking hunted birds and leaving their feathers strewn around the hunting sites – then it was likely that birds inhabiting that part of the forest might desert it. The *mauri* of a forest ensured that birds and fruits flourished while that of lakes, rivers, and streams ensured a plentiful supply of fish. These *mauri* were jealously guarded by being secreted in the forest, near the banks of streams or by the seashore.

The *mauri* of a *pā* was usually a stone that might be placed under the first palisade post to be erected or buried near the *tūāhu* or hidden at the foot of a tree in a nearby forest. The *atua* located within this *mauri* would normally be a war god under whose protection the *pā* would have been ritually placed. Loss of the *mauri* of a *pā* in battle would inevitably mean defeat for its inhabitants.

Mauri were sometimes buried by the rear post of *whare wānanga,* where they protected the house and its occupants.

Sometimes the *mauri* would sleep, or the *atua* be absent, in which event it had to be restored by religious rites and charms.

In some cases a *mauri* might be represented by a hill in the forest, or the sand on the beach. As an example, a whale-shaped hill near the beach at Mahia was regarded as the *mauri* of the whales that frequented that coast.

Birds (hunting), eels, fishing, hau, houses, life principle, souls, stones (sacred).

MAU TARINGA, see EAR PENDANTS.

MEALS. Except in times of food shortage there were usually two meals a day, the first after some hours of work in the morning, the second in the late afternoon or early evening when the labour for the day was done. Although women were busy all day with family duties, working in the cultivations, and gathering supplies of wood, they were required to do all the cooking. Some help might be given by male slaves, but the men of the tribe were thought to be too *tapu* to engage in such an occupation, cooked food being a pollutant of the *tapu* state.

Before the ovens were opened, the women plaited *kono* or *rourou,* simple baskets or dishes of green flax leaves, and when the meal was ready, vegetables were placed in these containers with flesh food such as fish, as a *kīnaki*, relish, on top. There were separate food baskets for those who were *tapu* and of high rank, but usually each basket contained enough food for up to four persons.

On ceremonial occasions, when a number of visitors was present, the cooked food was presented in a way more suited to the occasion. The meal would be brought on to the *marae* in procession, the women singing and swaying their bodies in time with the rhythm of the songs as they walked.

On less important occasions when only a few visitors were present, the entertainment was dispensed with. The baskets were placed on mats on the ground with the invitation, 'O friends, here is the sustenance of man.' The meal was eaten on the marae or in the porch of a house, never inside.

MEASUREMENTS. The limbs of the human body were employed as units of length. Some of the commonly accepted units of measurement were as follows:

The first joint of the thumb, the little finger, the width of the palm, the span of the fingers, the elbow to the tips of the fingers (likened to the biblical cubit), the span of the outspread arms (fathom), the length of the body and raised arm, etc. The fathom was termed a *maro*, and the one multiple unit for length, the *kumi*, equalled 10 *maro*. Although each unit had its distinctive name, none was constant because of variations in length from one person to another. When an exact standard of length was required, one person was selected as a measuring rod.

MEDICINE. While there is a different view now, the evidence is that Māori had a very small store of traditional knowledge about herbal remedies. Similarly, there was little knowledge about the treatment of even minor ailments. The reason was straightforward. Sickness of any kind was supposed to be visited on the sufferer as a punishment by the gods, or to be the result of attacks by evil spirits, or because of an infringement of *tapu*. Effective cures could therefore only be made by use of the appropriate 'magic' or *karakia*.

This changed with the coming of the Pākehā when Māori noted the efficacy of the treatment of illness by internal medicines, a practice that was quickly adopted and put into daily use. This development led to Māori finding their own herbal remedies and the establishment of the school of 'traditional' *rongoā Māori*, Māori remedies.

Diseases, sickness.

MEDIUMS (*ariā*). Lesser gods, spirits of the dead, deified ancestors, familiar spirits, and even the spirits of living men were represented by their *ariā*. An *ariā* may be termed a medium, form of incarnation, or material representation, and frequently takes the visible form of a bird or lizard. The hair was sometimes regarded as the *ariā* of the human *wairua*.

MEETING HOUSES, see HOUSES.

MEETINGS, see HUI.

Feasts, kōrero.

MEMORY. To compensate for the lack of a written language, Māori developed striking powers of memory. For example, the graduation tests of a student in the *whare wānanga* required that he should recite many *karakia*, some of great length, without a pause and without a mistake.

A tremendous body of history and lore of all kinds was preserved in the minds of some men. Elsdon Best records one Tūhoe *kaumatua*, elder, who was able to recite the genealogy of his hapū which included 1400 personal names and a great deal of tribal history. Another man was able to effortlessly dictate 406 songs.

MEN. The tasks in which men were engaged were strictly defined. Such *tapu* occupations as *waka*, canoe and *whare*, house-building, were universally confined to men, but the division of labour between men and women in most other tasks varied from tribe to tribe.

Hunting was essentially a man's job, but women sometimes assisted in setting the snares. In agriculture, women were required to help in clearing the ground and weeding, but men usually did the digging, and there were tribal variations as to whether women were permitted to help in planting.

Similarly, fishing *waka* were manned by men but women hunted for *kōura*, crayfish, and took part or the whole responsibility for catching fresh-water fish. The more *tapu* the task, the more strictly it was confined to men.

Women were subservient to their partners, though many of aristocratic rank wielded powerful influence.

Men were most given to personal adornment by *moko*, tattooing, hair dressing, and other means. They accepted the greater responsibilities in peace and war, and lived active lives but, wherever possible, left the heavy, monotonous tasks to their womenfolk.

Birds (hunting), man, tattooing, warfare, women.

MERE, see CLUBS.

Weapons.

METEORS (kotiri). Meteors were personified in the god Rongomai. Māori shared the Pākehā folk tradition that meteors were 'falling stars' but thought the reason for their fall was that they were pushed out of their *waka*, canoe, in the sky by their brothers. They were regarded as omens for good or ill.

Rongomai, stars.

MIDDENS. Piles of shells, buried in sandhills and uncovered by erosion, can be found in all coastal

Men at work, snaring rats, digging with the *kō*, fishing, fighting with *taiaha*, canoe building, and thatching the roof of a *whare*.

areas. These middens were the rubbish heaps of the people. Shells and debris were simply dumped as they accumulated round the earth ovens, but in some cases the shells were sometimes deliberately placed as a defensive measure. It was impossible to walk across the shells without disturbing them and making a noise.

Nowdays, the middens with their discarded shells, stone and bone fragments are mostly protected because they provide evidence which helps in reconstructing the life and economy of traditional Māori communities.

MIGRATION, THE GREAT. This is a now discredited theory that asserted that Māori came to Aotearoa in a fleet of *waka*, canoes, almost simultaneously. The theory was based on flimsy *whakapapa*, genealogical, evidence which attempted to align the generations of the *waka* captains and first arrivals so that they became contemporaries.

In recent years researchers have questioned these traditions, and have offered new and more likely theories to account for the settlement of Aotearoa, although it is likely that the reasons for migrating and the traditions concerning the composition of the crews and their adventures are common. The following sets out some of the more well-known Great Migration stories.

The 'Great Migration' tradition holds that fierce wars had broken out in the homeland Hawaiki, with over-population and shortage of food being the principal causes. For these and other reasons a great company of people set out some time in the 14th century A.D. in their picturesquely named *waka*, canoes – Te Arawa (The Shark), Tainui (Great Tide), Mataatua (Face of a God), Kurahaupo (Storm Cloud), and

An artistic depiction of the arrival of the Te Arawa migratory canoe at Whangaparāoa.

Tokomaru (Staff of a War God). In addition there were the Aotea, Takitimu, and Horouta, which sailed at about the same time, but did not accompany the main fleet.

Te Arawa was the first to leave, farewelled by the patriarch Hou-mai-tawhiti with the words: 'Follow not after the god of war in your country of the south; hold to the deeds of Rongo the peaceful. Haere, haere, haere atu rā!'

Tama-te-kapua, the son of Hou-mai-tawhiti, was the captain. He had abducted a famous *tohunga*, Ngatoro-i-rangi, and his wife Kearoa, in order to make use of his magic powers. Ngatoro-i-rangi brought the canoe to Te Korokoro-o-te-Parata, the throat of the sea monster, but later repented and saved it. Eventually the Arawa landed at Whangaparāoa in the Bay of Plenty, where the crew saw the scarlet blossoms of the *pohutukawa*, and threw their *kura*, red hair ornaments, overboard, to realise later that the supposed *kura* were but fragile flowers.

Most of the canoes arrived about the same time, and a quarrel arose over possession of a stranded whale found on the beach (Whangaparāoa means the bay of the sperm whale). An inspection was made of the *tūāhu*, sacred places, that had been set up on the shore and it was found that, while the posts set up by the men of Tainui were weathered and dried, those of the other canoes were still fresh and green. Tainui therefore claimed the honour of being the first arrivals – and the whale.

In fact the Tainui had arrived later than the others, but the crew had secretly passed the posts and flax of their *tūāhu* through the fire, giving them a weathered appearance.

Shortly after this the Arawa left the bay, leaving 140 men under the chief Taikehu to explore the north-west coast. The Arawa sailed to the island of Mōtītī, and then at Maketū the people set up their *tūāhu*. The descendants of Tama-te-kapua peopled the 'hot lakes' in the Rotorua district, while Ngatoro-i-rangi went to Lake Taupō. It is therefore said of the Arawa canoe that the *tauihu*, bow-piece, rests at Maketū and the *taurapa*, stern piece, at Tongariro, the figurative name for the Taupō district.

Tama-te-kapua became restless at Maketū, and journeyed to join forces with Taikehu at Tauranga. Then he went on to Hauraki and Colville, and made his home at the tip of the Coromandel peninsula, where he died. He was buried on Moehau *maunga*, mountain, where his sons said of him: 'Let him slumber here where his spirit can gaze far over the ocean and over the land of Aotearoa. And the winds that sweep across the great ocean of Kiwa, they shall ever sing his *oriori*, his wild lullaby.' Ngatoro and his wife ended their days on Mōtītī island.

The Tainui was built after the Arawa, and was also a double canoe. After leaving Whangaparāoa, Hoturoa, her captain, brought her to the Tāmaki isthmus, which was crossed by the portage. Other canoes also came to Tāmaki. The Tokomaru crossed the island first, but the Tainui soon followed, and sailed southwards to Kāwhia, where it was beached and later buried. Stone pillars that can still be seen projecting above the ground are said to mark the *tauihu* and *taurapa* of the *waka*.

A less fortunate end awaited Te Arawa. She was burnt by Raumati of the Tainui people, possibly in revenge for the abduction of the tohunga Ngatoro-i-rangi, and a long period of strife began. The descendants of Tainui settled in the Waikato district and were therefore neighbours of the Arawa.

The Mataatua was brought to her final resting-place at Whakatāne, although some say that the waka was taken north by Puhi and sunk in a stream in the Bay of Islands district.

The Tokomaru arrived at the east coast, rounded North Cape, and sailed down the west coast as far as the Mohakatino River. The Tokomaru's stone anchor was believed to have been kept there for hundreds of years, until at last it found a home in the New Plymouth museum. The descendants of Tokomaru spread northward to the Mōkau River, and formed the southern boundary of the Tainui people.

Little is known of the Kurahaupo canoe. The Ngā Puhi people say that it was petrified into a reef on the east coast, but the people of Aotea believe that it was wrecked at some time on its journey, and that the occupants were transferred to their canoe. This shipwreck was supposed to have taken place in the Kermadec Islands, which might help explain why the Kurahaupo people became scattered. Some are believed to have completed their journey in the Aotea, and that the Kurahaupo was afterwards repaired and continued its journey. One group of descendants inhabited the district where the canoe was supposed to have been petrified, on the east coast of the Tāmaki isthmus. A second group inhabited the country between the borders of Tainui and Aotea, while another group occupied the area from Whangaehu to Horowhenua.

Of the canoes which did not accompany the Fleet, but sailed about the same time, the Aotea, commanded by Turi, sailed from Ra'iatea, and was beached at Rangitahua (Sunday Island), where she was refitted. The Ririno sailed with her, but the two canoes parted company, and some say that the Ririno was wrecked on the Boulder Bank near Nelson.

The Aotea landed at the harbour that bears her name. Turi and his men continued their journey by land until they reached the Pātea River, where they settled, their descendants making their way up the Whanganui River.

Five canoes sailed under the command of Tamatea, but only two survived, the Takitimu and the Horouta. The Takitimu landed near North Cape, but was driven by a storm to Hokianga, where Tamatea and his people stayed for some years. The Takitimu later put to sea again and sailed to Whakatāne, where a number of the crew settled. Tamatea took the Takitimu to the Bay of Islands, where more of his crew settled, and then went to Waiapū on the east coast, where he found some of the men and women who had sailed in the Horouta. More people stayed there, but Tamatea-pōkai-whenua (Tamatea who travelled all over the land) could never stay in one place. He went to Te Waka a Māui, the South Island, and then returned north to Whanganui, Taupō and Whakatāne. Tradition says that finally the Takitimu was petrified into the range of mountains of that name in Murihiku, Southland.

This is how the country was settled.

Drift voyages.

MILKY WAY. Te Ikaroa was the personification of the Milky Way. Its position in the sky warned men of the approach of dawn and was also used to forecast the weather.

Stars.

MISFORTUNE. When a person or people suffered misfortune, the curious custom of *muru* was put into operation, and some of all of their possessions were taken as 'punishment'. The sinister Maiki brothers were said to be the cause of most ill fortune.

Muru.

MIST. Hine-pukohu was the personification of mist. She came to earth and was seen by Uenuku, who took her to be his wife. She stayed with him at night but returned to her home in the overworlds by day. Uenuku was so proud of her that one morning he detained her against her wishes, in order to show her to his people, and in consequence she left him. For the rest of his life Uenuku pursued her in vain, and at his death the gods took pity upon him and changed him into a rainbow.

During the creation, Hine-moana and Hinewai (the personification of misty rain) sent mist to cover the nakedness of Papa. It was on misty days that the *patupaiarehe*, fairies, roamed through the forest where they could be heard playing mournful tunes on their flutes.

Separation, Uenuku.

MOA. The giant bird known to the Māori as the *moa* still roamed the land when Māori first came to Aotearoa.

The *moa* was hunted and killed for its flesh, and its bones were used in the manufacture of fish-hooks and the reel or spool ornaments which are a distinctive feature of the earliest days of Māori occupation, popularly known as the Moa-hunter culture (see next entry).

Dinornis maximus, which was up to 3 metres in height, was probably extinct before the first Māori settlers arrived and of the several species hunted by the early inhabitants, the tallest was *Euryapteryx*, a little over 1.5 metres.

MOA-HUNTERS. Conventional early 20th-century scholarship said that the people who inhabited Aotearoa before the 'Great Migration' and even earlier were Moriori and were believed to be an inferior race of Melanesian origin. This theory has now been entirely discredited.

The first people are more properly referred to as *tāngata whenua* (people of the land, or original inhabitants) although this term has subsequently evolved to mean any Māori people belonging to a particular district.

The strongest evidence for the deserved demise of the Moriori theory came from a remarkable discovery on the Wairau bar in Marlborough in 1939. A local schoolboy found the grave of a 'chief' or leading man of a community that had existed before the later 'wave' of Māori migration. An analysis of the grave contents and the excavation and examination of other burials in the same locality showed these people to be, like Māori, of Eastern Polynesian origin. It also showed that the chief and his people had established a culture and lifestyle based on the hunting and exploitation of the moa.

The culture of the Moa-hunters, so named by the main investigator of the Wairau excavations, Dr Roger Duff of the Canterbury Museum, was presented in his 1950 publication *The Moahunter Period of Māori Culture*. Duff said:

> The term Moa-hunter . . . is applied to that particular phase of the ancestral New Zealand culture at which its divergence from the Hawaiki culture is not so great that its Eastern Polynesian origin cannot be clearly recognised, while the resemblance to Māori culture . . . is sufficient to establish it as ancestral to the latter.

The Moa-hunter theory has also been largely discarded, with modern scholars preferring to regard these first settlers as early Māori. A distinction of a kind has been made between the culture of these early settlers by describing them as belonging to the 'Archaic' period of Māori culture. The full flowering of pre-Pākehā Māori culture has been termed the 'Classical' period.

The Archaic period is important because it shows the slow and progressive evolution of Māori culture away from its Eastern Polynesian roots and on the way to developing a new tradition — Māoritanga.

Drift voyages, tāngata whenua.

MOANA, see OCEAN.

MOARI, see SWINGS.

MOE, see SLEEP.

MŌKAI. Slave, pet, or decoy parrot.

MŌKIHI, see RAFTS.

MOKO, see TATTOOING.

MONSTERS. The fabulous monsters of Aotearoa were many and varied. Numbered amongst them were the *maero*, the wild 'fairies' of Te Waka a Māui, a variety of repulsive and dangerous ogresses and, most important of all, the *taniwha* which were found in every part of the country, with varying degrees of shape, size and vindictiveness.

Maero, maraki-hau, taniwha.

MONTHS (*marama*). The moon was the standard by which time was measured in the Māori year. There were 12 months, each with its own name, which varied from tribe to tribe. The Takitimu calendar given here aligns with agricultural activities:

1. *Pipiri*	All things contracted by cold, including man.
2. *Hongonui*	Man now feels severe cold and depends on fire for warmth.
3. *Hereturi-kōkā*	The scorching effect of fire is seen on the knees of man.
4. *Mahuru*	The earth now acquires warmth, which is felt by vegetation.
5. *Whiringa-nuku*	The earth is now quite warm.
6. *Whiringa-ā-rangi*	Summer has arrived. The strength of the sun is felt.
7. *Hakihea*	Birds now sit in their nests.
8. *Kohi-tātea*	Fruits are now set. Man eats of first fruits.
9. *Hui-tanguru*	The feet of Ruhi now rest on the earth.
10. *Poutū-te-rangi*	Crops are now lifted.
11. *Paenga-whāwhā*	The haul of crops is now seen stacked on the borders of the fields.
12. *Haratua*	All crops are now placed in the storage pits; the tasks of man are finished.

The months were divided into approximately 30 'nights'. The following is the list of the Māori transliterations of the English months:

Hānuere:	January
Pepuere:	February
Maehe:	March
Āperira:	April
Mei:	May
Hune:	June
Hūrae:	July
Akuhata:	August
Hepetema:	September
Oketopa:	October
Nōema:	November
Tīhema:	December

Moon, nights of the moon.

MOON (*marama*). Rongo was the *atua* who controlled the moon, in addition to his function as god of agriculture. The double task was natural, because the moon was connected with fertility, causing seeds to grow, and *kūmara* tubers were planted only on the most favourable nights of the moon.

Rongo was the male element and was thought of as being the husband of all women. Hina was the female personification, and was known in two aspects – Hina-keha and Hina-uri (pale Hina and dark Hina), representing the full and new moon. Rona was also the deity of the moon, and as Rona-whakamau-tai she was, with Tangaroa, a tide controller.

Days, Hina, Hine-te-iwaiwa, months, nights of the moon, Rona, Rongomai, sun, tides, Waio-

ra-a-Tāne.

MŌRIŌRI. A discredited term for the earlier inhabitants of Aotearoa, but which is legitimately applied to the first inhabitants of Rēkohu, the Chatham Islands.

Drift voyages, Moahunters.

MORNING. The personification of morning is Hine-ata, the morning girl. The coming of morn ing is heralded by the planet Kopu, or Venus.

MOSQUITOES (*naeroa*, or *waeroa*). The crushed leaves of the Ngaio tree were used as a repellent for mosquitoes and sandflies.

Sandflies.

MOTHERS. At the birth of the baby, the mother was taken to the *kōhanga*, nest-house, but within a short space of time was able to resume her normal duties. She looked after her baby well, carrying it on her back or keeping it by her side in its basket cradle. As further babies arrived, the older girls took over a good deal of the work of looking after the younger ones, leaving the mother free to pursue her domestic duties.

Babies, birth, children, women.

MOTHS. Often regarded as representing *tāngata wairua*, the souls of men.

Souls, underworlds.

MOUNDS (ahu). Small mounds of earth were often formed in the *tūāhu* and used in connection with divinatory rites.

Individual *kūmara* plants were planted in moulded-up earth mounds, while mounds were also used as targets for the casting of darts or for spinning and jumping tops.

Darts, kūmara, tūāhu.

Māori woman carrying her baby on her back.

MOUNTAINS (*maunga*). The mountains of Aotearoa were formed when Māui's brothers trampled over and slashed at his 'fish' causing it to jump and buckle. Hine-maunga, who was one of the wives of Tāne, was the personification of mountains. In spite of the wealth of legend which clustered round mountains, the prin cipal ones were regarded as *tapu* and never climbed, as they were thought to be the homes of the gods.

Legend often gave mountains human characteristics. For example, Taranaki and Putauaki once lived in the centre of Te Ika a Māui with Ruapehu and Tongariro. But the mountains fought with each other and Taranaki and Putauaki were driven far away to the western and eastern edges of the land respectively.

Water.

MOURNING.

Death, hair, heads, laments, whare, widows.

MURU. The plundering or ritual stripping of property. *Muru* was an important method of redistributing goods in an economy in which there was little surplus. One of the chief ways of seeking *utu*, revenge or payment, was through *muru*. When someone acknowledged their offence, they would passively allow the seizure and destruction or redistribution of all their possessions.

Muru was a custom from which nothing was sacrosanct: weapons, garments, implements, ornaments, food and crops were taken by way of 'fines' from those who had suffered some misfortune. To be the victim of a *muru* raiding party was an honour, while to be ignored was an insult.

Although *muru* was a form of punishment, this does not entirely convey the meaning of the action taken against the victim, nor the high-spirited raid made by the plunderers.

It was the penalty paid for such things as carelessness resulting in a disabling accident, for the obvious disfavour shown by the gods, or for the death of a relative. For example, an elopement might be punished by a *muru* raid on the possessions of the families involved or on the possessions of their whole *kāinga*, village.

Abductions and adulteries were also offences that resulted in the imposition of a *muru* raid, even when the victim was also the victim of the actions of others.

It may be that the victims might console themselves with the thought that at some future date they might have the opportunity of restoring their plundered possessions at the expense of others.

Death, utu.

MUSIC. Music was part of the pattern of Māori life – it was a recreation and an outlet for the emotions in time of grief or rejoicing, in peace and in war.

Because there were few musical instruments Māori music was found in the *ngeri*, chants, the *waiata*, songs, the *oriori*, lullabies, the *haka*, and the *poi* dance, all of which were used to express various emotions.

Māori music had not developed to the stage of harmonies, nor of the primitive folk song of Western countries, but it was closely tied to daily life. Every *waiata* had a point and a definite object. An orator might use a *waiata* to drive home an argument or to sway the listeners to the speaker's point of view. Sometimes a *waiata* could move the audience to join in and sing too – for the most favoured *waiata* were those that were old and well-known songs.

If a person sang when alone, it was not merely to pass the time; there was always an object. For example a *waiata aroha*, a love-song, might be carried by the wind or by a bird to the object of affection.

A lament might even be carried to Rarohenga, the underworld, helping the singer relieve feelings of grief. Others might share the grief by learning the *waiata* and singing it on appropriate occasions.

Haka, musical instruments, songs.

MUSICAL INSTRUMENTS. Percussion instruments of the Māori were of a very primitive form and hardly related to music. Wooden gongs or 'drums' for example were used as warning devices rather than for music making.

Stringed instruments were unknown but wind instruments were common. They were played as solo instruments and, less frequently, as an accompaniment to *waiata*, songs.

The *pūtōrino* has been compared to a flageolet, piccolo, or flute. It was about 20 centimetres in length, had a single hole, and was used as a mouth instrument. The *kōauau* was more usually described as a flute and was probably the most common. It was made of bone, had several holes, and was played with the mouth.

The *nguru* was a nose flute, generally made of stone, with a curved end for the orifice, which was applied to one nostril, the other being closed with the thumb. The various forms of flute were difficult to play.

Special songs were composed for them, and it seems likely that words were often breathed into the music. Trumpets made from large seashells or wood were also known, but like the gongs were more in the nature of warning devices.

Flutes, gourds, haka, 'jew's-harps', music, poi, songs, trumpets.

MUTTONBIRDS (*tītī*). Vast numbers of *tītī* (sooty shearwaters) were collected from their extensive colonies on the shores of the mainland, and from offshore islands, especially in the Bay of Plenty, and around Rakiura, Stewart Island. The birds were usually taken at night when they returned from feeding at sea. The most common method was to dazzle the birds by the light of torches. Almost-fledged chicks were taken from their nesting burrows using fern sticks. The sticks were inserted into the burrow, twisted to entwine them in the chick's down and the plump young bird was then pulled out.

Adult birds were sometimes captured well away from the coast. Nets were set up on the crest of a ridge and fires lit at night to attract the birds. They flew into the nets, where they were killed with sticks. *Tītī* were an important item of stored food. They were roasted and then preserved in their own rich fat in gourds and other containers. In the far south *pōha*, large containers made of kelp and protected with bark covers, were used..

Baskets.

MUTU, see SNARES.

Birds (hunting).

MYTHOLOGY, see FOLKLORE.

Creation, gods, religion.

N

NAMES. In the case of children of high lineage a *tapu* name was given to the infant until the *tohi*, baptismal rite, when a new, permanent name was conferred. The *tapu* was lifted by the *tohi* ceremony, and the new name could be used freely, but until the baptism there was a severe restriction on the use of the *tapu* name. If the pre-baptismal name was a word in common use that word also became *tapu*, and severe punishment and even death was inflicted on any that might use it. Another word had to be substituted or invented. The names of very important chiefs occasionally became *tapu* in a similar manner.

Children were usually named after some incident that occurred about the time of their birth. A well-known instance of this appears in the Tawhaki cycle of legends when, some time before his son was born, Tawhaki sent his wife to bring in a large log of wood for the fire. In due course that baby was named Wahieroa (long log of firewood). But the name was also conferred in order to commemorate the treachery of his uncles, and to keep the flame of revenge alive.

Similarly a girl, Te Ao-mihia (the day welcomed), was named in memory of her grandfather, because he had welcomed the indications of a fine day for a fishing excursion, on which he was murdered. One of the most frequent sources of names was the death of a relative, even though the reason might be quite trivial. In other cases the name of an ancestor was chosen. Usually there was but a single name, but as it was frequently of some length, it was shortened, e.g. Tū-moana-kotere-i-whakairia-oratia (Tū-moana-kotere was hung up in the tree while he was still alive), which became shortened successively to Tūwhakairi, to Tūwhaka, to Tū.

The memory of famous ancestors was preserved in many tribal names, e.g. Ngāti Tūwharetoa, Ngāti Kahungunu, etc.

Every district, river, plain, mountain, and natural feature had its own name, and these were conferred in different ways. Some names were transplanted from Hawaiki, e.g. Arahura, Hikurangi, Motueka, Rangitoto, etc. which are names found all around the Pacific.

The earliest explorers were great name-givers, the most notable perhaps being Ihenga of Te Arawa. Many of the places he discovered were named in honour of relatives, and for incidents that occurred during his travels, for example Roto-rua-nui-a-Kahu (the second and big lake of Kahu-mata-mamoe). The first lake Ihenga had discovered was Roto-iti (the little lake) and the second, Roto-rua after his uncle Kahu.

Other incidents resulted in such names as katikati (nibbling), a place where food was nibbled. Many personal names enter into other place names, a great number commencing with O, which means The place of..., for example Ohau, the place of Hau. Natural features enter into other names, for example wai (water), motu (island), roto (lake), manga (stream or tributary), puke (hill), maunga (mountain), awa (valley), whanga (harbour). A great number of Māori place names as known now are abbreviations of longer names, and sometimes have become corrupted over the years. For example, the proper name for Rangitoto Island in the Waitematā harbour is Ngā rangi-i-totongia-a-Tamatekapua (the days of the bleeding of Tama-te-kapua).

The longest place name in Aotearoa is Taumata-whakatangihanga-kōauau-o-Tamatea-pōkaiwhenua-ki-tana-tahu (the brow of the hill where Tamatea who sailed all round the land played his flute to his lover). It is a location in Hawke's Bay.

Baptism, Aotearoa.

NAMU, see SANDFLIES.

NANAKIA. *Nanakia* were dangerous, malicious 'fairies' or beings. The normal meaning of the word is treacherous and crafty.

Fairies.

NATURAL PHENOMENA. These were always depicted in terms of personifications, guardians, and controlled beings, which gave vitality to all the manifestations of nature. A bewildering company of these personifications exemplified and controlled each natural phenomenon. Some control could also be exercised by the *tohunga* who, for instance, were credited with the power to reproduce solar and lunar haloes which could be used to convey messages to a distant place. Any measure of control was exerted by means of *karakia* that gave access to the gods, personifications often being the offspring of the *atua*.

Nature, personifications.

NATURE. Because Māori lived close to nature, climate and environment directly affected everyday life. The colder climate and absence of prolific fruit and vegetable growth modified clothing and agricultural activities when the first migrants arrived from Eastern Polynesia. This in turn regulated the times of war, because raids would be made during the growing season or when the harvest was gathered, but not during winter or planting time. Hunting and fishing were dependent on the fruitfulness of land and sea and Māori were conscious of this dependence on nature for their survival.

For this reason most activities were hedged about with religious restrictions designed to propitiate the powerful influences of the gods and to ritually ensure the success of any venture. Success in the future lay in the strict repetition of the circumstances and rituals that had brought success in the past.

On the more cosmic scale, Papa was the beneficent Earth Mother, Rangi the brooding sky from which came rain and sun, storm and mist, all of which affected food resources and personal comfort. The powerful departmental gods ruled over land, sea, and sky, and under them were the ubiquitous personifications of nature.

It was a living belief in the power of the supernatural that, in addition to fear, brought a practical element into the study of life-dependent subjects such as astronomy, hunting, fishing, agriculture and meteorology.

Agriculture, birds (hunting), fishing, garments, gods, natural phenomena, personifications, poutiriao, stars, Tāne.

NECKLACES (*mau kakī*). Breast ornaments and necklaces were made of a variety of objects and materials. Amongst the most interesting are spools or reels, which were sections of the bones of men and *moa*, or of drilled stones shaped as vertebrae with flanges. The central hole in vertebrae enabled them to be strung on cord and used as necklaces. The reel necklaces have been dated to the early years of the very first settlement of Aotearoa.

The strength and power of the sperm whale have always been admired by Polynesian people and not surprisingly, here in Aotearoa, sperm whale teeth were used occasionally as the centrepiece in a spool necklace. Sometimes an individual tooth, carved into a chevron pattern, was strung around the neck. Necklaces featuring *moa* bone carved in the shape of sperm whale teeth have also been found.

Necklaces might also be made from the teeth of dogs, human beings and of sharks. But the most important and universally used of all breast ornaments was the *heitiki* made from *pounamu*, greenstone.

Burial, ornaments, shellfish, teeth, tiki.

NEST-HOUSES, see WHARE.

Birth, mothers.

Paying out a seine net from two canoes joined together by a temporary platform.

NETS (*kupenga*). Legend tells us that at one time the art of netting fish was unknown until a chief named Kahukura, drawn by a persistent dream, travelled to the far north and saw the *patupaiarehe* catching fish by this method. He mingled with them in the darkness, delaying their work so that when morning came and the fairies fled before the light of the sun they left their net behind. Kahukura found the net in his hand and was able to pass the gift on to his people. While Kahukura's tale is an attractive one it is likely that, like the invention, the legend was brought to Aotearoa from the Hawaiki homeland. The clue is that the knots that were used in the making of the net were the ones used throughout Polynesia and in most other parts of the world.

The task of making and using a new net was highly *tapu* because the whole community relied on the success of such a venture. Large seine nets were usually made and used as a communal activity. In some cases related *hapū* might combine their labour to build a net. Each *whānau*, family, made part of the net, knotting the meshes of *harakeke*, flax or *tī kouka*, cabbage tree leaves, in their fingers, sometimes using a gauge to keep the size constant, but usually depending on the fingers to judge the size of the mesh. The mesh was bigger in the middle part of the net. When the various lengths were completed, they were tied securely together. A rope was attached to the top and bottom of the net and sinkers of stone in coarse, woven bags, and floats of light *whau* wood were tied to the ropes.

A wooden net float in human form.

A large seine net was stretched at full length on the ground with men standing by it. At a word of command they swung the net on to their shoulders and carried it to the canoe, where it was stowed carefully. In the case of the largest nets, two canoes would be fastened together to hold them. Men were stationed on high ground to watch the movement of a shoal of fish and pass the information on to the fishermen. When the fishing ground was reached the net was paid out overboard while the canoe was paddled ahead.

Except at the dedication of a new net, women assisted in hauling it ashore and gathering the fish. Some of the seine nets were enormous, and must have captured a vast quantity of fish. There is little reason to doubt that the largest examples were well over half a kilometre in length.

There were many other types of *kupenga* – small hand nets, landing nets, bag nets for taking shrimps and *īnanga*, whitebait, often placed across the mouths of rivers, or fastened with stakes to the bed of a stream. Many of the smaller nets had open mouths held in place with hoops of vine and with wooden handles. Bag nets used in rivers were many metres in length. A net used in catching the *kōkiri* was in the form of a bag that was pulled tight when the fishermen felt the fish nibbling.

Crayfish, eels, fishing, supplejack, whitebait.

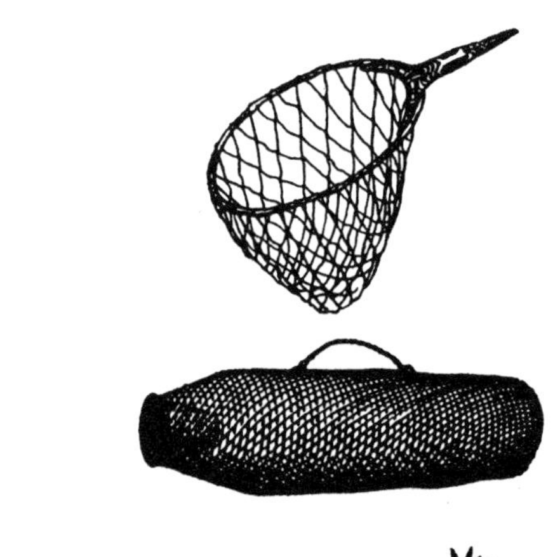

Top and centre: Two types of hand net. *Below*: A large seine net hung up for drying and mending. The making of large nets was an occupation for the whole tribe.

NEW ZEALAND, see AOTEAROA.

NGĀ. The plural form of the definite article.

NGAHERE, see FOREST.

NGĀHUE. An early explorer and companion of Kupe.

Greenstone, Kupe.

NGATORO-I-RANGI. Ngatoro was the *tohunga* who was abducted by Tama-te-kapua and brought to Aotearoa in the Te Arawa canoe. He was a powerful *tohunga*, and had many adventures in the new land. He climbed Tongariro mountain where he was rescued from freezing to death by his sisters in Hawaiki, who sent fire to him by way of Whakaari, White Island, and Rotorua, thus forming the thermal regions and the volcanoes in the centre of Te Ika a Mauī. Ngatoro was responsible for exploring and claiming a great deal of land for the Ngāti Tūwharetoa tribe.

Migration (Great), thermal regions.

NGAU PAEPAE. The rite of 'biting the beam' and which was an essential component in many *tapu* ceremonies.

Karakia, latrines.

NGERENGERE, see LEPROSY.

NGERI. A rhythmic dance with actions.
Dances.

NGURU. Nose flute.
Flutes, musical instruments.

NIGHT (*Pō*). In the traditional creation myth there were 12 *pō*, which were nights or periods of darkness, when Papa conceived and brought forth her offspring. Darkness and death were also associated, and the goddess of death was called Hine-nui-ō-te-pō, literally, the great girl of the night.

The hours of darkness were peopled with evil spirits and malign influences and no one dared venture abroad except as a member of a travelling party, or a band of hunters, who kept close to the cheering light of their fires or clutched their torches firmly. The only other reason for being about at night was a raid on an enemy position, when men were under the close protection of their tribal *atua* or war gods. Sentries also had to maintain a lonely vigil on the watchtowers.

The only tasks undertaken at night, therefore, were fishing, hunting for eels, and catching birds, and then only when torchlight provided the best opportunity for catching them; for example when a heavy frost left the birds stuck to their perches.

In the large meeting houses, where the central fires provided dim illumination, the early part of the evening was occupied by songs, dances and story telling.

Days, ghosts, Hine-nui-te-pō, Uru-te-ngangana.

NIGHTS OF THE MOON. Each night of the lunar month had a name. The year was divided into months, and the months into nights, these being the only divisions of time.

Though they differed from one tribe to another, the names of the nights were important, especially for planting and fishing. Some nights were favourable for these activities while others were not and the phases of the moon were carefully noted accordingly. Elsdon Best, the ethnographer who worked mainly amongst the Tūhoe people, recorded 30 names of the nights. He wrote, 'The moon dies on the Mutuwhenua night; its radiations of light are seen on the Whiro night; on the Tirea night it is actually seen; on the Ohua night it becomes round; on the Rakau-matohi night it wanes. There are ten nights of the ahoroa (moonlight) phase, five nights of decreasing light, and two of old age.'

Moon, months.

NITI, see DARTS.

NOA. Free from tapu.
Tapu.

NORTH ISLAND. Te Ika-a-Māui (Māui's fish), Te Ika-nui-a-Māui (Māui's big fish) or Te Ika-roa-a-Māui (Māui's long fish), were the names conferred on the North Island because of the legendary tale of how Māui fished up the land.

Because of its warmer climate, the earliest and principal settlements were on Te Ika a Māui, and the population was dense in such places as the fertile Tāmaki Isthmus and the Bay of Islands district.

According to tradition, the ancestor Toi landed in the Bay of Plenty in about the 12th century A.D., and most of the migratory canoes which followed made landfall in the same region. From here the first settlers travelled quickly round the coast before spreading inland. The climate was generally mild, and favoured the growing of *kūmara*, while forest, lake and shore provided a plentiful supply of food.

The only notable exception amongst the early arrivals was the Arai-te-uru canoe, which sailed down the eastern coast of Te Waka a Māui, the South Island.

Arai-te-uru, Ika a Māui (Te), Māui, South Island.

NOSE-PRESSING (*hongi*). Incorrectly termed 'rubbing noses,' the hongi is a form of greeting, performed by lightly pressing noses together, first on one side and then on the other. The action may be performed symbolically at a distance by doubling the forefinger and touching the tip of the nose. The hongi was also an expression of trust as the closeness of both parties made the use of hand weapons difficult, while the symbolic "sharing of breath" embodied in the action sealed the relationship between the participants.

Greetings.

NUKU. An early voyager who pursued the chief Manaia to New Zealand.

Manaia.

NUKUTERE. The migration canoe from which the Ngāti Porou people of the East Coast of Te Ika a Māui claim descent. Porourangi captained Nukutere.

NUMBERS. The following list shows how any specific number may be found. It is the ancient numerical system, which was not used with any degree of exactitude past 200.

The modern system is less complex and more exact.

1. tahi
2. rua
3. toru
4. whā
5. rima
6. ono
7. whitu
8. waru
9. iwa
10. ngahuru, or tekau (modern)
11. ngahuru mā tahi
12. ngahuru mā rua
13. ngahuru mā toru
20. tekau (the traditional word for 20, but now used for 10)
21. tekau mā tahi
22. tekau mā rua
23. tekau mā toru
30. tekau mā ngahuru
31. tekau ngahuru mā tahi
32. tekau ngahuru mā rua
33. tekau ngahuru mā toru
40. hokorua
41. hokorua mā tahi
42. hokorua mā rua
43. hokorua mā toru
50. hokorua ngahuru takitahi
51. hokorua ngahuru mā tahi
52. hokorua ngahuru mā rua
53. hokorua ngahuru mā toru
60. hokoturu
61. hokoturu mā tahi
62. hokoturu mā rua
70. hokoturu ngahuru takitahi
71. hokoturu ngahuru mā tahi
72. hokoturu ngahuru mā rua
80. hokowhā
81. hokowhā mā tahi
82. hokowhā mā rua
90. hokowhā ngahuru takitahi
91. hokowhā ngahuru mā tahi
92. hokowhā ngahuru mā rua
100. rau, or hokorima
101. hokorima mā tahi
180. hokoiwa
190. hokoiwa ngahuru mā iwa
200. ā rua rau, or kotahi rau (topu)
1000. mano

In the modern system kotahi is used for the one in 100 and 1000. Numbers 11 to 19 are formed by adding the numbers to 10, e.g. 15: tekau mā rima. Numbers 20 to 90 are formed by placing the number in front of the 10, e.g. 90: iwa tekau. A specimen number will illustrate the system — 9182 — e iwa mano ā kotahi rau e waru tekau mā rua.

Counting.

O

OBSIDIAN (*tūhua*). The main source of *tūhua*, obsidian or volcanic glass, in Aotearoa was Tūhua, Mayor Island. Other inferior deposits were found at Taupō and in North Auckland.

In the legend of the flight of *pounamu*, greenstone, it is said to have landed on Tūhua but was driven away by tūhua and māta (flint).

Sharp-edged flakes of obsidian were used for many small cutting tasks such as hair and fabric cutting. In a ceremonial role it was used for self-laceration in time of mourning.

Death, greenstone.

OCEAN (*moana*). Tangaroa was the god of the ocean and of fish and, as Tangaroa-whakamau-tai, was with Rona-whakamau-tai a controller of the tides. The ocean was known as Te Moana-nui-a-Kiwa (the great ocean of Kiwa), and was personified in Kiwa's wife, Hine-moana. Another figurative expression for the sea was Wai-nui (great water).

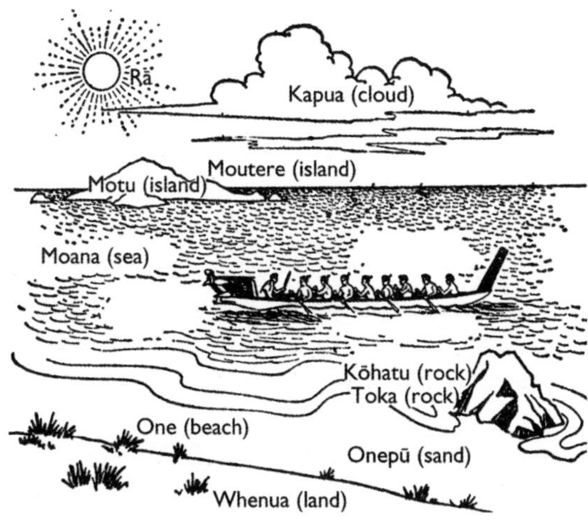

The ocean and the shore.

The ocean was the path between Aotearoa and the homeland and for that reason it occupied an important place in Māori thought. It was believed to be populated with monsters and wave children, and was sometimes referred to as Marae-roa-atea (the vast marae or space).

Hine-moana, Kiwa, laments, taniwha, tides, Tinirau, whitebait.

OCHRE, RED (*kōkōwai*). Red was the sacred colour throughout Polynesia and explains the sacred properties attached to this clay substance. Red ochre was an oxide of iron often found in muddy streams and swamps. One method of collection was by placing fern fronds in the water. The red, muddy deposit was subsequently dried, scraped off, and rolled into balls, the product being called kōkōwai.

So that it could be used as a paint, the kōkōwai was usually mixed with shark-liver oil before use. In view of the large quantities normally required, however, the red clay itself was usually ground up and mixed with oil. The use of shark oil gave the kōkōwai a very 'pungent' odour.

There were two practical and one aesthetic uses for kōkōwai. When mixed with shark-liver oil, it was a favourite adornment for the face, especially among men, and was also used for painting woodcarvings. It was said that a mixture of shark oil and ochre smeared over children protected them from sandfly bites. It was also a magical protection against the patupaiarehe, who were instantly repelled by it. To denote their sacredness, human bones were also paint-ed with kōkōwai. Uses such as this meant that kōkōwai had a tapu quality.

Separation.

OCTOPUS (*wheke*). In legend, the explorer Kupe was pursued from Rangiwhakaoma, Castlepoint, to Te Tau-ihu-O-te-waka, the Marlborough Sounds, by a giant octopus, which he finally overcame by spearing it in the eyes.

Wheke for eating were caught by hand amongst the rocks. The fisherman thrust his bare arm into the water, and when the wheke wound its tentacles round his flesh, it was withdrawn and removed by placing the other hand under its body.

OFFERINGS. It was customary to placate and propitiate the gods when engaged in occupations of any kind. Fowlers offered birds to Tāne, workers in the cultivations made offerings to Rongo, fishermen gave fish to Tangaroa, voyagers placated Tāwhiri-mātea, the god of winds, before the voyage and gave seaweed to Tangaroa at its conclusion. The first fruits of the harvest and the first fish caught were offered to the gods. Apart from such gifts, others of a symbolic nature, such as hair, blood, and human sacrifices were made. In some places special stages were erected to hold the gifts.

Another custom, in which local *atua* and spirits were propitiated, was that of *uruuruwhenua*. The gifts were twigs and clumps of vegetation, and the place where they were deposited was usually a *tipua*, enchanted, object such as a stone or a tree. These offerings upheld the *mana* of the *tipua*, and conferred good luck on the donor.

The *uruuruwhenua* rite in which a woman is laying an offering of a fern frond at the base of a tree.

Altars, ceremonies, demons, evil, fishing, kūmara, stars, travellers, warfare.

OHA, see DYING SPEECH.

OIL (hinu). There were a number of uses for oil, both animal and vegetable. Shark oil was used to mix kōkōwai. Oil was expressed from tītoki berries, scented with certain leaves and gums, after which bird skins were dipped in the fragrant oil and worn round the neck.

Ochre (red), scent.

OMA, see RUNNING.

OMENS (aituā). Unlucky or evil omens were *aituā*, a word used also in the sense of unlucky, or unfortunate. Omens were to be found in almost everything Māori came in contact with and, with their belief in *atua* and fear of evil spirits, meant that they had to walk circumspectly.

Unfortunately there were few lucky omens. An eel fisher, for instance, knew that he would secure a good catch if his nose itched. In warfare, fate would be kind or unkind in accordance with the appearance of omens such as the position or shape of a rainbow, the direction of a flash of lightning, or the performance of a war dance.

The endless number of evil omens included such diverse subjects as seeing a *morepork*, owl, by daylight, a *pīwakawaka*, fantail, flying into a house, stepping over fish in a canoe, seeing an albino *tūī*, or a large eel in the daytime, or abandoning the prepared site of a new house.

Dreams, lightning, meteors, rainbows, warfare.

ONE, see SAND. It also means beach, and mud, while *oneone* is earth or soil. Different types of soil had qualifying suffixes, e.g. *oneharuru*, sandy loam.

ORATORY. Māori were born orators and were usually able to hold their audience spellbound with their performance. Their speeches were full of legendary and historical allusions and were delivered whilst the speaker strode up and down the *marae*, using weapons such as *mere* and *taiaha* to emphasise the points he was making. Speeches might be interspersed with chants and songs as a *kīnaki*, or relish to the words.

Speeches.

ORIGINS. Legend and folklore were rich in stories that explained the origin of natural phenomena, plants, animals, and mankind. The gods came from the mating of earth and sky; the departmental gods in particular were responsible for the creation of everything in their own domain, frequently by mating with various personifications; while the remaining gods were active in similar pursuits. From their wars and adventures other origins arose, e.g. quarrels first came from the wars of the gods; finally, legends of later heroes and demi-gods explain many origins, such as Māui's jealousy of his brother-in-law Irawaru resulting in the making of the first dog.

Gods, natural phenomena, personifications.

ORIORI, see LULLABIES.

ORNAMENTS. While both men and women were fond of personal adornment, men were the most vain about their appearance. As a rule they wore their hair long while women kept theirs short. The long hair was tied in one or more knots and decorated with feathers and combs.

The same trend was shown in tattooing. Men were frequently tattooed full face and on the buttocks, while women's *moko* was confined to the lips and chin, occasionally to the forehead, and less frequently to other parts of the body.

Men occasionally wore a long feather threaded through the septum of the nose, a practice still found in other parts of the Pacific.

Anklets made of woven flax and of strings of shells and bracelets of the same materials were mostly favoured by young women. Ear pendants were made of stone, greenstone, and shark's teeth, while flowers, albatross and gannet down and sometimes living birds were worn in the ear. The principal neck ornament was the *heitiki*, but there were also necklaces of shells, teeth, and bone spools.

Sachets of scented grass and of birds' skins were impregnated with fragrant oil and hung about the neck or from a belt.

Faces were liberally painted with *kōkōwai* and on occasions, blue mud. Ornaments worn by both men and women are described elsewhere in greater detail.

Ear pendants, feathers, hair, necklaces, ochre (red), painting, scent, tattooing, teeth, tiki, whales.

OVENS (*hāngi* and *umu*). Food steamed in an earth oven had a delicacy and flavour that cannot be equalled by any other method of cooking. The oven consisted simply of a pit dug in the earth, varying in size with the amount of food to be cooked. A typical family oven would be about a metre in diameter and nearly as deep. Permanent ovens were lined with plaited flax bands.

Short lengths of dry wood were placed in the pit, with stones on top and the whole set alight. By the time the wood was burnt the stones were red hot. The embers were raked away and the stones spread evenly over the bottom of the pit. Green leaves, fern fronds, and other vegetation was placed on top of the stones, and the food on top of the vegetation.

A layer of kūmara might be put in first if they were available, then any green vegetables – fern fronds for example – and lastly flesh food like fish, wrapped in leaves. Another layer of vegetation was placed on top and then liberally sprinkled with water that trickled down to the hot stones and was turned to steam. Matting was placed on top, earth scattered over it and patted firm to trap the steam within. The process of cooking began. The food steamed quietly for several hours until the oven was opened and the meal began.

Cooking, food.

OVERWORLDS. In some late collected traditions the sky was divided into 10 strata. This division of the sky into 10 overworlds was ascribed to Tāne, and they became the scene of the adventures of heroes such as Rupe and Tawhaki, which might originally have occurred in distant countries, and then been transferred to the supernatural realms.

In his commentary on Māori life, *Te Ika a Māui*, the Wanganui-based missionary Richard Taylor wrote that the lowest was the abode of rain; the second of spirits; the third of winds; the fourth of light; while the tenth was the habitation of the gods.

The 10 overworlds were said to be *ngā rangi tūhaha* (the bespaced heavens). The lowest was Rangi-nui, the great Sky Parent. The sun, moon, and stars moved on his body. Through the sides of the hanging sky, sea voyagers forced their way. According to some tribal beliefs, the soul of man painfully ascended the storeys of the sky, assisted by the *karakia* of the *tohunga*, and aimed to attain at least to the comfort of the eighth heaven. The lower storeys, with wind, storm, and rain, were not regarded as fitting places for the souls of the dead.

In the adventures of Tawhaki it is shown that at least one of these heavens closely resembled the earth in appearance.

The next stage of evolution was the 12-heaven concept, where guardian and tutelary spirits engaged in the preservation of an ordered universe, and the summit was regarded as the home of the Supreme being, Io, and his attendant spirits.

There is a great contrast between the 10-storeyed heaven and the 12-storeyed one. The latter was a religious conception, with detailed knowledge of the upper rather than the lower overworlds.

Once past the first visible heaven, we come to Rangi-tāmaku, notable for the *whare kura*, the prototype of such temples on earth, where the sacred stones were kept. Snow, rain, lightning, and storms abounded in the lower heavens, and the winds ranged up to the eleventh overworld. Tāwhiri-rangi, a sacred house, was provided in this overworld for the purification of spirits who were worthy to stand before Io in the twelfth heaven. The portals of the summit were closely guarded. *Apa*, or celestial beings, guarded the doorway and allowed only a few chosen gods or spirits to enter. In this heaven, Te Toi-ō-ngā-rangi (the summit or citadel of the heavens), there were three sacred houses: Matangi-reia, the temple of Io, in which was kept the *wānanga* (knowledge) until it was given to Tāne; Rangiatea, the building where the *whatukura* or sacred stones were kept; and Whakamore-ariki, where lived the spirits who guarded the treasures of Io.

The inhabitants of the 12 overworlds, apart from Io and the gods, were the *apa* (*whatukura*, *māreikura*, *poutiriao*, etc.). Each heaven was guarded by 12 of these spirits, who also controlled the forces of nature.

Because most of these traditions were collected late in the 19th century, it is likely that they have been very much influenced by missionary teachings – replacing the underworld of Rarohenga with the ascent of the heavens being one example.

Gods (wars of), Hawaiki-nui, māreikura, Rangiatea, Tāne, Tawhaki, Tāwhiri-mātea, whatukura.

P

PĀ. The traditional meaning of the word *pā* was a fortified village, as distinct from a *kāinga*, or unfortified village. The meaning behind the word *pā* is to defend. As a verb it means to block up, obstruct, dam, prevent, or assault, while as a noun it is a weir, screen, blockade and principally, a stockade or fortified place, or the inhabitants of such a place.

When an attack was threatened, the occupants of the nearby *kāinga* would immediately retire to the shelter of the *pā*, taking with them supplies of food and water and valued possessions.

The defences of these Māori fortresses varied according to the terrain. In some parts of the country *pā* were sometimes not necessary, either because warfare was less common (extremely rare), or because the people could retire to the shelter of the forest. Warfare, however, was a constant of Māori life and for that reason a sturdy, defended retreat was necessary.

The many *pā* that were constructed made clever use of ramparts, ditches, cliffs, and stockades. Wherever possible the builders used natural defences, placing their *pā* on islands, steep river banks, hills, and at the edge of precipices, so that the fall of the ground made it difficult or impossible for invaders to reach them on one or more sides.

A coastal *pā* built on a hill. The concentric rings of stockades and the tall watch-towers provide a strong defence. The cultivations are below, with children playing in the stream and on the banks while the warriors keep watch on the hilltop.

Pā in isolated positions such as on deep-sided promontories, with stockades along the edge, were almost invulnerable to attack except at the entrance, which was well fortified and defended. Sometimes natural defences were improved, and a steep hillside cut back to make a precipice.

When *pā* were built on hills, the ground was terraced, with a stockade on the outer edge. There might be several of these stockaded terraces. Palisades were erected at the outer edge of the terraces, with ditches behind and raised ramparts, supplemented by fighting stages and watchtowers, provided excellent platforms for defence.

Before the enemy attacked, access to various parts of the *pā* was easy, but when the ladders were drawn up, the bars of the gateways slid into place, and temporary bridges removed, the defenders were in a strong position.

The entrances or gateways were strongly made, and even when broken down, they led into a maze of narrow defensive works where the enemy was at the mercy of stones thrown from above, and long spears which could be thrust between the palisades. The gateways were set at different places in the stockades, and attackers ran the gauntlet between the defensive rings even when the outer one was broached. For example, the rampart defenders were armed with long spears to reach any enemy who had scaled the outer palisades, or who had broken through, only to find themselves in a deep ditch facing yet another palisade ring.

In the flat areas in the centre and on the highest portion, the *tihi* of the *pā*, the *whare* were located. Their thatched roofs were the most vulnerable part of the *pā*, for if they were close to the stockade they could be set on fire by torches or burning darts thrown from outside.

Food and water were problems for the defenders, especially having a reliable water supply in time of siege. This might be overcome by having covered or fortified trenches leading to springs or wells, and cisterns might be dug within the perimeter. On riverside *pā* ingenious constructions were made, by which vessels could be lowered into the water at the end of a rope.

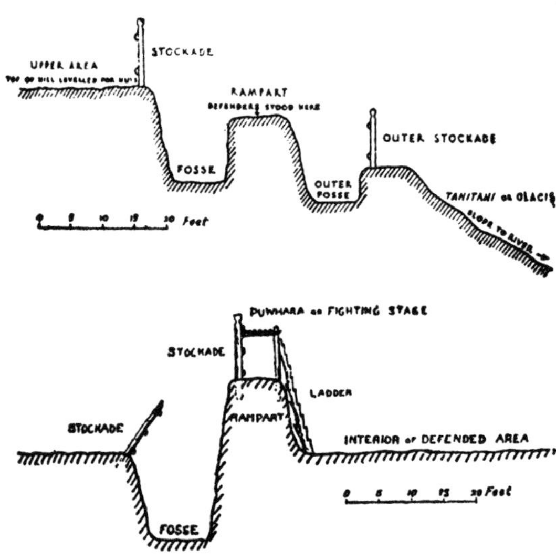

Diagrams of the defence system of a *pā*.

The defenders could be starved out, and stockades could be pulled down with strong ropes, scaled with ladders, or sometimes by piling brushwood against the timbers and simply burning the defences down. Sapping was sometimes resorted to, and island *pā*, in shallow lakes, were assaulted by means of causeways as well as by canoes.

A successful attack was a costly operation and recorded traditions seem to suggest that many *pā* were overcome by treachery rather than force of arms.

Darts, gateways, kāinga, palisades, spears, terraces, warfare.

PADDLES (*hoe*). Canoe paddles were graceful and pointed, tapering gently from the knobbed handle to the blade, with a slight curve at the junction. They were about 1.5 metres in length. The leader of the crew, who chanted a song to give the time for the strokes, wielded a carved or painted paddle as a badge of office. The long steering paddles usually had a carved design such as a *manaia* on the handle end.

PAE. Perches.

Birds (hunting).

PAEPAE, see DREDGES, FISH, and LATRINES.

PAHŪ, see GONGS.

PAIKEA. According to tradition Paikea, an ancestor of the Ngāti Porou *iwi*, came from Hawaiki on the back of a whale.

PAINTING. The painted *kōwhaiwhai* designs that appeared in Māori architecture were principally on the rafters, battens, and ridgepoles of important houses, and to a lesser extent on skirting boards, wall plates, and the planks under the roof of porches. Decoration was more often applied by carving, but the painted designs were striking, in contrasting colours of red, black, white, and brown. The characteristic curvilinear pattern is said to represent fern fronds.

Materials used for colouring were mainly red ochre, blue earth, and white clay. Charcoal was occasionally crushed to provide a black pigment. The natural whiteness of timber was often used instead of a paint.

Cave paintings mainly using charcoal are known in several parts of the country, but were not a common practice. Caves, rock overhangs and shelters in the central parts of Te Waka a Māui sometimes had paintings which appear to date from the earliest times of Māori settlement.

On some occasions paint was used for facial decoration. In most cases this consisted of simply daubing the face with *kōkōwai*, red ochre mixed with shark oil. Men were more given to face painting than women, but young women sometimes stained their cheeks with blue earth and the red pigment of berries. In some *iwi* high-born women were permitted to paint a blue cross on the cheeks and forehead.

Art, houses, ochre (red), peace, tattooing.

PAKANGA, see WARFARE.

PAKIWAITARA, see FABLES.

PALISADES (*tūwatawata*). The outer stockade was termed a *pekerangi*, and the main stockade a *kātua*. There might be several concentric stockades round a *pā*, the outer one being lighter than the inner ones where the fighting was often fiercest.

The stockade consisted of heavy posts firmly set in the ground and supported by lighter palisades of split timber. The posts were of various sizes, and spaced irregularly. Larger posts might be as much as 10 metres in length, a metre in diameter and buried to a depth of several metres. Smaller posts were buried to a depth of one to two metres.

Intervening *tūwatawata*, often with sharpened points, were spaced and terminated about a half metre from the ground. This allowed the defenders to thrust spears between and under the palisade timbers. Palisade timbers were lashed to a rail that in turn was fastened to the inner side of the posts to make it more difficult for the enemy to pull them down with ropes. The average height of the stockades was about 3–4 metres.

The heavy timbers were erected at the edge of the ramparts, usually vertically but sometimes angled inwards or outwards depending on the terrain and the arrangement of the associated defences.

An immense amount of labour was expended on the erection of the posts of palisades. The timbers had to be dragged up steep inclines, holes dug with a sloping side and the posts slid into position and dragged upright with ropes. One working song associated with palisade building has been recorded:

Here is the stockade;
Here is the vine being bound;
Here am I, the bait, within.
E-e-e-i-a-e!

Posts were sometimes surmounted with images carved into the form of figures or faces expressing defiance, but more often the heads of slain

Storming the palisades of a *pā*. A section of the stakes has been torn down with ropes, but the inner and more strongly fortified stockade has yet to be taken. From the fighting stage at the back, the defenders will harass the attackers from above with spears and stones. The warrior in the foreground, who is fighting naked, has his buttocks closely tattooed with the *rape* design.

enemies were simply spiked onto palisade posts to act as a deterrent.

Gateways, pā, stages (fighting), visitors, watch-towers.

PANI. The goddess of agriculture, especially of the *kūmara*. She was known as 'the mother of the *kūmara*' because she was supposed to have given birth to the tubers in miraculous fashion.

Kūmara.

PANIA. A 'sea goddess' in popular legend she was probably a *ponaturi*, sea fairy, who married a mortal and eventually returned to her own people, where her grieving husband sought her in vain.

PAPA. The Earth Mother, whose full name was Papa-tū-ā-nuku (the earth extending afar). Her husband was Rangi, the Sky Father, and together they were the parents of the gods. After the separation of earth and sky, Papa was turned over on her face so that she could no longer see her husband, lest she continue to grieve for him. Tāne then adorned his mother with plants and trees, and finally created from her body the first woman.

Creation, earth, female element, fire, gods (wars of), Hine-moana, night, Rangi, separation, Tāne.

PARĀOA. Sperm whales.

Whales.

PARE, see CHAPLETS.

PĀTAKA, see STOREHOUSES.

PĀTĪTĪ. A modern striking weapon made from a tomahawk axe.

Clubs.

PATU, see CLUBS.

PĀTUA. *Pātua* were baskets made of *tōtara* bark.

PEACE. As the god of the peaceful arts of agriculture, Rongo was also the god of peace, peacemaking, and the ratification of peace treaties. An enduring peace was sometimes known as a *rongo taketake.*

There was also the expression *tatau pounamu* (greenstone door), which was used to describe a firm and enduring peace that may not lightly be broken. A chief who proposed such a peace would say, 'Let us erect the greenstone door at such and such a place as a sanctuary for the helpless, where our women and children may roam unharmed by man.'

Peace was no less important than war for the continuation of the life and prosperity of the tribe, and the conclusion of hostilities was a time for rejoicing. When the tribes gathered to announce and cement the peace, there were ritual observances to be performed, and the name of Rongo, which was forbidden in war, was invoked. Young women of high rank with painted faces took part in the ceremonial dance, followed by the men. After the recitation of the proper *karakia* the event was brought to a climax by the sharing of a feast.

Io, Rongo, warfare.

PEKA, see DARTS.

PEKAPEKA, see BATS.

PENDANTS, see ORNAMENTS.

Burial, ear pendants, necklaces.

PERSONIFICATIONS. Māori had a genius for the concept of personification and both legend and daily life were richly endowed with personifications, tutelary beings, and spiritual entities of all kinds. Personifications and their personal manifestations helped explain the natural world. For example, the erosion of the shoreline was the evidence of the unceasing war between the sea, as represented by Hine-moana, and the sand of the shore as represented by Hine-one.

The number of personifications was endless: Tonga caused headaches; Korokoro-ewe, presided over childbirth; Hine-whaitiri was the thunder girl; Upoko-roa, the personification of comets; Pare-arohi, the quivering, heated air of summer; Rakahore, rock and Te Rara-taunga-rere, the fruitfulness of trees.

Disease, female element, fire, Hina, Hine-moana, insects, kūmara, language, lightning, meteors, natural phenomena, plants, rain, sand, sandstone, seasons, shellfish, space, stars, stones, sun, trees, water, weta, winter.

PERUPERU, see WAR DANCES.

PIGEONS (*kūkū, kererū*). The name *kūkū* was given because of the soft, cooing cry of the birds. In the legend of Māui, the young man hid his mother's *maro*, and when he pursued her to the underworld, he put it around him. The white feathers and colours of the apron were transformed into the glowing breast of a pigeon. In this disguise Māui entered the underworld and perched on a tree, eventually turning back into human shape when he was recognised by his parents.

The large *kūkū* was the most important bird for food purposes. It was captured by snares, spears, and, on frosty nights when the birds were too cold to move rapidly, by hand.

Birds (hunting), Rupe, snares, spears.

PIKAUNGA. A load, or to carry on the back.
Burdens.

PĪRORI, see HOOPS.

PĪTAU, see SPIRALS.

PITS (*rua*). The most common use for pits was as storage places, where food supplies such as the *kūmara* were kept. The place name Ngāruawāhia provides an example, for it was the place where 'the store pits were broken into' to provide food for a large company of visitors.

Small pits were also dug and baited as traps to catch rats.

In some areas the sites of some unusual pit dwellings were discovered which might be a variation on the usual *whare puni*, or sleeping house, which often had a sunken floor, with earth piled against the walls to help keep the house warm at night.
Houses, rats, storehouses.

PIU, see SKIPPING.

A *rua kūmara*, or store pit for *kūmara*.

PIUPIU, see SKIRTS.
Garments.

PLACE NAMES, see NAMES.

PLAITING. Māori were skilled at plaiting ropes for many purposes, and had names for plaits of from two to five strands, some being round, some flat, and some square. There was even a nine-strand flat plait. Dried flax leaves provided suitable material for plaiting.

The origin of plaiting is ascribed to Māui when he instructed his brothers in the art of making round, square, and flat ropes in order to snare the sun, during a successful attempt to delay its journey across the sky and to lengthen the hours of daylight. A later legend tells how plaited ropes of various sizes and design were invented to trap Hotupuku, the enormous *taniwha* of the Kāingaroa plains.

Mats, baskets, sails, belts, fans for fanning the fire, packs and shoulder straps for carrying loads, and sandals were made from strips of flax. Plaiting and weaving were distinct crafts, although the term weaving is often used as a synonym of plaiting. The error is probably due to both crafts using the same process, that is, the interlacing of two sets of cords or threads to form what may be regarded as a textile. But the methods of obtaining the results are different.

In plaiting all the threads or cords needed are fixed along a commencement edge, from which they are directed obliquely right and left to form a crossover pattern. There is, however, a form of plaiting in which the crossings are at right angles to the commencement edge.
Baskets, mats, ropes, weaving.

PLANTING, see CULTIVATIONS, and AGRICULTURE.

PLANTS. Papa, the Earth Mother, was provided with growing plants by Tāne to cover her nakedness after the separation. In the Māori cosmology myths, Tāne mated with many personifications to produce these plants. For example with Apunga he fathered small plants, Rerenoa became the mother of epiphytes, Tutoro-whenua, the mother of the *aruhe*, bracken rhizome, Tauwhare-kiokio, the mother of tree ferns, and other personifications parented the various species of trees.

Creation, Papa, separation, Tāne, trees.

PLATFORMS, see STAGES.

PLUNDERING, see MURU.

PŌ, see NIGHT.

POI. The *poi* was a ball with an outer covering of woven flax fibre, or dried *raupō* leaves, stuffed with *raupō* down. It was frequently decorated with *tāniko* patterns, dog's hair, or feathers. *Poi* were light and strong, and were attached to the ends of long cords, much longer than the modern *poi* cord.

Poi were used by women and girls when they danced the *haka poi*. The dances were performed standing, or else seated in a long row on the ground – a favourite position for the canoe dance in which the bodies swayed backwards and forwards to the rhythm of the canoe song, the *poi* being used to tap out the regular beat of the paddles.

Performers were very skilled at making the *poi* dance deftly in their hands. As a rule two *poi* were used by each person, and could be made to flutter like birds or provide a rhythmic accompaniment as they were bounced on arms and legs to the beat of the song. Many traditional *waiata poi* have been preserved.

Dances, tāniko.

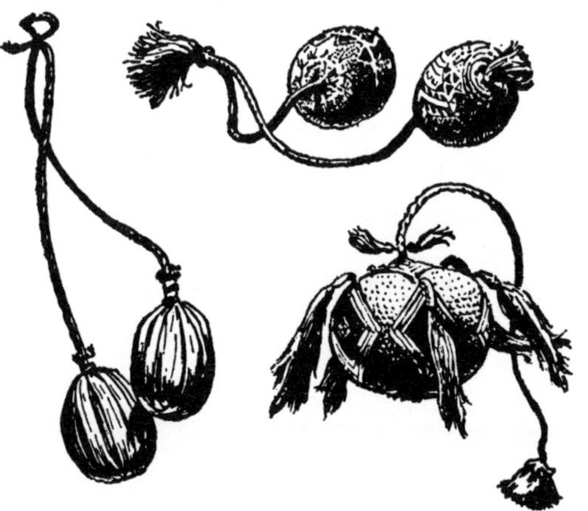

Several forms of *poi*. The two *poi* on the left, with *raupō* leaf coverings, are the usual type.

POISONS. Fortunately there were few poisonous plants in Aotearoa. The *karaka* and the *tutu* provided wholesome food and drink when properly prepared, but in their natural state were poisonous. The bite of the *katipō* spider was also poisonous, though rarely fatal. The common cures for poisoning were to bury the victim up to the neck in the expectation that the pressure of the surrounding earth would help expel the poison; immersion in water or suspension over a smoking fire. A combination of any of these 'remedies' might also be tried.

Berries, karaka.

POLYGAMY. The majority of marriages were monogamous, but it was the custom for important *rangatira* to take more than one wife. In addition to his free wife or wives, he might have several slave wives, who had a hard existence being forced to carry the burden of the work for the chief's family. The first wife was called *wahine matua*, and ranked above all the others. But the children of all wives, slave or free, inherited a portion of their father's cultivations and personal property. *Punarua* describes the second wife, or having two wives (as well as 'in pairs'), while *punatoru* is the state of having three wives.

The first marriage of a chief was usually made for political reasons, but later marriages were a matter of personal choice. There was also a desire for sons and if the first wife was barren she often suggested that her husband take a second wife. One further incentive to polygamy amongst chiefs was that wives were a form of capital, because of their industry in the plantations and at weaving.

Marriage.

PONATURI. Sea fairies. These strange creatures lived under the sea by day but came ashore at night to sleep in large houses. They were dangerous to mankind, but were creatures of the darkness and could be destroyed by light. There are several legends which tell how companies of them were destroyed when they were inveigled into remaining in their houses until after dawn. When light entered the *whare* they were killed.

Fairies, Rātā.

POPULATION. It is thought that at one time there was a relatively large Māori population in Aotearoa, but it is impossible to determine its size, even within broad limits. Early European visitors made estimates varying from 100,000 (Cook) to 200,000 (Williams) and even more, but these were deductions made from the limited observations to which they were restricted, usually in coastal areas. The dense population of the temperate and fertile areas such as the Bay of Islands may well have given the impression that the total population was much greater than was the case.

In spite of constant warfare – in most cases better described as skirmishing – it is likely that the population grew steadily for several centuries with the founding *whānau* quickly expanding to *hapū* and eventually loose confederations of *hapū*, tribes or *iwi*.

This growth was checked with the arrival of the Pākehā in the early 19th century. The introduction of diseases such as tuberculosis, influenza and measles to which Māori had no immunity, and the deadly impact of muskets and gunpowder, led to such devastation that by the end of the century Māori were regarded as a dying race.

During the 20th century however there has been a remarkable recovery and at the start of the 21st century, people claiming Māori descent are estimated to make up some 12–15 percent of the population, with the proportion continuing to grow.

PORCHES (*mahau*). Houses were provided with a *mahau*, a front porch or veranda, the larger ones being some 3 metres in depth, and the smaller ones as little as 1 metre. The central ridgepole was supported by a post at the front, and the overhanging roof provided shelter in wet weather.

The side walls and the roof of the house projected as far as the low board which marked the front line of the veranda, making a sheltered enclosure. In the large houses the rafters of the porch were painted, the wall slabs carved, and the spaces were filled with reed patterns. The base of the front post was carved, usually in the form of a figure, and surmounted above the roofline by another carved human figure, a *tekoteko*.

The *mahau* was used as a sheltered gathering place where hand games might be played or for people to just sit and talk.

Houses, tekoteko.

POROPOROAKĪ, see SPEECHES.

POSTS (*pou*). Posts were employed for a number of purposes, such as the raising of storehouses from the ground for protection from scavenging animals, supporting the ridgepole of a house, and the strengthening of stockades. A *pou rāhui* was a post set up to mark a place where trespassers were not permitted.

Boundaries, houses, palisades, rāhui, storehouses.

PŌTAKA, see TOPS.

POTATO, SWEET, see KŪMARA.

POU, see POSTS.

POUNAMU, see GREENSTONE.

POUTIRIAO. Supernatural beings said to be the guardians of the universe, regulating all the forces of nature. Some were gods, and some lesser spirits. They were powerful, and were appealed to by the *tohunga* in cases of sickness, to cast out the harmful *atua* and restore the sufferer to health. This is another 'late-collected' tradition that does not fit comfortably with the more widely accepted view of the Māori spiritual hierarchy, suggesting that the origins of the concept are post-contact with Pākehā.

Stars.

POUTOTI, see STILTS.

POUWHENUA. A wooden weapon resembling a *taiaha*, but with a spear point replacing the tongue. They were not adorned with hair or feathers.

Taiaha.

PRESENTS. The presentation of gifts such as garments, greenstone pendants, weapons, and food was a custom that placed the seal upon peace and goodwill, and did honour to the recipients. The ceremonial presentation of gifts was associated with important occasions, such as birth and baptism, betrothal and marriage, but only for those who were of high rank. The gifts made to infants and young people were preserved by the parents and presented to them permanently on the occasion of their marriage, becoming treasured heirlooms that often passed from one generation to another. There was a formal procedure to be observed. The gifts were not placed in the hands of the recipients, but laid on the ground in a particular way. Garments, for instance, were placed with the neck towards the recipient, and weapons were laid down butt foremost. Feasting, games and entertainment usually followed the presentation of gifts.

Food was given on occasions when one tribe visited another, and it was common practice for a traveller to bear a small parcel of food to give to his hosts when visiting another *kāinga*.

Āhua, feasts, offerings.

PRESERVATION OF FOOD. Unlike the tropical homelands, in Aotearoa the colder climate permitted only one harvest a year. As there were seasons for harvesting, bird hunting, and the gathering of berries, it was necessary to preserve food for the winter months, and a great deal of time was devoted to this essential task. Roots were prepared in several ways, and stored in pits or caves lined with dry bracken fern, fish were *pāwhera,* dried in the sun, while birds were roasted and stored in gourds and other containers in their own fat. In preparation for the lean months the *pātaka*, storehouses, were filled with a variety of foodstuffs.

Birds (preserving), cooking, eels, fern root, fish, food, gourds, muttonbirds, rats, stages, storehouses, whitebait.

PRIESTESSES (*ruahine*). Although most *tohunga* were men, women of high rank possessed such *mana* and *tapu* that they were initiated into some of the mysteries of the priesthood.

Tohunga.

PRIESTS, see TOHUNGA.

PRIMAL OFFSPRING. The *atua* who were the sons of Rangi and Papa are sometimes referred to as the primal offspring. Some accounts say there were 70 children, but the list may contain repetition of some names in alternative forms.

The first-born was Uru-te-ngangana, who personified light in various forms. The need to introduce light into the darkness between the Sky Father and the Earth Mother was one of the first and most urgent acts of creation, giving rise to the separation of the primal parents.

The principal gods were those in charge of the major manifestations of nature, and are known as departmental gods. All the *atua* exercised functions of guardianship and control, and many of them were well-known personifications, but the functions of others is not now known.

Gods, Haumia-tiketike, light, Papa, Rangi, Rongo, separation, Tāne, Tangaroa, Tāwhiri-mātea, Tū-matauenga, Uru-te-ngangana, Whiro.

PRONUNCIATION. The consonants *h, k, m, n, p,* r, *t* and *w* were pronounced as in English. *Ng* is pronounced as in singing, and the *wh* sound has been described as the English *f* sounded without letting the upper teeth touch the lower lip.

In addition there are five vowels, pronounced as follows:

a:	ah
e:	eh (the e in ten)
i:	ee
o:	aw
u:	oo

There are short and long vowels, the long vowels sometimes being indicated by a macron, or by doubling the vowel. There is less stress on syllables than in English. The first syllable of most words, and the third syllable of words beginning with *whaka*, are slightly accentuated.

Māori is a musical, flowing language and the pronunciation can best be discovered by listening and practice.

Language.

PROVERBS. Māori speech was rich in proverbs and imagery. Many contained allusions to names and events in legend and tribal history, the meaning of which is not apparent unless one is versed in such subjects, for example the proverb *E kore a Para-whenua e haere ki te kore a Rakahore* (Para-whenua will not go anywhere without Rakahore).

Rakahore is the origin of rocks, and Para-whenua the personification of water. The meaning is that streams could not flow, nor springs appear, if it were not for rock that lies below the surface of the land.

Others carry a message that is self-evident. Some examples are given below:

A mischievous child: *He tamaiti wāwāhi tahā* (A child breaks the calabash).

The permanence of marriage: *He hono tangata e kore e motu; kapa he taura waka, e motu* (The joining of man will not be broken as a canoe rope will break).

Mourning for the dead: *Waiho kia tangi ahau ki tāku tūpāpaku, āpā he uru tī e pihi ake* (Let me weep for my dead; it is not as though he were a cabbage tree which springs up again.)

The beauty of a woman: *Me te mea ko Kōpū ka rere i te pae* (Like the planet Venus as it appears above the horizon).

Women and war: *He wahine, he whenua, ka ngaro te tangata* (For women and for land men are destroyed).

Bravery: *He umauma tangata, he umauma rākau* (The breast of a man, the breast of timber).

Peace and war: *He toa taua, mate taua; he toa piki pari, mate pari; he toa ngaki kai, mā te huhu tēnā* (A warrior dies in battle; a hunter on a high cliff; a food cultivator of old age).

Food: *E hoa mā! Ina te ora ō te tangata* (O friends! Here is the sustenance of man).

Eloquence: *Me he korokoro tūī* (Like the throat of a tūī).

PUAKA. Traps.

Birds (hunting), rats.

PŪ, see TRUMPETS.

PUHI. The eldest daughter of highborn parents was sometimes a *puhi*, a term with several meanings such as virgin, betrothed woman, or (principally) a much-courted, unbetrothed young woman.

She was a virgin of high lineage who was held

A *manu* or kite, made from *raupö* stretched over a framework of *toetoe* stalks (see page 98). *Te Papa, Wellington, New Zealand [B.042421]*

The nocturnal *kiwi* was an important food item and dogs were used in its capture. Its feathers were highly valued in the making of prestigious cloaks (see page 99). *Te Papa, Wellington, New Zealand [F.002793/02]*

A stone kūmara god (see page 101), said to have been brought from Hawaiki by the first Māori settlers.
Auckland War Memorial Museum

A *kuta* or maro (apron or kilt) made from rushes (see page 111), from Taranaki. *Auckland War Memorial Museum*

This early reconstruction shows the immense size of the extinct *moa*. It is now thought that rather than standing upright, as shown in the photograph, the bird normally carried its head and long neck in a U-shape, much as its close relatives the emu and ostrich do today (see page 120). *Te Papa, Wellington, New Zealand [C.000073]*

A greenstone *pekapeka* or ornament (see page 133) from the North Cape district. *Auckland War Memorial Museum*

A *tāhei* or necklace (see page 126) made from the seeds of the *tawāpou* tree, from Kaitaia. *Auckland War Memorial Museum*

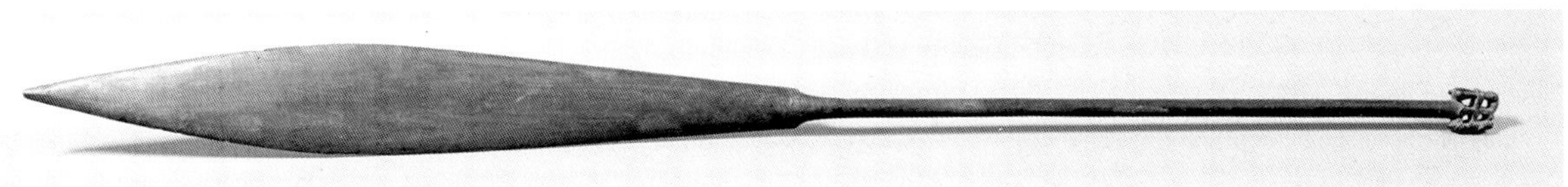

Hoe or paddles (see page 136) were usually about 1.5 metres long and were used by paddlers facing in the direction in which they were heading. The end of a paddle was usually decorated with a manaia, or bird motif. *Auckland War Memorial Museum*

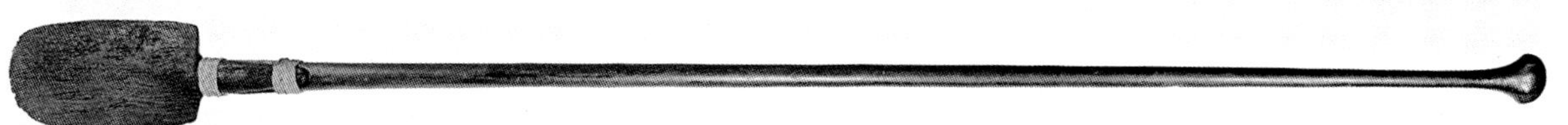

A *kāheru* or digging stick made of *mānuka* (see page 162), from Motiti Island, Bay of Plenty. *Auckland War Memorial Museum*

Top: A *poi* made from *tāniko*, with a fringe of dog hair sewn onto the netted area and a cord made from flax fibre. Above: A *poi* decorated with tassels of black and white hair and *pāua* shell (see page 141). *Auckland War Memorial Museum*

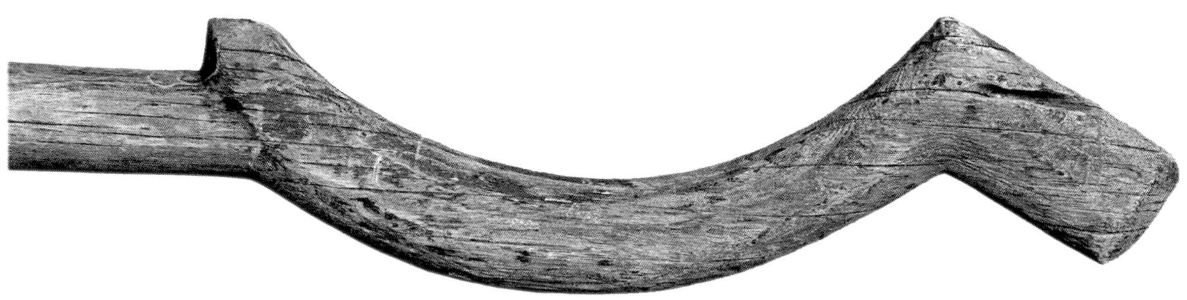

The handle of a *kō* or digging stick (see p 162), from Kaiaua, on the Hauraki Plains.
Auckland War Memorial Museum

A *matarau* or spear for catching eels (see page 163), from the Urewera district. (This is a post-European contact reproduction of an implement that was much used in former times.)
Auckland War Memorial Museum

A *pātaka* or storehouse (see page 168), which stood at Te Waerenga, on the shore of Lake Rotorua, photographed at Auckland War Memorial Museum. *Auckland War Memorial Museum*

An *amo* (front support of a bargeboard) from a *pātaka* or storehouse; these were often carved in great detail to demonstrate prosperity and fertility (see page 168). *Auckland War Memorial Museum*

A *kūwaha* or porch of a *pātaka* or storehouse from Māketu in the Bay of Plenty. Storehouses varied in size from small boxes to buildings many metres in length (see page 168). *Auckland War Memorial Museum*

The *taiaha* or spear was used in close-quarter fighting: the flat blade or rau was for striking, while the head or arero, carved in the shape of a tongue, was for piercing the enemy's body. The feathers attached to the head were shaken to distract the enemy's attention (see page 172). *Auckland War Memorial Museum*

A carved *tekoteko* in the form of a lizard (see page 179). *Auckland War Memorial Museum*

Like the *taiaha*, the *tewhatewha* is a two-handed weapon used in close combat. The pointed end was for thrusting, and the flat projection at the other end was used as if striking a blow with the back of an axe, with the blade adding force to the blow (see page 180). *Auckland War Memorial Museum*

A *tekoteko* (see page 179) from the gable of a house at Waimarama, Hawke's Bay. *Auckland War Memorial Museum*

A *pūtātara*, or large shell used as a trumpet (see page 191) and fitted with a wooden mouthpiece.
Te Papa, Wellington, New Zealand [F.004298/2]

A *turuturu* or weaving spike (see page 203), the stick of authority for Wi Te Puna of Ngāti Tūwharetoa. *Auckland War Memorial Museum*

A *pūkāea*, made from two hollowed-out pieces of wood lashed together to form a long cylinder. It was used to sound the alarm in times of war (see page 191). *Te Papa, Wellington, New Zealand [Γ.004323/1]*

A wooden wahaika or short club (see page 203) from the Rongowhakaata tribe. It was collected by Captain Cook and taken to England. *Auckland War Memorial Museum*

in respect, and accorded a number of privileges. Her high estate came from her noble birth, and by the wish and respect of her people. She possessed a great deal of influence, was not permitted to engage in heavy labour or normal domestic duties, including cooking, but was allowed to work at weaving. She was pampered, provided with slaves and attendants, and was frequently permitted to live with her attendants in a house of her own.

On the other hand she was hemmed in with restrictions on account of her personal *tapu*. She was not allowed to co-habit with young men, and had duties to perform in the removal of *tapu* during religious ceremonies. *Puhi* were eagerly courted by young men, who might come from a great distance in the hope of impressing her and her family with their suitability as a potential husband. There have been many examples in legend and history of notable women who were *puhi* in their younger days, and who exercised a great influence on the history of their people.

Betrothal, courtship, Hinemoa, marriage.

PŪKĀEA, see TRUMPETS.

PUNGA, see ANCHORS.

PŪNGĀWEREWERE, see SPIDERS.

PUNIPUNI, see HAND GAMES, PUZZLES.

PŪREREHUA, see BULLROARERS.

PŪTĀTARA, see TRUMPETS.

PŪTŌRINO, see FLUTES.

Musical instruments.

PŪWHARA, see STAGES, WARFARE.

PUZZLES (*kai*). The word *kai* is used for puzzles, riddles, guessing games, and competitions. An example of such guessing games is *tutukai*, a game in which one person has to find a pebble as it is passed rapidly from the hand of one player to another.

Hand games, riddles.

R

RĀ. see SUN, SAILS.

RAFTS (*mōkihi*). Small rafts made of bundles of very light flax stalks lashed together were used for crossing lakes and rivers. They were popular too with small children, who used them for playing in the water.

Children playing on small rafts made of the flower stalks of the flax plant.

RĀHUI. A form of *tapu*, and a mark, frequently in the form of a post set in the ground, to warn people against trespassing, usually against a *tapu* placed on a forest, stream, or other source of food. A place might be made *tapu* in this way on the death of a chief. The visible sign of the *rāhui* would be a stone, hair, cloak, post, a bunch of fern, or other object.

Birds (hunting), hair.

RAIN (ua). The origin of rain was supposed to be the tears of Rangi the Sky Father when he was separated from the Earth Mother, Papa, and wept for her. Te Ihorangi was the personification of rain, and Hinewai of light rain. Kahukura, a personification of the rainbow, heralded the coming of rain and insulting remarks were sometimes addressed to him in order to offend him and send him on his way.

Māori protected themselves against rain by weaving rough flax capes with overlapping layers to shed water. Travellers built temporary shelters for protection from rain. On rainy days the porch of whare served as an open-air shelter. Cooking sheds, *kāuta*, were built for the use of women in wet weather.

Separation.

RAINBOWS (āniwaniwa). There were several personifications of the rainbow, notably, Uenuku, Kahukura and Haere. These deities also served as powerful war gods. A popular legend tells of the adventures of Uenuku, who sought in vain for his departed celestial wife, Hinewai (misty rain). The gods eventually took pity on him and he was changed into a rainbow.

A rainbow standing in the path of a *taua*, a war party, was regarded as an evil omen and when it was seen the raid would be abandoned.

Gods (wars of), Kahukura, mist, rain, Uenuku.

RĀKAU. Trees, timber, and sometimes weapons were all described as *rākau*.

Trees.

RĀKAU WHAKAPAPA, see STICKS, MEMORY. Also called *kapeu whakapapa*.

RAKIURA, the Māori name for Stewart Island.

Stewart Island.

RAMA, see TORCHES.

RANGATIRA. Chiefs, nobles or 'gentlemen'.

Chiefs, social classes.

RANGI. In Māori mythology Rangi was the Sky Father whose full name was Rangi-nui-e-tū-nei (great heaven standing above). His wife was Papa, the Earth Mother. Because their coupling blocked out the light they were separated by their offspring. (Tāwhiri-mātea, the god of winds and storm, remained faithful to his father.) Rangi was adorned by Tāne with the sun, moon, stars, and clouds.

Creation, overworlds, Papa, separation, Tāne.

RANGIATEA. This was the name for the topmost overworld or 'heaven', where the sacred *whatukura* stones were kept on the altar. It was also the name of the first *whare wānanga*, house of learning, which was an extremely *tapu* building. This first *whare wānanga* was said to have been built at Ra'iatea (Rangiatea) in the Society Islands; it remains a *tapu* island known throughout most of Polynesia.

Hawaiki, Io, overworlds, schools of learning, stones (sacred).

RĀPAKI, see KILTS.

RAROHENGA, see UNDERWORLDS.

RĀTĀ. Rātā was the hero of many legendary adventures, the most famous being his attempt to avenge the death of his father Wahieroa. He started on this quest by building a *waka*, canoe, but forgot to placate the forest god when cutting down a tree to build the *waka*. Three times he felled the tree, but three times it was raised to its former position by the Tini o te Hakuturi, the birds, insects, and spirits of the forest.

Rātā eventually discovered what was happening and made amends for his error. He quickly completed the *waka* with the help of the creatures and set off with his followers for distant lands. There he killed a dangerous ogre by throwing a red-hot stone into its mouth.

Eventually they came to the place where Matuku, the slayer of Wahieroa, lived, and trapped this unpleasant person in a noose. As the noose fell on him, Matuku's legs grew thin, wings took the place of his arms, and he was transformed into the *matuku* bird, a bittern, who flew away through the noose and fled to the swamp, where these birds have lived ever since.

Rātā was not yet satisfied. He discovered that his father's bones had been stolen away by the *ponaturi*, sea-fairies. He spied on the *ponaturi* at night and learned the charms that were being recited by their *tohunga* whom he then killed. Rātā then secured his father's remains and returned to his home. When his people were attacked by the *ponaturi* in revenge and were in danger of defeat, Rātā repeated the *karakia* he had learned from the fairy *tohunga* and so won the day.

Fairies, ponaturi, sandstone.

RATS. The almost extinct native *kiore*, rat, was introduced by Māori from Polynesia. It thrived on a rich diet of berries, especially in winter, when it became fat and plump and was most sought after as food. The *kiore* was grey or brown in colour, and lived in holes in the ground or in hollow trees. They were creatures of habit and kept to the same paths when foraging, making 'runs' which stretched for miles through the forests usually following ridge lines. Cleverly designed traps and snares were set along these paths and the *kiore* were caught in good numbers.

The various types of trap showed a great deal of ingenuity in their construction. Those that were placed on the runs were not baited, but consisted of a narrow entrance through which the rat squeezed and was then unable to escape. Others, which were baited with berries, had a supplejack spring and a noose in which the rat was caught.

Pits with undercut sides were also dug. Berries were placed at the end of thin sticks that projected over the pit. The rat ate the berries and, unable to turn round on the thin stick, fell into the pit, from which it could not escape.

The *kiore* were plucked or skinned and cooked in *hāngi*, earth ovens or sometimes in vessels made from the tough base of a *nikau* frond. They were also cooked in wooden containers with hot stones, and then preserved in their own fat.

Cooking, food.

RAU MANU, see FEATHERS.

RAUPŌ, see REEDS.

REED PATTERNS (*tukutuku*). The most frequent house decoration was the use of *tukutuku*, patterned panels, placed between the *pou* or sidewall supporting posts.

The materials used for making *tukutuku* were the smooth, round, yellow stems of the *toetoe* grass, varied occasionally by the insertion of brown bracken stems, all tied to thin, horizontal laths. The materials used for the lashing were thin strips of *harakeke*, flax leaves, which were sometimes dyed, yellow *kiekie*, and other leaves. These lashings with their several colours added to the attractiveness of the designs.

The making of *tukutuku* panels was normally undertaken by two women seated on either side of the panel, taking care to preserve the symmetry of the design. Elaborate geometrical patterns were worked out, giving a characteristic appearance to the work in contrast to the freedom of line of the adjacent carvings, and a number of designs were introduced. The panels were fixed in position against the outer thatching of the walls in between the carved *pou* slabs.

Houses.

Women standing on either side of a reed panel as they fashion a geometrical design which is typical of *tukutuku* work. The four posts to the left indicate that a superior cloak is also being woven.

REEDS (*raupō*). The common *raupō*, bullrush, had many uses such as thatching for the walls and roofs of houses, stuffing for *poi*, and pollen which was made into cakes for food. The roots of the plant were also eaten.

Food, houses, poi, thatch.

REHUA. The god of kindness. He was associated with forests. When Tāne visited him in the heavens Rehua gave him the *tūī* birds that were concealed in his hair. That is how the *tūī* came to earth.

REINGA, TE. The place where the souls of men go down to the spirit world. It is at the northern end of Te Ika a Māui, the North Island. The souls descend the cliff and leap from a *pohutukawa* tree into the water, through which they pass to Rarohenga, the true spirit world or underworld.

The place of spirits is also known as the Reinga. The name means 'the leaping'. Te Reinga is also called Te Wairua-rerenga (the leaping place of spirits).

Soul, underworlds.

RELATIONSHIP. To help explain the relationship between all members of an *iwi*, tribe, who came from a common ancestor – and the importance of genealogies that were remembered with astonishing accuracy – a brief table of kinship terms is useful. The following table lists the terms most commonly used. It is noted that the same terms are used for the collateral as well as the direct line, which is an evidence of the homogeneity of the *whānau* or family. Exceptions to this rule are the terms *pāpara* and *kōkara* for true father and mother respectively, and *irāmutu* used only for nephew or niece. In most cases in the list the addition of *kēkē* to the Māori word shows that the relationship is definitely collateral (descended from a different line).

Genealogies.

RELIGION. Māori religion was instinctive in every activity. Spirits, demons, *taniwha*, protective family spirits, and the souls of departed ancestors were found everywhere, and had to be placated. Nothing could be done, in peace or war, which did not have religious or superstitious significance. Anything that was done without respect for the laws of *tapu*, or the influence of *atua*, could contaminate the perpetrator, with disastrous results.

	DIRECT LINE	COLLATERALS
Grandparents	*Tīpuna, tūpuna*	
Grandfather	*Tipuna tāne*	Grand uncle
Grandmother	*Tipuna wahine*	Grand aunt
Parents	*Mātua*	
Father	*Matua tāne*	Uncle
Mother	*Whaea, whaene*	Aunt
Elder brothers of male	*Tuakana*	Cousins
Elder sisters of female	*Tuakana*	
Younger brothers of male	*Tēina, tāina*	
Younger sisters of female	*Tēina, tāina*	
Brother of female	*Tungane*	
Sister of male	*Tuahine*	
Children	*Tama* *Tamaiti (s)* *Tamariki (pl)*	Nephews and Nieces
Son	*Tamāroa*	
Daughter	*Tamāhine*	
Grandchildren	*Mokopuna*	
Grandson	*Mokopuna tāne*	Grand nephew
Granddaughter	*Mokopuna wahine*	Grand niece

Warfare, agriculture, hunting, fishing, travel and the elements and the dangers of the environment, territorial boundaries and the treachery of men and women are the vital concerns around which Māori religion was at its most elaborate. Backed by the sanction of *tapu*, Māori religion was of sufficient force to provide for the ultimate sanction of death and had sufficient authority to even counter the privilege of aristocracy.

Māori religion also linked to the vivid imagery and drama of dreams and myths, providing comforting spirits to support the grieving and rituals for protection against the unpredictable, the uncontrollable and the unknown.

The influence of the *tohunga* was paramount, the power of the *atua* irresistible, and the *karakia* and ceremonies of the priesthood of vital importance. All these powers and influences were equally binding on the *tohunga*. Amongst some tribes it is said that the priesthood had evolved a purer, esoteric religion, based on an acknowledgement of Io, a monotheistic deity similar to the Christian tradition of God.

Charms, gods, Io, magic, nature, tohunga.

REPTILES. *Ika*, fish, and *mokomoko*, reptiles, were originally under the guardianship of Tangaroa, but after the war with his brother Tāne, the fish fled to the sea and the reptiles to the land. It was Tāne who decided that reptiles should be viviparous, with one exception being made in the case of the egg-laying *tuatara*. *Mokomoko*, lizards, were feared as the emblem of death. Reptiles and insects were supposed to have come to Aoteoroa in the mythical canoe Mangarara.

Eggs, lizards, taniwha, tuatara.

RIDDLES (*kai, panga*). Guessing competitions, puzzles, and riddles were always popular. For example the following is a good specimen of the riddles told by children:

'What is a *kiri*, full of holes, joined together, raised up in front and at the back, with a head and eyes, and with its tongue sticking out?' The answer is a canoe.

Kiri usually means skin, but is also the term for the outer covering of a hollow object. In the riddle, the holes are those bored round the top edge by which the top strakes are lashed in place, the raised ends are the *tauihu*, bow, and *taurapa*, stern pieces, while the head, eyes, and tongue can be found on the carved figurehead.

Puzzles.

RITES, see CEREMONIES.

RIMURAPA, see KELP, BULL.

RIVERS. In legend, rivers were endowed with human characteristics, and raced each other from the mountains to the sea. They were also the homes of feared monsters known as *taniwha* who in most accounts lived in deep holes at the foot of cliffs.

The banks of most rivers were ideal settlements because of their strategic situation and their accessibility to fishing grounds and eel weirs. To an aquatic people equipped with canoes the rivers were highways of travel.

Wide rivers were crossed by swimming and on rafts; swift mountain torrents were negotiated at an angle by treading water while the current carried the traveller downstream and diagonally across until the farther bank was reached; holding onto a long pole allowed larger streams to be crossed by several people at once. All river fords were well known.

Rafts, swimming, taniwha.

ROASTING, see COOKING.

ROCKS (*kōwhatu, kōhatu*). Rakahore, the guardian of shellfish, was also the personification of rocks. The rocks of the seashore help to guard the land against the ravages of the sea, personified as Hine-moana. They provided landmarks for fishermen, and were frequently given names.

Hine-moana, stones.

RONA. The woman in the moon. A popular legend tells how Rona went to fetch water at night for her children. When the woman stumbled over a root because the moon was hidden behind a cloud, she cursed it. Enraged, the moon descended to earth and seized her. Rona caught at a ngaio tree to try and save herself. But it was pulled up by the roots, and now she can be seen in the moon, together with the *ngaio* tree and her two hue or calabashes. In a sense she personifies the moon, and is known as Rona-whakamau-tai, Rona the tide controller.

Echoes, moon, tides.

RONGO. The departmental god responsible for agriculture and cultivated foods. He was also the god of peace and some boys were dedicated to him in the *tohi* rite, as others were to Tū-matu-aenga, the god of war.

Those who worked in the cultivations were under the *tapu* of Rongo as they planted, weeded, and harvested the crop. Objects such as stone representations of the god were often kept in the māra, garden, as *mauri* in order to preserve the fertility of the kūmara garden, for Rongo was closely identified with this plant. His full name was Rongo-marae-roa.

There is an interesting association of Rongo with Tāne in the name Rongo-mā-Tāne, a being or atua who combined the essential qualities of fertility and reproduction.

Gods, gods, (wars of), kūmara, mauri, moon, peace, Whiro.

RONGOMAI. A war god who was the personification of meteors. The dark marks on the face of the moon were called 'the ovens of Rongomai'.

ROOTS, EDIBLE.

Fern root, kūmara, taro.

ROPES. Ropes and cords were used for drawing together the roof and walls of a house and holding them permanently in position, and in the construction of fishing nets, snares, skipping ropes, and other common objects. They were usually made from *harakeke*, flax fibre, and were plaited in many different ways. *Aka*, or vines, were sometimes used as ropes, and the aerial roots of the kiekie were useful for weaving fish traps and similar receptacles.

Flax, houses, pā, plaiting, vines, swings.

RORE, see SNARES.

RŌRIA, see 'JAW-HARPS'.

ROUROU. Baskets or woven flax platters containing food.

Baskets.

RUA, see PITS. The word also means two.

RUAHINE, see PRIESTESSES. The word also means old woman.

RŪAUMOKO. The god of earthquakes and volcanic fire. There are a number of variations of the name, which is sometimes contracted to Rū. He was the youngest of the gods, and remains at Papa's breast, or in her womb, where his movements are responsible for the earthquakes that shake the body of his mother.

Earthquakes, fire.

RUNNING (*oma*). Both men and boys competed in running races, a valuable form of training for the future warrior. A fast-running young warrior would be chosen for the honoured post of challenger before a fight.

Races over long distances were generally held as a test of endurance rather than of speed.

Children preparing for a race, while the older people are watching. Several other juvenile sports are illustrated.

RUPE. Also known as Māui-mua, and brother of the celebrated Māui. When searching for his sister Hine-te-iwaiwa, he transformed himself into a pigeon and flew up to Rehua to seek assistance from the god of kindness. As he may be regarded as a personification of the woodpigeon, the *kūkū* or *kererū* is occasionally called *rupe*, but the name was not in common use and was apparently imported with the legend from the Hawaiki homeland.

S

SACRIFICES, HUMAN. The custom of offering human sacrifices was not an integral part of Māori religious ceremonial.

Human sacrifices might be made to the gods only on the most important occasions, such as the building of the largest houses and canoes, or when people were in desperate straits, as when in danger of defeat. In this case it was a placatory gesture of last resort in an attempt to secure the help of the gods. It should be distinguished from the offering of the heart of 'the fish of Tū' to the tribal war god. When danger pressed this closely a member of the tribe might volunteer or be chosen for the sacrifice if there was no slave available and it was not possible to kill an enemy.

Important feasts and ceremonies might sometimes be underlined with a feast of human flesh, but the killing of a slave for that purpose was to provide a *kīnaki*, 'relish', for the celebratory feast rather than for any religious reason.

Offerings, warfare.

SAILS (*rā*). The great ocean-going *waka*, canoes, which brought migrating Māori ancestors to Aotearoa were probably equipped with one or more masts and huge lateen-type sails such as those still found in some parts of the Pacific. Early European explorers of Aotearoa found Māori still using masts and sails in their larger *waka*, although the practice seems to have mostly died out soon after the Māori arrived here and the need for long ocean voyages had diminished.

The usual sail was in the form of a narrow, inverted triangle, and was plaited from *harakeke*, flax, *kiekie*, or *raupō* leaves. One fine specimen is held by the British Museum in London. It is about 12 metres in length, tapering from 2 metres to less than 0.5 metres and is made from several pieces joined together. Feathers were attached to the upper edge and a metre-long, plaited streamer floated from the upper rear corner. When hoisted, the sail was lashed to the mast with the other long side being fastened to an angled spar. When not in use the sail was furled and the mast and spar lowered into the *waka*.

Canoes.

SAND (*one*). Personified in Hine-one. She protects the land from the attack of Hine-moana, the ocean girl.

Hine-moana, mauri, one.

SANDALS. Māori went barefoot for the most part, although sandals were sometimes used in very rough country. These sandals were plaited from the tough leaves of the *tī kouka*, cabbage tree, and tied to the feet. *Harakeke*, flax, was also used for sandal-making but was less durable. A combined sandal and shin guard that protected the lower leg was sometimes used, particularly when journeys were undertaken in snowy conditions or involved crossing thorn-infested country.

A sandal from the Whanganui district.

SANDFLIES (*namu*). Māori life was often made unpleasant through the presence of the biting insects, mosquitoes and sandflies. Children were sometimes smeared with shark oil to protect them from attack, while adults used a combination of shark oil and *kōkōwai*, red ochre, or in some instances, mud. When the insects were particularly active, meals might be eaten while standing in the smoke from the cooking fires.

An entertaining fable tells how the *namu* and mosquito tribes attacked mankind. The *namu* made the attack by day and were repelled, but the wily mosquitoes waited until night and were successful.

SANDSTONE (*hōanga*). Hine-tū-a-hōanga was the personification of sandstone. She had two sisters, Hine-one and Hine-tū-a-kirikiri, who were the personifications of sand and gravel. Hine-tū-a-hōanga was said to be the mother of Rātā, who cut down a tree in order to build a *waka*, canoe. There is a symbolic significance in the names because Rātā means sharp. He asked his mother to help him sharpen his *toki*, adze, which he whetted on her backbone.

Sandstone was used for grinding stone adzes and other implements. Stone of varying grades was employed, *matanui* and *matarehu* being the terms used for coarse and fine grain.

Rātā, stones, Tutunui.

SCENT. Women and girls were fond of wearing scent sachets suspended round their necks or hung from belts at the waist. The sachets consisted of tiny bags, woven from scented grass and stuffed with scented moss and fragrant leaves.

There were several names for the scent sachets, each coming from the materials used in their manufacture, e.g. *hei piripiri*, a neck ornament in which the native burr (bidibidi) or *piripiri* provided the scent. Oil was also squeezed from *tītoki* berries and placed in containers with fragrant leaves and gum.

SCHOOLS OF LEARNING (*whare wānanga, whare kura*). For a people with no written form of language, the preservation and passing on of knowledge from one generation to another was a matter of high importance. The *whare kura* was the building in which such knowledge was taught, while the term *whare wānanga* was usually applied in a metaphorical sense. There is a similar dual meaning in the English word school, used for a building in which information is imparted and in the expression 'school of thought'.

Many subjects were taught and therefore required different 'schools', although clear-cut distinctions in subjects were not always observed. In some tribal areas the *whare wānanga* was divided into two houses of learning, the *kauwae runga* (upper jaw) where celestial knowledge was imparted, and the *kauwae raro* (lower jaw), or terrestrial knowledge. Elsewhere the *whare wānanga* was the school where religious, occult, and celestial knowledge was taught; the *whare kaupo* was reserved for the teaching of tribal history; and the *whare maire* for evil, low-class, or destructive magic.

Tai-whetuki belonged to the evil god Whiro. It dealt with black magic and was the origin of the *whare maire*. Other names were the *whare takiura* where high-class magic was taught; and *whare pūrākau*, the store of legendary knowledge.

Tāne brought knowledge to mankind, but he had to fight Whiro for it. He first obtained the plan or pattern of the house of learning, which was named *whare kura*, and with it built a similar house in which the *wānanga* (sacred knowledge), was held.

It is said that his next deed was to climb up through the heavens, until after many adventures. he reached the uppermost heaven where he obtained the three baskets of knowledge and the two *whatu kura* or sacred stones of the gods. The baskets and stones were eventually deposited in the *whare kura* that he had prepared for their reception. The place of this celestial *wānanga* was Rangiatea, which has subsequently always been a name held in the greatest reverence throughout Polynesia. The first *whare wānanga* on earth was at Te Hono-i-wairua (the assembling of souls), said to be in the far-off homeland of Irihia.

High-born chiefs and *tohunga* gained their knowledge through attendance at the several houses of learning in various parts of the country. Great pains were taken to ensure that there would be no changes in the oral transmission of knowledge. Any change would have been dishonouring to Tāne and to the *wānanga* that he had obtained, but more importantly would affect the efficacy of that knowledge. As a result many of the carefully preserved *karakia* contain words and expressions of such antiquity that their true meaning has been lost.

Instruction was given by the most knowledgeable *tohunga* and a strict *tapu* pervaded everything in the school. New entrants were required to leave their clothing outside and put on special cloaks during the classes. Sessions of the *whare kura* were held during the winter months when the workload was lighter.

Baskets of knowledge, houses, Io, karakia, kura, magic, mākutu, Rangiatea, stones (sacred), Tāne, tapu, tohunga, Whiro.

SEASONS (*tau*). The seasons of the year were thought to be regulated by various personifications. Hine-raumati, the summer girl, and Hine-takurua, the winter girl, were married to the sun, the former being in charge of food and forest products, the latter of fish. In the warm weather the sun clings to Hine-raumati, but abandons her for Hine-takurua when the days grow shorter. Spring is personified in *mahuru*.

Various tasks were regulated by the seasons, whose commencement and ending might be signalled by the rising of certain stars, the arrival and departure of migratory birds or the flowering of trees and plants.

The names of the seasons were: autumn, *ngahuru*; winter, *takurua* or *hōtoke*; spring, *mahuru*, *aroaro-mahana* or *te koanga*; summer, *raumati*.

Months.

SEAWEED (*rimu, rimurimu*).

Food, Hine-moana, kelp (bull).

SECOND SIGHT (*matakite*). There were rites that conferred the gift of second sight on those that possessed the necessary *mana* and desired such an uncomfortable gift. It was part of the training of most *tohunga* and there were others, including women, to whom it came naturally. The spirit or soul of a *tipuna*, ancestor, was said to take possession of the seer's body, and by omens and dreams and in other ways warned him or her of forthcoming events, usually of a disastrous nature.

Matakite also used their powers to find lost objects or persons.

Dreams, omens.

SEINE NETS, see NETS.

SEPARATION OF RANGI AND PAPA. This was the central event in the Māori creation myth. When the primal children became discontented with their life in eternal darkness, enclosed in the narrow space between Rangi the Sky Father and Papa the Earth Mother, they revolted. Tū-matauenga wished to kill the parents but Tāne proposed that they should be separated. This met with the approval of all except Tāwhiri-mātea, god of the winds. He loved his father and remained with him after the separation.

One after the other the gods tried to thrust Rangi away from Papa and failed. Tū-matauenga cut off his father's arms, and the blood that flowed on to Papa was the cause of red ochre in the earth.

Tāne finally succeeded, and threw Rangi far away, supporting him on poles that might be seen as the winds or rays of sunlight. Light then entered the world but the parents grieved for each other; Rangi's tears fell as rain on the earth and the rising mists were a token of Papa's love for her lost husband.

Although light and space had entered, earth and sky were bare, and it fell to Tāne to clothe them – the earth with trees and vegetation, and the sky with sun, moon, stars, clouds, and the red glow that covers it when the sun sets.

Divorce, earth, gods (wars of), light, Papa, Rangi, space, Tāne.

SEX. In the Māori natural world, Tāne was the male or procreative force. He was the symbol of fertility and in his quest for the female element he mated with many personifications which controlled the forces and manifestations of nature.

Finally he formed a woman of earth and she gave birth to the first true human being. The male sex was therefore said to be of divine origin and the female sex, human. For this reason the male line of descent was always regarded as more important than the female line.

The idea of sex permeated Māori society as shown in the creation myths and as reflected in traditional Māori art. Māori spoke freely of sexual matters in general conversation between the sexes and in front of children.

The only barriers to free relationships between the sexes prior to marriage were those of social class and a prohibition on relationships between close cousins. After marriage, however, any promiscuous intercourse was severely curtailed. There was a great deal of personal modesty and women sometimes committed suicide because of the slightest violation of their privacy. *Puhi*, specially chosen, high-born young women, were required to guard their virginity.

The absence of restriction in sexual matters does not imply an easy, conflict-free approach to love where, as many legends show, courtship could be a time of great emotional stress. There was often an idealisation of the loved one and much doubt as to the success of a courtship. The story of Tūtānekai and Hinemoa is one example. However it is also clear that there was no repression of sexual desire. The object of courtship was the acknowledgement of mutual attraction and its expression in sexual intercourse.

Phallic worship was not practised by Māori but much power was credited to the organs of generation and reproduction, hence their presence on many *pou whakairo*, carved figures. Flutes and the handles of bailers were often carved in the shape of the phallus and phallic stones were apparently used in some ceremonial rites.

Female element, man, marriage, Tāne, trees, Tiki.

SHARKS (*mako, mangō*). There were a number of different species of shark, all of which had descriptive names, for example the *mangō-pare*, hammerhead shark and the *mangō-ripi*, thresher. They were mostly caught by hook and line although there are accounts of sharks being lured alongside a *waka*, when a loop of rope was slipped over their heads to capture the creature.

Sharks were prized for their flesh. The fish were gutted and *pāwhera*, hung up and dried for future use. Shark teeth were used in necklaces and ear pendants and for setting in *māripi* or cutting knives. *Hinu*, oil from shark livers, was mixed with *kōkōwai*, red ochre, and used as paint or for personal adornment.

The fighting qualities of the shark were admired by Māori and a famous warrior might be likened to one.

Fishing, knives, ornaments.

SHELLFISH. According to legend, shellfish were the offspring of the personifications or guardians of the ocean, and were cared for by Hine-one, the sand girl.

The huge shell middens found in all coastal areas around the country show the importance of shellfish as a staple food item. Collecting them was one of the tasks assigned to women. *Pipi* and *titiko*, mud snails, were gathered from the beach while wooden levers were used to prise other shellfish such as *pāua*, abalone, from the rocks.

Women waded over muddy lake bottoms feeling for freshwater *kākahi*, mussels, with their bare feet.

Dredges were sometimes used in the taking of shellfish such as scallops and horse mussels which were found in mud or sand. Some species of fresh-water mussels were gathered by means of a wooden rake, to which a *harakeke,* flax, net was attached.

Shellfish were cooked by placing them in an

open space on the ground in the middle of a ring of fire or embers, where the heat opened the shells, or by the conventional method of steaming in the *hāngi*. The flesh of *pipi* and similar shellfish was sometimes smoke or sun-dried and threaded onto flax stalks for winter storage.

Sharp-edged shells were used for cutting and scraping tasks while other shells served as rudimentary spoons and ladles. Other uses were found as ornaments, being threaded into necklaces or, as with the iridescent *pāua* shells, polished, cut into discs, and used as eyes in carvings.

Cooking, dredges (fish), fish, fishing, Hine-moana, pāua, rocks, Tutunui, swimming.

SICKNESS (*mate*). Māori were generally robust and healthy and more in danger of losing their lives from wounds than from sickness. They were singularly free of sickness and disease, although some afflictions have been recorded: a form of leprosy, goitre, boils, skin diseases, eye infections and worms, for example, while it can be concluded that common complaints such as stomachache, headache and toothache, were also present.

For some of these complaints there were charms to be recited but no medical treatment of any kind. The treatment accorded to the sick was without sympathy and the few cures that were applied are thought to have been probably worse than the affliction. Sufferers were regarded as *tapu* and were taken from their *whare* and placed in rough shelters. It was believed that sickness was caused by offences against *tapu*, which brought punishment from the *atua*, by the attacks of the guardians of disease, and by malignant spells. It was therefore considered that cures needed to depend on magical formulae. The magic that was used as a cure was usually wielded by a lower class of *tohunga*.

There were several magical methods of diagnosis involving the pulling of flax leaves and the cooking of food to neutralise the sickness *tapu*, but the principal method, both of diagnosis and of cure, was by water. In cases of sickness induced by malignant spells, patients were immersed in water and *karakia* directed to the gods for their recovery and for the death of those who had bewitched them.

There were a number of minor ailments that were treated by common-sense methods. Warts were pared down and bound with leaves, boils were cut and squeezed, urine was rubbed into goitre swellings, herbal purgatives were given for constipation and various seeds or leaves were used to cure diarrhoea. Sufferers from toothache most often had to rely on the doubtful efficacy of chants.

In general the harsh conditions of life brought an early death to the frail and ailing and only the fittest survived.

After Pākehā arrived the Māori population was decimated by severe epidemics of diseases such as measles, tuberculosis and smallpox, to which they had no immunity. The epidemics were compounded by changes that occurred in their mode of life, dress, food, and living conditions. The widespread use of herbal remedies did not come into fashion until after Pākehā settlement.

Āhua, death, disease, evil, latrines, leprosy, magic, massage, medicine, poutiriao, tapu, whare, wounds.

SIGNALS (*waitohu*). Messages were conveyed to a distance by means of smoke signals, by arm signals, and by means of trumpets. There is little information about the former, but *rotarota* or arm signals were used in some districts. The commonly understood signals were as follows: raising the arm and throwing it outwards twice meant that the intention was to go in the direction indicated; to strike the buttocks twice, that the person signalling would stay where he was; to place the hand on top of the head indicated that the distant person was to come to the signaller; to raise the arms and place the hands against the forehead was to inquire whether it was safe to advance; to raise the right arm three times and touch the head showed that it was dangerous to advance; while to raise the right arm, touch the head, and fold the arms was a sign that it was safe to advance.

Gestures, natural phenomena, trumpets.

SINGING, see SONGS.

SKIPPING (*piu*). Several players usually took part in skipping games, one at each end of the rope, and one or more jumping in the middle. There were special songs to be sung to the rhythm of the rope as it turned.

SKIRTS (*piupiu, rāpaki*). The *piupiu* consisted of strips of flax hanging from a belt. The green leaves were scraped and dried, so that they curled into tubes. The *rāpaki*, mat, was made of dressed flax.

Garments, kilts.

SKY (*rangi*). The sky was personified in Rangi, the Sky Father, whose body was clothed with clouds, whose ornaments were the sun and moon, and whose tears fell as rain.

Overworlds, Rangi.

SLAVES (*taurekareka, mōkai*). Slavery was an integral part of the Māori social system, lightening the burden of life for the women of the owner's household. The lot of the slave was a miserable one, being subject to the whims of their owners, relegated to the most menial tasks and liable to death and the *hāngi* at any time.

Men and women who were captured in battle were doomed to slavery and sometimes took their own lives and their children's to escape the dishonour and misery of such a life. Fierce passions were roused in warfare and some captured prisoners never became slaves, being killed by the griefstricken women who had lost their men in the fighting and wanted revenge.

Nevertheless, though they were degraded and despised, and given hard tasks, those who reconciled themselves to their fate as slaves often lived contented if unadventurous lives. What prevented slaves from running away was the knowledge that they were dishonoured people because in being captured their personal *mana* had been destroyed. Sometimes they went to war and fought for their captors.

Slaves serving *rangatira* with food.

The children of female slaves who married men of the *rangatira* class were regarded as free-born though they could seldom aspire to a higher rank.

Marriage, meals, polygamy, sacrifices (human), social classes, warfare.

SLEDGES. The simpler forms of sledge were flat pieces of timber about a metre in length. The more elaborate ones were carved, with an upward-curved tip in front, and a cord to which the rider could cling. Some were made to hold two riders, and had projecting pegs to serve as handgrips. The undersides were rubbed with shark oil, and water might be poured on a slope to make it slippery. The run often ended in a stream or a pool of water. Small children sometimes used the head of a *tī kouka* cabbage tree or the leaves of the *nīkau* palm for the same purpose.

SLEEP (*moe*). In the *whare*, men, women, and children slept side by side with their heads toward the wall and their feet toward the central passage and the fire. They lay on mats spread

A boy riding on a stepped toboggan.

over piles of bracken fern or other brushwood. When travelling and sheltered by a *wharau*, shelter, they lay side by side with their feet toward the fire; but when conditions were less crowded there was comfort in lying with the back to the fire. Travellers who had no shelter or fire slept in a squatting position so that their coarse cloaks would act as a tent and shed the rain.

Tohunga were able to cast people into a deep sleep by means of magic spells, and there are examples of this in legend and history. It was thought dangerous to make a sleeper wake suddenly, for his *wairua*, soul, might have wandered far from his body and might not be able to return quickly.

Day, dreams, houses, mats.

SMOKE. Sleeping houses had little or no ventilation, the principal object being the conservation of heat. Smoke from a fire in the centre of the building was allowed to find its way out as it could, and it is not surprising that there were cases of asphyxia, even though Māori apparently developed a tolerance for foetid atmospheres at night. In the Whanganui district, men and

The interior of a *whare*, showing the sleeping arrangements. Families slept together in the *whare puni*, with their feet towards the fire.

women who were overcome by charcoal fumes were supposed to have been visited by malevolent *patupaiarehe*.

The only concession to the need for ventilation was that the front post of the house was slightly longer than the back one. The smoke could therefore drift slowly along the ceiling below the ridgepole and find its way out through the front porch. A few large houses had some sort of primitive smoke vent, termed *pihanga*, in the roof, but this term was usually applied to the window in the front wall, which was shut tight at night.

Smoke was used for signalling to friends at a distance but the method or details of the practice have been lost.

Signals, snares.

SNARES (*māhanga, rore, mutu*). The making of snares was *tapu* work and reserved for men. The cords used in making the traps were made from the leaves of *tī kouka*, cabbage trees, rather than *harakeke*, flax, because they were stronger and more durable. The snare materials were held over a smoky fire to preserve them and give them a weathered appearance, because it was believed that this would not excite the suspicion of prey such as birds. Some of the leaves were burnt to propitiate the appropriate *atua*, gods. Snares were all of ingenious construction and of many different types. Those used for catching rats were made from strong vines such as *kareao*, supplejack.

Birds (hunting), rats.

SOCIAL CLASSES. There is some dispute now about the structure of traditional Māori society. The three strata of Māori society were chiefs (*ariki* and *rangatira*), commoners, and slaves – but there is another proposition that there were only 'gentlemen' (*rangatira*) and slaves. There is a good deal of support for this point of view.

Māori were proud of their ancestry, and respect was paid to the first-born children of noble rank. There was a *tūtūā* class, which was thought to be composed of the *teina*, junior members of an extended *whānau*, family, who married into *teina* branches of other families, but there was always a reluctance to accept this classification, and a natural tendency for everyone to claim the rank of *rangatira*.

Misfortunes often reduced the status of those who belonged to the *rangatira* class to that of *tūtūā*.

Slaves were not free-born members of the tribe, but were captives taken in war, as were their offspring; yet the children of slave wives and *rangatira* husbands were free-born and lost the stigma of slavery. The *tohunga* was not a member of a social class, but of a profession. He was certainly a *rangatira*.

Although it is not possible to be specific, there was some differentiation of degree or rank among both men and women which sprang from a combination of descent and personal *mana*.

Chiefs, slaves.

SONGS (*waiata, pātere, oriori*). The melodies sung in characteristic Māori harmony and which are so popular today bear no resemblance to traditional Māori music. Traditional *waiata*, sung with an ear for the minutest difference in tone, would appear to many Pākehā as monotonous recitative, but there was a wealth of tonal significance within a narrow range.

Songs were sung with the whole being, body, hands, legs, arms, and facial expression all having their part.

There was great variety in the different types of song. *Karakia* were sung or intoned in somewhat the same manner as church rituals such as the catechism. However, within the broad classification of *karakia* came many different forms of charms, spells, incantations, invocations, and prayers. *Waiata* is the name for songs with some modulation, even approaching melody. They included love songs, laments, songs of longing, welcome songs, etc. Others, termed *tau*, occupied an intermediate position between *waiata* and *karakia*, being intoned with some degree of modulation.

Haka were dances accompanied by song where

there is a good deal of action associated with the words and music. *Rangi* were songs accompanied by a musical instrument such as a flute.

Waiata which tended towards rhythm, as in the dances or songs with actions, subordinated the melody. The *waiata* that were most distinctively melodious in the Western sense were the laments and love songs.

Songs with very little rhythm were also extremely varied; there were songs usually sung by one person only, or by one person and a chorus, watch songs, love songs, laments, lullabies, taunting songs, all had their own distinctive character.

Action songs, dances, haka, incantations, karakia, laments, lullabies, music, musical instruments, palisades, poi, tattooing, warfare.

SOOT. The pigment used in tattooing was made from soot obtained by burning the resinous heartwood of the *kahikatea*, the gum of the *kauri*, or the curious vegetable caterpillar. The soot was mixed with water to form a paste.

Tattooing, vegetable caterpillars.

SORCERY, see MAGIC.

SOULS (*wairua*). The *wairua*, soul, which was first given to the earth-formed woman Hine-tītama, represents the divine element in mankind. It is conferred before birth and, apart from excursions from the body during sleep and unconsciousness, remains with it till death.

The soul is immortal and at death makes the long journey to the Rarohenga, underworld. If there seems to be reluctance for the *wairua* to depart, it is speeded on its way by a special ceremony performed by the *tohunga*. For the most part the *wairua* seems to make its way to Te Reinga at the far end of Te Ika a Māui, there to plunge down from the leaping-place of spirits before eventually making its home in Rarohenga where it is welcomed by those who have gone before.

Other teachings say that the spirits of the dead guide the *wairua* through the waters of the ocean until it comes to the figurative temple of Hawaiki-nui, where it makes its choice of a final resting place.

No one returns from Rarohenga in mortal form, but apparently the soul can escape in the shape of a butterfly or moth, which is known as a *wairua atua*, or in insubstantial form as a ghost (*kēhua* or *kikokiko*). *Kēhua* and *kikokiko* prefer night to day, and were greatly dreaded.

Tipua, enchanted, objects are also supposed to be animated by the souls of departed ones.

In spite of belief in the immortality of the soul, powerful *tohunga* were said to be able to destroy the *wairua* of living people. All animate objects such as animals and trees possessed a *wairua*.

Although the conception of the *wairua* as the immortal spirit of man was a lofty one, the belief that malevolent ghosts and evil spirits were the *wairua* of the dead allowed a certain baseness to pervade the original teaching, and may have accounted for a later development of a belief in the *ata* and *awe*.

The *ata* of a human being was his divine shape, image, or reflection (terms which can also be applied to the *wairua*), while the *awe* was a conception of a purified spirit which also occupied the body of a man. These are sometimes confused with *mauri*, which was a life spirit or principle, but it died with the physical body. It is not possible to define these conceptions exactly and in terms of Pākehā thought, nor to put them in watertight compartments, for in some ways *wairua*, *ata*, and *awe* are synonymous.

Death, demons, dreams, ghosts, Hawaiki-nui, mana, mauri, overworlds, second sight, sleep, theft, underworlds.

SOUTH ISLAND. Te Waka a Māui, Māui's canoe, i.e. the canoe with which he fished up Te Ika a Māui, 'Māui's fish' or the North Island. The other common names for the South Island are Te Wai Pounamu, the Greenstone Water and Te Wāhi Pounamu, the Place of Greenstone. Te Waka a Māui is used consistently in this book to correspond with the constant use of Te Ika a

Māui for the North Island but the other Māori names for the South Island are equally valid.

While many traditions point to the first settlement from Hawaiki as being on the northern island, other traditions and the archaeological evidence support a southern island settlement of greater antiquity.

For example, some traditions record Māui as making his landfall on the southern west coast amongst the rugged fiords of that coastline; the Arai-te-uru canoe, carrying the *kūmara* and *hue*, gourds, was wrecked at Moeraki on the opposite coast and its crew settled there. Kupe and Ngāhue are said to have made their discovery of *moa* and *pounamu*, greenstone, at Arahura near modern Greymouth.

The advantages of the southern island were in its mineral resources and the apparently more numerous *moa*, the giant, fleshy, flightless bird that was hunted out very quickly. Later the land became a refuge for weaker tribes pushed out of the northern island by relentless warfare. Though much more closely populated in earlier years, there was never a great number of Māori in the southern island, the warmer climate of the north and its advantages for horticulture being preferred.

The early explorer James Cook recorded the name of the island as Te Wai Pounamu (the water of greenstone) but some argue for Te Wāhi Pounamu (the place of greenstone) as being more likely.

Arai-te-uru, Te Ika a Māui, Māui.

SPACE (*ātea, wātea*). Māori possessed a conception of the infinite extent of space as illustrated in genealogies in which Wātea, the personification of space, is said to have given birth to the successive ages of Kore (nothingness) and Pō (endless night) before the separation of Rangi and Papa.

In a variation of the usual legend of creation, it was not Tāne but Wātea, space, who separated Rangi and Papa. As such it aligns with modern belief. The wind children lived and played on the Mahora-nui-ātea (the great spreading out of space).

Creation, separation.

SPADES (*kō, kāheru*). Neither the *kō* nor the *kāheru* was a true spade, though the latter, fashioned in wood as a single piece, more nearly resembled a spade in shape. It had a long shaft and an elongated, paddle-shaped blade. The *kō* was provided with a detachable footrest lashed to the lower end. Both the footrest and the upper portion of the handle were sometimes carved. Elaborately carved models were made for ceremonial purposes.

Māori did not use these implements for turning over the soil, but simply lifted and loosened it, after which it was pulverised with smaller tools. Working together, men frequently used several *kō* in a row to ease the task of breaking in new ground.

Implements (agricultural).

SPEARS. In warfare the spear was a useful weapon. It was seldom thrown, although the throwing of whip spears or darts was a favourite pastime. Thrown spears were avoided by the agility of the warriors, or parried by hand.

The longest spear used in battle was the *huata*, which was sometimes more than 6 metres in length. It was used in the attack or defence of a *pā* as it could be thrust through the palisades. At other times it might be used in open warfare but it was awkward, requiring two men to wield it.

Some spears were barbed with detachable heads while others had two or more points. Others were pointed at both ends. The *tao* or common stabbing spear was about 2 metres in length and was held about the middle of the handle where it was nicely balanced. It could also be used as a staff.

Warriors were trained in the use of spears, and were instructed in various kinds of thrust and parry. The spears were also used as striking weapons.

Spears were made of *mānuka* (a favourite timber, being strong, light, and resilient), *maire*, *hīnau*, *rimu*, and *kahikatea*; the latter timber split readily and was therefore easily worked. The wood was adzed, trimmed, scraped, and smoothed with sandstone, after which it was polished by being rubbed on the trunk of tree fern or other suitable surfaces.

Finally it was oiled and the wooden tip hardened by fire.

Bird spears were long and slender and sharply pointed. Fish spears were used to take flounders and eels. They had a short handle, to which a number of pointed tines were lashed. Spear fishing was usually done at night by the light of torches. In spearing eels the technique was to pin the slippery fish to the bed of the stream and to thread a strip of flax through its gills before lifting it out of the water.

Birds (hunting), boys, darts, eels, fishing, pā, warfare, weapons.

SPEECHES. The making of *whaikōrero*, speeches, and listening to them, was a social convention of great importance to Māori, as is common with all oral societies where the spoken word carries great weight.

Whaikōrero were an essential ingredient in every social ceremony, in the greeting and farewell to guests, as a prelude to peace and war, in baptism, betrothal, and marriage ceremonies, and at the funeral *tangi*. Important matters that affected the welfare of the people were debated at length, and all of free birth could participate. Classical *whaikōrero* made use of a great deal of repetition and historical allusion.

The speaker – nearly always male – put all his energy into his oration as he strode up and down with quivering *mere*, gesticulating hands, and expressive features. The more important speakers shrewdly reserved their orations for the end when the subject under discussion was reaching a critical stage and a judgement could be made as to the likely outcome.

Farewell speeches were termed *poroporoakī*, and were made both by those who were taking their departure and those who were remaining. They provided an opportunity for chiefs of renown to give advice to their people.

Dying speeches, kōrero.

SPELLS, see KARAKIA.

Charms, incantations.

SPIDERS (*pūngāwerewere*). Spiders entered into mythology because there were spiders' webs stretching from earth to sky, providing a pathway for those who were bold enough to tread them. The various species of spiders were known and named, with the *katipō* spider being most feared because of its poisonous bite.

Poisons, spirals.

SPIRALS (*pītau*). The single and double spirals in *whakairo*, carvings, are a characteristic Māori development as an artistic motif. It is significant that *pītau* means the young, succulent shoot of a plant, especially the circinate frond of the fern, as well as a perforated spiral design in carving. This is confirmed by some informants who said that the *pītau* was derived from the young, closely-curled fronds of the tree fern.

Others said that the design was based on the web of the spider (*wharepūngāwerewere*) which is exactly a spiral. This motif, complete to its connection of supporting lines radiating from the centre, is copied in the open fretwork designs of the war canoe *taurapa* and *tauihu*, stern and bow pieces.

While the origin of the Māori spiral is not satisfactorily understood, it is known that other Polynesians used it to a limited extent and that it is a common design pattern in other parts of the Pacific, especially in Melanesia.

Carving.

SPIRITS, see SOULS.

Evil, gods, mauri, overworlds, personifications, second sight, souls.

SPIRIT WORLDS. The *wairua*, souls of men, descended to the underworld, the Rarohenga, where they were cared for by Hine-nui-ō-te-pō, the goddess of death.

SPOOLS, see NECKLACES.

SPRING (*mahuru, aroaro-mahana*), see SEASONS.

STAGES (*whata*). *Whata* is the name used for platforms and small storehouses erected on one or more posts, while *pātaka* was the word for more important, elevated storehouses. The platforms were used for a variety of purposes, such as the drying and storing of some types of food, the keeping of human bones, fishing nets, and anything edible which might suffer from the depredations of dogs and rats. In other cases they might be used to store the highly tapu possessions of a chief.

Sometimes they were built in the shallow waters of a lake or estuary, but normally the removal of the notched log ladder that gave access to the platform kept the contents unharmed. A primitive form of platform was made by cutting off the branches of a tree and laying a platform on top. Human bones were kept on platforms of this type until the time came for them to be hidden or buried.

At important feasts, enormous, many-tiered platforms known as *hākari* stages were erected in order to display food and other gifts to visitors.

Feasts, stages (fighting), ladders, palisades, storehouses.

STAGES, FIGHTING (*pūwhara*). Fighting stages were erected on the top of the ramparts of a *pā* behind the palisades. Often they were large platforms some 10 metres high, up to 15 metres long and 2 metres wide. Elsewhere, the tops of the earth ramparts, defended by a stockade and a trench, were used as a fighting platform. On the stages the warriors were equipped with long spears and large stones and darts which could be hurled down on the enemy below.

Warfare, watch-towers.

STARS (*whetū*). In the beginning of time, after the separation of earth and sky, Tāne went in search of the stars in order to adorn his father Rangi. The *whānau mārama*, children of light, were being cared for by Uru-te-ngangana, the eldest son of the primal parents and the personification of light.

Uru gave them to Tāne, who gathered them together in a basket and conveyed them to Rangi in the canoe Uruao. The basket hangs in the sky and is called Te Ikaroa (the long fish), the name given to the personification of the Milky Way. Māori regarded them as a family, calling them variously *whānau ariki* and *whānau mārama* to indicate their importance. They jostle each other in the basket, and if one falls out it becomes a 'falling star' or meteor. The stars are the younger relatives of the sun and moon.

Another name for the stars was *rā ririki* (little suns) an accurate surmise made by Māori, but this belief was likely to have been confined to the *tohunga* experts who studied the stars.

The knowledge of the astronomer was important for ocean navigation and subsequently when the rising of stars and constellations was seen to mark the seasons of planting and harvesting. The appearance of the stars was carefully studied to determine whether the growing season would be fruitful or not and offerings were made to the stars to ensure a plentiful harvest. They were also observed in order to foretell weather conditions. The rising of an important star, or of a constellation such as Matariki, the Pleiades, was greeted with songs and feasting.

The stars were important to welfare, and even those who did not belong to the brotherhood of experts and priests had an intimate knowledge of them. They had a large number of names for planets and stars, which they were able to recognise at once, but much of that knowledge has been lost and in most cases it is too late to link the stars with the large number of star names

Dittmer's conception of Maunganui, where Tāne obtained the stars from his brother Uru-te-ngangana, in order to adorn the Sky Father.

that have been preserved.

Day, meteors, Milky Way, sun, whitebait.

STEWART ISLAND. Rakiura (glowing sky), or Te Punga ō Te Waka a Māui (the anchor of Māui's canoe). This most southern region was one of the more thickly populated areas of the country and in its isolation developed distinctive traditions. It was a place famous for *tītī*, muttonbirds, which provided a rich and plentiful article of diet.

Māui, South Island.

STICK GAMES (*tītī tourea, tī rākau*). Throwing sticks was one of the most popular pastimes for old and young. There were many ways of playing these games, and from many positions – standing, sitting, or kneeling. Young women found that it made them supple and graceful in their dances; it was equally important to young men, because it trained them to be quick with hand and eye.

The sticks were about a metre long. Many people could play at one time, or the game could be confined to two players. Sometimes as many as 40 people would take part, 20 on each side, throwing the sticks from one to another simultaneously, or successively.

At times the object of the game was to throw the sticks thrown backwards and forwards without touching, at others the sticks were made to touch each other in passing, the rhythmic tapping of the sticks keeping time with the *tī rākau* song.

In another form of the game, players who missed a catch would fall out until the last player was left as the winner. When this game was played among men it might go on for weeks or months at intervals until all but one player had dropped out.

Boys.

STICKS, GENEALOGICAL (*kapeu whakapapa*). Sticks up to a metre in length with projections on one side were used as an aid to memory when reciting genealogical tables, much in the way that rosary beads are used.

Genealogies.

Two separate stick games are depicted here. A small group is seated on the left, throwing sticks to the time of the chant. The large group on the right is engaged in a game in which the players fall out one by one as they fail to catch a stick.

A memory stick with a number of projections serving as aids to the recital of genealogies.

STILTS (*poutoti*). Small children played on simple stilts made from the stems of saplings, or a branch of a tree with a convenient step formed by another branch at right angles. Older children and adults used poles with separate footrests lashed to them. The users became adept at the sport, and the footrests were often more than a metre from the base of the pole. They were used for crossing streams in sport, and young men sometimes wrestled on stilts.

Stilt walkers waded through streams on tall stilts.

STOCKADES, see PALISADES.

STONES (*kōhatu, kōwhatu*). The personifications of rock, gravel, and sand were closely related, and formed the defences of the earth against the sea. There are a number of legends to account for solitary stones, the usual account being that a human being has been transformed to this shape.

In the absence of any form of metal, stone of all kinds from greywacke to greenstone was used, principally as adzes, clubs, beaters for pounding food, and occasionally for bowls. The manufacture of a stone implement or weapon was long and laborious, from the first rough shaping, chipping, bruising, and grinding, to the final polishing. Stone bowls were a rarity because they were so difficult to make, and their place was taken by wooden bowls and troughs, gourds, and plaited baskets.

Hard stone was used for the bits in a primitive form of drill, and also for weights, as this tool had no cap by which pressure could be exerted. Stones were heated and used in the *umu* or *hāngi* and also to heat water by dropping them into containers.

Adzes, boundaries, bowls, clubs, cooking, greenstone, knucklestones, mauri, necklaces, offerings, ovens, rock, sandstone, stages (fighting), stones (sacred), thunder.

STONES, SACRED (*whatu kura*). When Tāne brought the sacred *wānanga* (knowledge) to earth for the benefit of mankind it was contained in the three baskets of knowledge which also held the two *whatu atua* (stones of the gods). These stones had been kept at the *ahurewa*, altar, in the sacred house Rangiatea. On earth the stones were similarly kept at the *ahurewa* at the rear post of the first *whare wānanga*, or *whare kura*. They were highly *tapu* and possessed great *mana* and magical powers.

These *whatu atua* were the prototypes of the *whatu kura* which were always buried by the rear post of the various schools of learning. They were *mauri* – a shrine or dwelling place of the gods – and imparted *mana* to the teachers and pupils of the school, and assisted in the imparting of knowledge. Smaller stones were also kept there and brought in contact with the *whatu kura*, and employed in various ways. They were held in the mouth by students to aid concentration, and sometimes swallowed, but in other schools they were presented to the pupil when he had passed the final tests, and were regarded as a kind of graduation diploma. All such stones were highly *tapu*, and this *tapu* extended to the stone seats in the school, which were used by both pupils and teachers.

Baskets of knowledge, boundaries, mauri, schools of learning, Tāne.

STOREHOUSES (*pātaka*, *rūa*). There were three methods of storing food and other objects – in elevated *pātaka*, storehouses, *whata*, small, elevated platforms (see Stages) and in caves or underground stores often cut into hillsides and known as *rua* (see Pits).

Pātaka were usually elaborately carved and unlike ordinary houses had plank walls. They were supported on one, four, or more posts, to help protect the contents from rats and damp. The *pātaka* varied in size from small boxes to house-shaped buildings many metres in length. Because they represented the fertility and wealth of the community to which they belonged, *pātaka* decorations often reflected such themes.

Undecorated *pātaka*, more numerous than the richly carved ones, were sometimes called *whata* although this term was usually reserved for elevated storage platforms. A ladder, consisting of a notched log, gave access to the taller *pātaka*.

As houses were kept free of personal property, the *pātaka* were also used for storing garments, ornaments, weapons and tools, as well as preserved foods.

A tall *pātaka* on a single post. The stepped pole is a ladder which gives access to the storehouse.

Ladders, pits, stages.

STORMS. When a storm at sea seemed imminent, the crew manned the long steering paddles, readied their bailers, and stowed all their gear. The anchor was lowered as the head of the *waka*, canoe, was turned into the wind, the lashings of the top strakes checked and protective awnings erected so that the canoe and crew might ride out the storm. However for most journeys the shores were hugged fairly closely and canoes usually ran

Tamatea.

TAMA. Can mean son, nephew, eldest son, boy, girl, man. There are also several derivatives, such as *tamatāne*, son; *tamawahine*, daughter, girl, female; *tamaiti*, child; *tamariki*, children; *taitama*, young man; *taitamahine*, young woman.

TAMAITI. Child.
Children.

TAMA-NUI-TE-RĀ. The personified form of the sun.
Sun.

TAMARIKI, see CHILDREN.

TAMATEA. Tamatea-pōkai-whenua (Tamatea who travelled all over the land), to give him his full name, was, in some *whakapapa* lists, the captain of the Takitimu canoe, and one of the notable early explorers of Aotearoa where his adventures are recorded in many place names.

He travelled to Te Waka a Māui, the South Island, before returning north to Kapiti, Whanganui, Taupō, the east coast and Hokianga.
Names, Takitimu.

TAMA-TE-KAPUA. The captain of the Arawa canoe. He had rather an adventurous career, commencing with his abduction of the *tohunga* Ngatoro-i-rangi and his wife. After staying some time at Maketū, he went on to travel in the Hauraki district where he eventually died and was buried on Moehau mountain on the Coromandel Peninsula.
Arawa.

TĀ MOKO, see TATTOOING.

TĀNE. The departmental *atua* Tāne was the life-giver, the fertiliser and the sustainer, the god of nature and of trees, the active element in life, and the one who brought knowledge to the earth.

The god had many qualifying names. One group is descriptive of his first great exploit in separating Rangi and Papa. As Tāne-mahuta he is the origin of trees, and as Tāne-mataahi, of birds. As Tāne-te-waiora he is the source of health and well-being, as well as the creator of the life-giving lake Waiora-a-Tāne.

As an instance of Tāne's powers of fertility, it appears that amongst many others, he was the father of the gods of the *weka*, *kiwi*, *kākā*, *tūī*, *kākāpō*, *kākāriki*, and all dark-coloured birds, while as god of trees and timber, he was responsible for the personifications of the grub, butterfly, and many different kinds of insects and spiders.

Tāne clothed the earth and the sky. Above all, he is known as the forest god. When he visited his brother Rehua in the heavens, he longed to take the *tūī* that nested in Rehua's hair back with him to earth. He was advised first to plant trees to provide food for them. He planted the *kahikatea*. In the third year they fruited and he was able to bring the *tūī* to earth.

His greatest deeds were concerned with bringing the baskets of knowledge to mankind. As god of light he opposed Whiro, god of evil and darkness. He ascended up through the overworlds or heavens where he found a pattern for the school or *whare wānanga*. He copied it and called it the *whare kura*, a name that has subsequently been given to all houses of instruction. Tāne continued his climb followed by Whiro, who attacked him in several ways.

He was greeted by his brother Rehua, submitted to purificatory rites and was given the sacred baskets of knowledge, which he brought to earth, a running battle taking place all the way until Whiro and all his followers were driven down to Rarohenga, the underworld.

Tāne was also engaged in several other battles with some of his brothers, but will perhaps best be remembered because it was his strength that lifted Rangi away from Papa, bringing light into the world and creating room for the gods to move.

Baskets of knowledge, creation, day, earth, eggs, evil, female element, gods, gods (wars of), Hine-ahu-one, Hine-nui-ō-te-pō, Hine-tītama, Io, light, mountains, overworlds, Papa, Rangi, Rehua, reptiles, Rongo, schools of learning, separation, stars, stones (sacred), sun, Tāwhiri-mātea, trees, Tū-matauenga, Waiora-a-Tāne, water, winds.

TĀNE, see MAN.

TANGAROA. God of fish and of the sea. Māori differed from other Polynesian societies in not giving Tangaroa first place amongst the *atua*. Although in one early Māori legend he was the first husband of Papa, the normal version is that he was one of the primal offspring, and that he and Tāne fought against Tāwhiri-mātea and were defeated. One of his special qualities is that of tide controller, under the name Tangaroa-whakamau-tai.

Fish, gods, gods (wars of), greenstone, Hina, reptiles, tides, Tinirau.

TĀNGATA WHENUA. 'People of the land', or the original inhabitants. This is a traditional term that was used by Māori for the very first people to occupy Aotearoa.

Kupe, Moa-hunters.

TANGI. As a noun, the name given to the activities and ceremonials surrounding death and as a verb it carries the meaning, to weep. The wailing and weeping of the *tangi* are not confined to mourning for the dead. The *tangi* is also a means of expressing emotions, such as when people meet each other after a prolonged absence. This palpable expression of grief is therefore not only for the one who has just died but for all those who have departed for the after-life since the last meeting of friends.

The *tangihanga* ceremonial includes *whaikōrero*, speech making and feasting. But it is thought to be a cause of ill luck if the weeping continues as the guests depart.

Burial, death.

Mourners at a *tangi*, lacerating their breast and cutting their hair.

TĀNIKO. Decorative forms of weaving in geometrical patterns of different colours.

Cloaks, dyeing, garments, weaving.

TANIWHA. Taniwha were 'fabulous' monsters that usually took the form of giant lizards or fish. Their origin came when Tāne mated with

Hine-maunga, the mountain girl. Their offspring was Pūtoto, whose descendants were *taniwha*, reptiles, and insects, and the personifications who were responsible for rocks, sand and gravel. Some scholars think that the *taniwha* represents a cultural memory of the crocodiles of tropical lands.

Māori believed that these fearsome creatures populated the whole land. Every *kāinga*, village, seemed to have its own *taniwha*, which lived in springs, rivers, lakes, caves, and mountains. A popular home for *taniwha* was in deep-water holes beneath a cliff.

There are occasional stories of *taniwha* kept as pets, but as a rule they were dangerous beings which attacked human beings ruthlessly. Notable warriors who killed *taniwha* and cut open their bellies usually found bones, whole bodies of men, women, and children, as well as scattered limbs, tools, weapons, and treasured ornaments, and even whole *waka*, canoes. There were also *taniwha* of the deep sea and in one tradition, a flying *taniwha*.

Arai-te-uru, lizards, magic, marakihau.

TAO. Short stabbing spears. The word is also used to describe cooking in a steam oven.

Cooking, ovens, spears.

TAPU. Sacred; under religious or superstitious restriction, a condition which refers to places, persons, and things. Other meanings given are: 'beyond one's power, inaccessible; ceremonial restriction, quality, or condition or being subject to such restriction'. 'Sacred' is given as a modern

Pekehaua, the *taniwha* of Te Waro-uri, is captured in a cage and brought to the surface of the pool now known as Taniwha Springs.

Tutae-poroporo, a large *taniwha* of the Whanganui River. He was killed when he swallowed a box containing Ao-kehu, the *taniwha* slayer, who then cut his way out of the monster's body.

definition, and while this term may not have the exact connotation of the Pākehā word, it yet conveys a good deal of what is meant in addition to the restricted meaning 'forbidden'.

Williams's *Dictionary of the Māori Language* provides a useful summary, so far as any summary can serve: 'Under religious or superstitious restriction; a condition affecting persons, places, and things, and arising from innumerable causes.' As such *tapu* acted as the strongest social control in traditional Māori society.

Belief in *tapu* was the most important of all aspects of Māori life and thought, because it affected everyone directly and indirectly from birth to death.

It was a religious belief and condition, and the force which governed the whole of life, taking the place of law, i.e. as a social regulator, as well as of religion. It is so vast a subject that only a few of its effects can be stated here.

Tapu emanated from the gods, and any infringement of this condition, or of the rules and conditions pertaining to it, resulted in sickness, calamity, and death, because the mana and protection of the gods was withdrawn. Anyone violating tapu contracted a hara, error, and was certain to be overtaken by calamity. As a rule, elaborate ceremonies were necessary to remove *tapu* and make anything (or anyone) *noa*, (common or safe).

Tapu was so important that life was controlled by these restrictions, and the higher the estate of a man, the more he was subject to them. For example tohunga, especially after taking part in religious ceremonies, were so tapu that no one could approach them, and food had to be served to them on a stalk to avoid the possibility of actual physical contact and a breach of *tapu*.

References under other headings show how widespread the restrictions were. They lay heavily on buildings, canoes, nets, and other objects that were under construction. This was to underline the importance of the work and designed so that all the proper rituals were observed and therefore guarantee the success of the task or venture. Places as well as people could be protected against evil influences by *tapu*. Forests and fishing grounds could be reserved by the imposition of *tapu* in the form known as *rāhui*. *Wāhi tapu*, sacred places within *kāinga*, villages, were so designated to restrict access except for particular purposes. *Tūāhu*, 'altars', where *tohunga* might carry out their duties fell into this category, as did the communal turuma, latrine, which was restricted for health reasons.

A *tapu* chief eating with a fern stalk to avoid touching his head.

Tapu-removing rites (whakanoa) had to be conducted with great care. A certain degree of tapu always pertained to a house, which accounts for the fact that cooked food, a pollutant of the tapu state, was never eaten indoors. The roof of a whare was especially *tapu* (as was the head of man), and rainwater was never collected from it, even though the defenders of a *pā* might be dying of thirst.

Burdens, burial, cultivations, disease, experts, fasting, feasts, female element, fire, fishing, hair, houses, mana, meals, men, names, nets, ochre (red), puhi, rähui, sacrifices (human), sickness, snares, travellers, water, women.

TARO. This food plant is found throughout the Pacific. In Aotearoa it was confined to Te Ika a Māui, the North Island, and although it was not a staple article of diet like the kümara, this introduced plant nevertheless became a very useful food source.

It was a perennial, the roots and leaf stalk of which could be eaten. Taro was cultivated in swampy, sandy soil, and protected from the wind by brush fences. Crops were small, and the roots were something of a delicacy. For that reason it was also know as a *kai rangatira* or food for chiefs.

Cultivations, underworlds.

TĀRUKE. Crayfish pot.

Crayfish.

TATA, see BAILERS.

TATUA. To count; door.

TATTOOING (*tā moko*). The art of tattooing was believed to have originated in the underworld. The story of Mataora and Niwareka tells how Mataora went to the Rarohenga in search of his wife Niwareka. So that he would look like the other men there, he painted the moko (pattern of the tattoo) on his face, but was laughed at because it washed off so easily. Finally his father-in-law consented to tattoo him in the proper manner, and when Mataora returned to the world, he brought back the knowledge of this art.

In remote times it is thought that the moko was confined to crosses and straight lines, but during the centuries of occupation in Aotearoa the

A fine example of tattooing, depicted by Dittmer, who shows the similarity of the designs with those of the kindred art of wood carving.

characteristic curvilinear patterns were developed in the same way as designs in wood carving.

Tattooing was such a painful process that it was not commenced until maturity, when the skin had hardened. In fact, the incising of the lines was a sign of maturity in both men and women.

It is thought to have had no connection with tribal distinction or rank, but was purely decorative. However, men of rank almost always possessed a full facial *moko* which became, as it were, their 'signature'.

In women, the chin and lips were usually tattooed, sometimes the forehead, and occasionally the breasts, while rather more frequently bands were tattooed on ankles and wrists. Men were tattooed heavily on the face, body, thighs and buttocks.

The painful operation of tattooing. The *tohunga*, or expert, is tapping the chisel with a light mallet. A calabash and a stone bowl contain the pigment, and there are bunches of soft fibre to wipe away the blood as the chisel pierces the skin.

The operation caused the blood to flow freely as the chisel cut through the skin. Owing to the pain of the operation, and the swelling of the lacerated flesh, only a small portion of the design could be done at a time. When the lips and cheeks were tattooed they became so swollen that the patient had to be fed by means of a funnel.

Tattooing experts, who were well paid for their services, performed the operation in the open air. Onlookers sang songs to take the sufferer's mind off the ordeal. The expert used a sharp chisel, like a miniature adze, often made from the wing bone of a *toroa*, albatross, mounted in a carved wooden handle, and tapped with a small mallet. The sharp chisel edge cut right though the skin, making a groove bounded by ridges of flesh. Combs, or chisels with teeth, were used for the more intricate punctured incisions, and to fill in the solid coloured areas, but the main characteristic of the *moko* in Aotearoa was that the flesh was cut right through – carved – to form the basis of the pattern. As the blood flowed it was wiped away with wisps of soft flax fibre.

The pigment used in tattooing was called *kauri*, and was made by burning *kauri* gum, certain heart timbers and vegetable caterpillars, and mixing them with water. A common pigment was made by feeding charcoal to dogs, and using the excrement.

Art, belts, carving, plaiting, soot, spirals, vegetable caterpillars, weaving.

TĀTUA, see BELTS.

TAU, see SEASONS.

TAUA, see WAR PARTIES.

TAUMATA. A resting place, or the brow of a hill.
Names.

TAUMATA ATUA, see KŪMARA GODS.

TAUMAU, see BETROTHAL.

TAUPUNIPUNI, see HIDE AND SEEK.

TAUREKAREKA, see SLAVES.
Mōkai.

TAWA. The berries of the *tawa* tree were cooked on the embers of the fire. They could be stored for some time, and were appreciated by inland tribes, where the people could not obtain *karaka* berries, which grow only near the coast.

TAWHAKI. A demi-god or hero of many fabulous adventures, who was finally regarded as a god, with control over thunder and lightning. The stories of Tawhaki and his grandson Rātā are mytho-poetic legends based on discoveries of and voyages to distant lands.

Tawhaki is said to have fought with the *ponaturi*, and later, when his celestial wife returned to the heavens, he climbed the vines that stretch from earth to sky, and discovered her in a land singularly like his native earth, where he remained, and manifested himself in the lightning.

There is a cycle of Tawhaki stories, beginning with his grandfather Kaitangata, his father Hema, his son Wahieroa, grandson Rātā, and great-grandson Whakatau-pōtiki, all of whom are famous characters of legend.

Lightning, names, Rātā.

TĀWHIRI-MĀTEA. God of the winds. After the separation of Rangi and Papa, Tāwhiri-mātea took the side of his father and declared war on land and sea, and was victorious. The only god who could withstand him was the god of man, Tū-matauenga.

Tāwhiri-mātea fathered most of the natural phenomena of the sky – wind, snow, frost, ice, rain, hail, mist, and clouds.

Gods (wars of), separation, winds.

TAWHIRIRANGI. Said to be one of the canoes that brought Kupe and Ngāhue to Aotearoa.
Kupe.

TE. The singular form of the definite article.

TEETH. Necklaces were often made of shark, whale, dog and human teeth, or representations of such teeth carved in bone and strung together on a cord. The teeth of deceased relatives were prized and preserved in this way. Shark teeth were set in cutting implements because of their sharp, serrated edges.

In humans, because of the staple diet of coarse, gritty food such as fern root, teeth became badly worn. The wear (and probably tooth decay) was so excessive that at the age of 40 or thereabouts, teeth had deteriorated to such an extent that it was probably a contributing factor to the relatively short lifespan of traditional Māori.

Burial, ear pendants, fish-hooks, knives, necklaces, ornaments, sharks, whales.

TEKA, see DARTS.

TEKOTEKO. The carved wooden figure on the gable of a house. It took the form of either a head or a complete figure.
Carving, houses.

TEMPLES. Although there were no temples in the conventional Pākehā sense of a place in which to worship, large *whare* were sometimes used for imparting sacred and esoteric lore. The true 'temple' was the sacred, small, open space known as the *tūāhu*.

Hawaiki-nui, houses, Rangiatea, tūāhu, whare wānanga.

TERRACES. When a *pā* was built on a hill it was necessary to excavate trenches, build up ramparts, and provide flat spaces where *whare* could be built. There were usually a number of such terraces and the serrated outlines of hills indicate the site of such *pā*. Trenches were dug and lined with palisades at their outer edge, the walls being strengthened with layers of bracken, while in some cases a stone facing was built to strengthen the construction.

Pā, palisades.

TEWHATEWHA. The *tewhatewha* was a wooden striking weapon, up to 1.5 metres in length, with a flat projection at one end resembling the blade of an axe. The other end was blunt or sometimes pointed and might be used for thrusting. But the flattened portion was the lethal part of the weapon. It was used as if one were striking a blow with the back of an axe instead of with the edge of the blade. The blade portion of the weapon lent weight to the blow at delivery. A bunch of feathers was suspended from a hole in the lower part of the blade, and these were fluttered in order to confuse the opponent.

Taiaha.

THATCH. The roofs of important houses were neatly lined with the stalks of *toetoe*, lesser houses with *mānuka* sticks or *tōtara* bark. On the roof, long rods of *kareao*, supplejack, were laid on the battens, and the first layer of thatch, which was composed of bundles of *raupō*, laid on them. The ends of the bundles were butted. Further rods and bundles of *raupō* were fastened on top of the inner layer. A final, outer layer was composed of more durable materials, such as brushwood, and the bundles overlapped to shed rain. They were held firmly in position with rods and creepers. *Raupō* thatch was also applied to the outer walls of a *whare*.

Houses.

THE. Singular, *te*; plural, *ngā*.

THEFT. Stealing was not unknown, but a thief ran considerable risks. When a theft was discovered and the thief was not known, the victim would take the *āhua* of the stolen object to the *tohunga*, who would cause the *wairua* of the thief to materialise. He then brought the powers of *mākutu* to work to bring punishment on the offender. The punishment varied with the gravity of the offence, the anger of the victim, and the powers of the *tohunga*, but in extreme cases the result was death. An appropriate punishment was a spell that caused the thief's fingers to contract, and prevented him from stealing again.

Āhua, evil, mākutu, muru, utu.

THERMAL REGIONS. Takiwā-waiariki (district of hot springs) was a name given to the thermal regions. Volcanic activity in Aotearoa originated with the *tohunga* Ngatoro-i-rangi, who ascended Tongariro and, when in danger of death from the intense cold, called on his sisters in Hawaiki for help. They sent the gods of fire, who travelled under the sea, emerging first at Whakaari, White Island, then at Rotorua, and finally burst from the top of the mountain and saved the *tohunga*.

Wherever they appeared on the surface of the land in their journey, they left signs of thermal activity behind them. The geological fault where thermal activity is most pronounced marks the passage of the ancient fire gods.

Ihenga was the discoverer of the land of geysers and boiling mud pools. When he first saw the drifting steam he thought that it was smoke from cooking fires, but soon discovered a land of wonder. Māori found the warmth of the hot-water pools comforting in a colder country than their homeland, and Rotorua and its environs were quickly settled. The hot pools were used for bathing, boiling springs for cooking food, and *whare* were built over ground made warm by thermal activity.

Ngatoro-i-rangi.

THROWING STICKS, see STICK GAMES.

THUNDER. Thunder was personified in the female Hine-whaitiri. In several religious rites a powerful *tohunga* was able to conjure up thunder by striking stones together, and invoking Hine-whaitiri and other personifications.

Lightning, Tawhaki.

TĪ, see CABBAGE TREES.

TIDES (*tai*). An esoteric belief in the cause of tides was a colourful rendering of a scientific truth. Tides were thought to be caused by Tangaroa-whakamau-tai (Tangaroa the controller or establisher of tides), a secondary name for the god of the ocean, and Rona-whakamau-tai, a secondary name for the personification of the moon. In the fixing and controlling of the tides they were assisted by Hine-moana, the goddess of the ocean. It was said that far out at sea there is a ridge known as the Tuahiwi-nui-a-Hine-moana (great ridge or backbone of Hine-moana) which, in conjunction with the activities of the deities, also affected the tidal flow.

A more popular and simple belief was that somewhere in the depths of the ocean there lived a monster called Te Parātā whose breathing caused the ebb and flow of the tides. It was in the throat of this monster that the Arawa canoe was almost engulfed on its voyage to Aotearoa.

Hine-moana, moon, Rona, Tangaroa.

TIKI. Tiki was the first mortal man, formed by Tū-matauenga, and endowed with life. There are so many versions of the Tiki myth that they become confusing. According to some he was a god, but it seems clear that the general belief was that he was a person. The esoteric meaning of most of these legends is that while Tū-matauenga represents the male principle, Tiki represents the *ure*, or male organ. Whatever may be Tiki's origin and relations with the first woman whom, in some legends, he is said to have created and mated with, it is certain that he represents the male element in sexual relations, and has a definite phallic significance. The confused nature of the Tiki traditions suggests that, as in other parts of the Pacific, these traditions were tightly suppressed by early missionaries because of their explicit nature.

The neck pendant or amulet known as a *tiki* is still a most highly prized possession. It is essentially an image of the human form and is made of polished *pounamu*, greenstone. The manufacture of the images was a long and laborious task. The hands of the figure were three-fingered, the legs usually drawn up, and the head turned to one side. There was a theory, no longer tenable, that it represented the human embryo, whereas all such images were those of particular ancestors, and thus were preserved from one generation to another.

The turned head and drawn-up legs give compactness to the figure, and avoid the danger of projecting parts being broken off. If *tiki* are studied it will be seen that they are roughly rectangular in shape, with notches for the neck. The head and face are at an angle, ingeniously fitting the figure to a rectangular form. Tiki were often made from *toki*, adze blades, which supports the conjecture that its shape was determined by the material that was available, and that its resemblance to an embryo is accidental. Certainly after contact with Europeans many *pounamu toki* met this fate as the popularity of *tiki* as collector's items grew and the need for adzes was diminished by the availability of steel.

Wood carvings of men were called *tiki*, the greenstone neck ornament being differentiated by calling it a *heitiki* (*hei* meaning neck ornament). It is interesting to note that although Tiki was the first male, most *heitiki* were female figures. It is now believed that this was only because the female figure was easier to carve in greenstone than the male, and that earlier theories about the fructifying significance of the image were exaggerated, and its symbolism as an embryo without foundation.

Eels, man, Tū-matauenga.

TIME. Māori used a time scale that worked on a daily, rather than an hourly, basis. There were names for day and night, midnight and dawn. The passage of time throughout the night was known by the position of the stars, and through day by the sun. There were special expressions or words for yesterday, today, tomorrow, last night, and one, two, and three days past and to come.

The year was divided into 12 months, and each month into about 30 nights, while there was some system of intercalation, now lost, designed to correct the calendar to correspond with the solar year. The rising of various stars and constellations provided the necessary check on the lunar system.

Day, moon, months, night, seasons, stars.

TINI Ō TE HAKUTURI. Spirits of the forest.

Fairies, Rātā.

TINIRAU. The son of Tangaroa, the god of fishes. Tinirau was connected with fish, and especially with whales. His place of birth may have been Te Puna i Rangiriri, a spring in the midst of the ocean where fish originate. Tinirau married Hina-uri (Hine-te-iwaiwa), and when the *tohunga* Kae baptised his son, Tinirau sent Kae home on the back of Tutunui, one of his pet whales. Another legend says that he was the guardian of whales. Te Puna a Tinirau (the spring of Tinirau) is a name sometimes given to the blow-hole of a whale.

Fish, Hina, Tutunui.

TIMA, see IMPLEMENTS, AGRICULTURAL.

TIPUA (or TUPUA). Demons, supernatural objects, or anything which appears to have supernatural qualities.

Charms, demons, mana, offerings, souls, travellers.

TĪ RĀKAU, see STICK GAMES.

TĪ RINGA, see HAND GAMES.

TĪTĪ, see STICK GAMES, MUTTONBIRDS.

TOA, see WARRIORS. The word also means brave man and bravery and, as an adjective, brave, victorious, and male.

TOETOE. Feathery pampas grass, the stalks of which were used for darts in boys' games, and in the decoration and thatching of houses.

Houses, reed patterns, thatch.

TOHI, see BAPTISM.

TOHORĀ, see WHALES.

TOHUNGA. Basically a *tohunga* was simply a skilled person, or an expert. There were many *tohunga* Māori, with special gifts and qualifications, such as *tohunga whaihanga*, an expert in building, *tohunga whakairo*, an expert in tattooing and other patterns, *tohunga whakairo rākau*, an expert in wood carving, etc. This aspect of the work of the *tohunga* is described under the heading Experts.

In all such tasks there were certain rituals and religious practices to be observed. A *tohunga* was therefore regarded as a priest, and when his training and knowledge were directed towards occult matters, he was without question a priest

A *tohunga* chanting a *karakia* over *kūmara* tubers.

or a wizard, with magic powers under his control. As a matter of convenience, priestly *tohunga* may be divided into four categories, though in practice a priest might well be skilled in more than one department of knowledge.

The *tohunga ahurewa*, or *tohunga tūāhu*, was a priest trained in the highest, most sacred knowledge, in the lore of the 'upper jaw' of the *whare wānanga*, skilled in ritual and forms of invocation to Io, and in all the knowledge that pertained to this sacred lore.

The second class of priests was those who specialised in knowledge of the *atua*, both tribal and departmental. They occupied a very important position in the tribe, and their knowledge of ritual and *karakia* was essential to the welfare of their people. They presided at ceremonies connected with hunting, agriculture, warfare, peace-making, birth, betrothal, marriage, and death. It is difficult to draw any close distinction between the first and second classes of the priesthood.

The third class was skilled in history as well as legend. They were repositories of genealogies and chants which were handed on from generation to generation unchanged.

The lowest type of priest was those who dealt with demons and evil spirits. They were powerful and greatly feared, because they were the earthly media of the *atua*, and were able to exercise control over earthly and unearthly forces. *Tohunga ka mākutu* and *tohunga kēhua* could be included in this category.

In each of the four classes, there were 'wizards'. Their proximity to the gods gave them supernatural powers, which resulted also from long periods of training, and physical and mental hardship. They were natural leaders and advisors in tribal councils, and those who were *ariki* by descent exercised great power.

Altars, canoes, ceremonies, charms, death, disease, divination, experts, gods, Io, karakia, mana, natural phenomena, priests, schools of learning, second sight, stars, tapu, theft, wānanga, warfare, war parties.

TOI. According to tradition, Toi-te-huatahi came from Tahiti in the Paepae-ki-rarotonga canoe in search of his grandson Whatonga in the 12th century A.D. He settled at Whakatāne, where Whatonga eventually found him. Because he was forced to eat the forest products of the new land, he was given a new name, Toi-kai-rākau (Toi the wood-eater). His descendants married the descendants of the crew of the Mataatua, and from them came the tribes of Maunga-taniwha, Ngāti Awa, and Tūhoe.

Aotearoa, drift voyages, Kurahaupo, Whatonga.

TOKE, see EARTHWORMS.

TOKI, see ADZES.

TOKOMARU. There were two famous canoes of this name:

• The canoe belonging to Manaia, but which was more properly named Tahatuna. The main body of its descendants comprised the Āti Awa tribe.

• The second Tokomaru was commanded by Whata. There is some confusion between the two canoes, and there is a theory that the first Tokomaru returned to Hawaiki, and then made the voyage to Aotearoa a second time.

TOMBS. In a few isolated places, buildings made of timber contained dead bodies which were placed inside in a sitting position. Eventually the bones were removed and put in caves, or in boxes on tall poles in the village. In North Auckland, carved boxes containing bones have been discovered in caves.

Death.

TONGUES. The protruding tongue and rolling eyes (*pūkana*) expressed defiance, and the outthrust tongue is one of the simplest and most common features of Māori art. It is obviously a symbol of defiance, and vigour appropriate to a war-loving people. In childhood at least it is an almost universal way of expressing contempt, and appears in carving art where defiance seems most necessary, e.g. on defence stockade figures, canoe prows, carved gateways, *tekoteko, koruru,* and as a general feature of both the interior and exterior of meeting houses.

TOOLS. Most tools were used skilfully. A great deal of care was lavished on some implements, carving often being featured on tools of a purely utilitarian type. Adzes and chisels were used for wood-working, and the representation of an ancestor was sometimes carved on the handle to increase the mana of the implement.

Adzes, birds (hunting), chisels, fishing, drills, implements (agricultural), spades, tattooing.

TOPKNOTS. The single or multiple topknot was a method of dressing the hair adopted only by men.

Hair.

TOPS (*pōtaka*). Top spinning was one of the most popular sports among old and young. Whip-tops were made of wood, stone, or pumice. Gourds were used for humming tops. A small gourd was dried, the interior removed, and a stick threaded through it vertically to provide a peg and the handle, round which a cord was wound. Holes were bored in the sides of the gourd to produce the humming sound.

Whips were made of strips of flax tied to a handle. The flax was wound round the top, which was thrown down and kept spinning by whipping. Games were played on the *marae pōtaka*, which was a level piece of ground carefully flattened, and dotted with small mounds over which tops jumped as they were kept spinning with the whips. The player who kept his top spinning the longest time and was successful in getting it to jump over all the mounds was declared the winner. Sometimes two parallel lines were drawn, one on each side of the *marae pōtaka*. Two boys would play against each other and try to whip their tops over the opponent's line. They were allowed to whip the other's top as well as their own.

Some of the tops had grooves in them, so that they hummed as they spun over the *marae*. If the top turned steadily, and seemed to stand still, it was called a sleeping top. Two players were needed to set the gourd humming tops spinning, one to hold the top upright, and the other to set it spinning with the cord. Fighting tops had small shells stuck in them and were whipped to make them bump against the other tops and cut them to pieces.

Lullabies.

TORCHES (*rama*). Muttonbird hunters used strips of flax bound round pieces of *tōtara* bark, about a half metre in length, to provide torches to attract the birds and to enable them to see what they

Old and young join in whipping tops over the mounds on the *marae pōtaka*. Different types of tops in wood and stone are illustrated above.

were doing when they brought the birds out of their burrows.

To make the torches, dried grass and broken pieces of bark were packed inside and saturated with fat. Such a torch would burn for a long time, probably for three or four hours. It was whirled round the head from time to time to increase the flame.

In Te Ika a Māui, the North Island, *rimu* heartwood was used, being split into laths and tied into bundles. Periodically, the ash had to be knocked off. Other torches, used in fish and bird-hunting expeditions, were made of *tī*, cabbage-tree leaves, *mānuka* bark, dried *kareao*, supplejack vines, and *kahikatea*, heartwood.

TORERE, see DRAUGHTS.

TOROA. The captain of the Mataatua canoe.

TOYS. Māori children had few toys, but many games that could be played with natural objects, such as stones, flax leaves, sticks, and vines. The

The torch carried by Ihenga when he invaded the fairy *pā* on Ngongotaha.

most ingenious toy was the *karetao* or jumping jack, a puppet figure with articulated limbs. Small canoes were made from flax leaves and provided hours of amusement. Knuckle stones were popular, and hoops were made of *kareao*, supplejack vine.

Games, hoops, jumping jack, knuckle stones, tops.

TRAPS.

Birds (hunting), fishing, rats.

TRAVELLERS. Journeys through hostile territory required great care. Where possible *waka*, canoes, were used as a quick and easy method of travel. Some expeditions went far afield and from one island to another, especially as *taua*, war parties, or when visits were made to distant families and connections by marriage.

There was also a considerable amount of travel for trading purposes where supplies such as fish, eels, greenstone, *kūmara*, etc. might be bartered. However, these transactions were not commercial ventures but reflected a long-standing relationship between *iwi* or *hapū* groups where the products of one would be exchanged for those of another.

There were well-defined trails through forests, and these usually kept to the crests of the ridges in mountainous country. Rivers were crossed by canoes, rafts, fords, bridges formed from strategically felled tree trunks and by swimming.

When a party left its own tribal territory it came under the influence of other gods and was surrounded by inimical forces. Preparations had to be made to avoid the evil that might otherwise fall upon the travellers. A sacred fire was lit into which all the travellers threw a hair. Food was then cooked at these fires and each person carried a portion of the food with him in his belt, protecting himself against gods and evil spirits.

As the storyteller holds the children enthralled, their toys lie discarded on the ground. They include a kite, stilts, foot ropes for climbing, *poi*, knuckle stones, a top, hoops, a jumping jack, and a draught board.

A *taua* proceeding through the bush in single file.

Taua were forbidden from eating while they travelled as it was regarded as a bad omen. They had to stop to eat. The *tapu* attached to this practice had to be removed at the end of the journey.

Offerings of leaves, twigs and branches were made to *tipua*, enchanted, objects such as a particular stone or tree to secure fine weather and good fortune for the journey. When important chiefs were leading the party, hospitality from neighbouring villages and plentiful food supplies were assured, and etiquette demanded that the gifts be accepted. Messengers frequently brought supplies to the party on the march from the local villages.

The Māori method of walking was a 'pigeon-toed' trot with a short stride that was almost a shuffle. As a result well-used paths and tracks were extremely narrow. It was a silent method of progress that nevertheless covered the ground quickly. The heavy-boned Māori frame was also well adapted to carrying large loads.

Magic, rivers.

TREE CLIMBING (*whakaeke rākau*). Tree climbing for boys was a sport that provided good training for the future, when many of them would become bird hunters and would need all their skill in a dangerous occupation. Near the pā there would usually be a tree from which the branches had been stripped and which provided a pole for practising. It was easy to climb a tree provided with convenient branches, but a special method was devised for getting up the smooth bole of a branch-less tree. A short rope with two loops was slipped over the feet, which were pressed against the trunk. Another rope was looped round the tree and held in the hands. The cord was moved upwards 30 centimetres or so at a time, and provided a purchase as the feet were moved up. By this method the lowest branches of the tree could soon be reached.

Birds (hunting).

TREES (rākau). Tāne-mahuta was the creator of trees, with which he clothed the body of his mother Papa, and provided food for his children the birds. There is an amusing fable telling how, on his first experiment, he planted the trees upside down, and later had to reverse them when he discovered his mistake.

Individual trees were his offspring and were born during his quest for the female element.

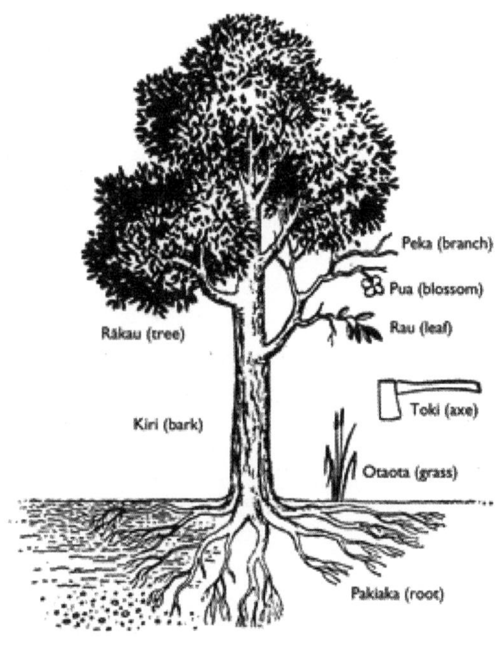

The parts of a tree.

The union of Tāne with Mumuhanga produced the *tōtara*, with Te Pu-whakahara the *maire* and *pūriri*, with Tū-kapua the *tawai*, etc. Tāne is not only the god of the forest, but of all the living things that it contains.

The *tapu* of the forest was strictly preserved. When a tree was felled to make a canoe, build a house or to provide posts for stockades, or any of the other uses to which timber was put, it was necessary to seek the aid of the *tohunga* in order to propitiate Tāne for the loss of one of his 'children'.

Felling a large tree with stone adzes was a difficult task. The usual method was to cut a scarf in the trunk, in which a fire was kept burning with the charred wood being adzed out from time to time.

A simple form of battering ram was set up to reduce the work of cutting through the trunks of the very large trees needed for building canoes. Horizontal poles were erected up close to the trees in order to support a heavy piece of timber to which a large adze blade or chisel was attached. Two men slid the pole across the scaffolding and gradually cut into the trunk, forming a narrow groove. The platform was raised and another groove cut above it, the wood between the two grooves being removed with adzes. The whole process had to be repeated many times.

A more effective and complex instrument of this kind was in use in some districts. The ram was attached by a long cord to the ends of a stout pole on the other side of the tree, forming a gigantic bow which, when the ram was drawn back, hurled the chisel-ended stake against the tree.

The following list gives Māori and English names of the well-known trees of Aotearoa, some of which provided berries for food:

akeake:	*akeake*
akepiro:	*akepiro*
akirākau:	golden *akeake*
haekaro:	*haekaro*
haumangōroa:	*haumangōroa*
heketara:	*heketara* or daisy tree
hīnau:	*hīnau*
horoeka:	lancewood
houhere:	ribbonwood, lacebark or hoheria
houpara:	*houpara*
hutu:	*hutu*
inaka:	grass tree
kahikatea:	*kahikatea* or white pine
kaikawaka:	mountain cedar
kaikōmako:	*kaikōmako*
kāmahi:	*kamahi*
kānuka:	tree *mānuka*
karaka:	*karaka* or New Zealand laurel
karo:	*karo*
kauri:	*kauri*
kawaka:	New Zealand arbor vitae
kawakawa:	*kawakawa* or lofty pepper tree
kohekohe:	*kohekohe* or New Zealand cedar
kōhūhū:	*kōhūhū*
kohutuhutu:	tree fuchsia
kōtukutuku:	*kōtukutuku* or tree fuchsia
kōwhai:	*kōwhai*
kōwhai ngutukaka:	red *kōwhai*, parrot's bill or kaka's beak
māhoe:	*māhoe* or whiteywood
maire:	*maire* or sandalwood
maire-tawake:	*maire-tawake* or black *maire*
makamaka:	*makamaka*
makomako:	*makomako* or wineberry
mānatu:	lowland ribbonwood
mānawa:	mangrove
mangeao:	*mangeao*
mānuka:	*mānuka* or teatree
māpau, *māpou* or *matipo*:	usually *matipo*
mataī:	*mataī* or black pine
miro:	*miro*
neinei:	spiderwood
nīkau:	*nīkau*
ngaio:	*ngaio*
pāpāuma:	broadleaf
parapara:	*parapara* or bird-catching plant
patē:	*patē*

poataniwha:	*poataniwha*
pōhutukawa:	*pōhutukawa*
pōkākā:	*pōkākā*
ponga:	treefern
porokaiwhiria:	pigeonwood
puka:	*puka* or shining broadleaf
pukatea:	*pukatea*
punawētā:	Māori may
pūriri:	*pūriri* or New Zealand oak
putaputāwētā:	Māori may
ramarama:	*ramarama*
rangiora:	*rangiora*
rātā:	*rātā*
raukawa:	*raukawa*
raurākau:	*raurākau*
rewarewa:	*rewarewa*, Māori or New Zealand honeysuckle
rimu:	*rimu* or red pine
rōhutu:	*rōhutu*
tainui:	*tainui*
tānekaha:	celery pine
taraire:	*taraire*
tarātā:	*tarātā* or lemonwood
taupata:	*taupata*
tawa:	*tawa*
tawāpou:	*tawāpou*
tāwari:	*tāwari*
tāwheowheo:	common quintinia
tawhero:	*tawhero*
tawhiwhi:	*tawhiwhi*
tī or *tī kouka*:	cabbage tree
tītoki:	*tītoki* or New Zealand ash
toatoa:	mountain celery pine
toro:	*toro*
tōtara:	*tōtara*
tōwai:	*tōwai*
tūrepo:	milk tree
tutu:	*tutu* or 'toot'
whārangi:	*whārangi*
whau:	*whau* or New Zealand mulberry
whauwhau or *whau whaupaku*:	New Zealand fig or five-finger.

Forests, gongs, offerings, Rātā, Tāne.

TRENCHES, see TERRACES.

TRIBES (*iwi*). A tribe began with a *whānau* or family that, if some strong leader of good birth and *mana* arose, would become a recognised self-supporting group. If everything prospered, in the course of time the *whānau* would grow into a *hapū*, and might eventually reach the strength and status of a loose confederation deemed an *iwi* or tribe, containing many *hapū* and *whānau*. The *hapū* or *iwi* would probably take the name of the ancestor who welded the original *hapū* into a cohesive unit. It was the *hapū* that operated as the principal political and social organisation in Māori society.

The welfare of the individual *iwi* and its *hapū* was the most important factor in everyday life. The welfare of the group almost always overrode that of the individual, and although there might be *whānau*, family, ownership of fishing grounds, canoes, lands, etc., ultimately they belonged to the people as a whole. Most marriages occurred within the *hapū* of an *iwi*, but occasionally an important union was made between high-born men and women of different tribes for the preservation of peace, or to form an alliance against a common enemy.

In addition to the *iwi* there was another, rarely recognised division, that of the *waka* (canoe), although it is also said that this division is probably post-European contact in origin. Māori attached great importance to the *waka*, canoes, in which their ancestors first came to Aotearoa, and the loyalty of the *iwi* to their '*waka*' was paramount because among other things it embodied identity and therefore claims to land.

The *waka* was not a social unit but it had political importance. For example, it proved the blood relationship of the *iwi* who were descended from it and that common ancestry might influence alliances in peace and war.

Tribal names were formed by prefixing *Ngāti*, *Ngāi*, *Ngā* and *Āti*, all of which mean offspring, to the name of the eponymous ancestor. The accompanying table sets out the disposition of some of the main iwi.

Ancestors, boundaries, families, hapū, Migration (Great), whānau.

TROUGHS (*waka*).
Birds (hunting and preserving).

TRUMPETS (*pū*). There were several forms of *pū*, all of which were used for signalling, and not as musical instruments. All kinds of *pū* were employed for sounding the alarm, and for various signals in time of war. Each type had its own name. Long, wooden *pūkāea*, trumpets, were made from two pieces of wood, hollowed throughout their length, and lashed together. This *pū* had a bell-shaped mouth, and in some cases one or more projections in the barrel which affected the sound. A temporary *pū* of much the same shape was made by winding flax leaves in a long spiral.

The most commonly used *pū* was the *pūtātara* (or *pūtara*), made from a large, tropical shell found in the far north of Te Ika a Māui. The point of the shell was cut off, several holes were drilled in it, and a mouthpiece lashed in place by cord threaded through the holes. *Hue,* gourds, were also fitted with wooden mouthpieces and used for signalling.

CANOES	TRIBES	DISTRICTS
Tainui	Waikato tribes, Ngāti Haua, Ngāti Maniapoto, Ngāti Maru, Ngāti Paoa, Ngāti Raukawa, Ngāti Tamatera, Ngāti Toa, Ngāi Tai (Bay of Plenty)	Waikato, King Country, Hauraki, Cambridge, Coromandel, Kawhia
Tokomaru	Ngāti Tama, Ngāti Mutunga, Ngāti Rahiri, Manukorihi, Puketapu, Āti Awa, Ngāti Maru	North and Central Taranaki
Kurahaupo	Taranaki, Āti Hau (Whanganui), Ngāti Apa, Rangitāne, Muaupoko, Te Aupouri, Te Rarawa	Taranaki, Whanganui, Manawatu, Rangitikei, Horowhenua, North Auckland
Aotea	Ngāti Ruanui, Ngā Rarau, Āti Hau	South Taranaki, Whanganui
Te Arawa	Ngāti Pikiao, Ngāti Rangitihi, Ngāti Rangiwewehi, Ngāti Whakaue, Tūhourangi, Ngāti Tūwharetoa	Maketū, Mātātā, Rotorua, Taupō
Mataatua	Ngāti Awa, Tūhoe, Whakatōhea, Whānau a Apanui, Ngāiterangi, Ngāti Pūkenga	Whakatāne, Urewera, Bay of Plenty
Takitimu	Rongowhakaata, Ngāti Kahungunu, Ngāi Tahu	Poverty Bay, Hawke's Bay, Wairarapa, South Island
Horouta	Ngāti Porou	East Coast of North Island
Mamari	Ngā Puhi, Te Rarawa, Te Aupouri	North Auckland
Mahuhu	Ngāti Whātua	Kaipara, Auckland

TŪ, see TŪ-MATAUENGA.

A shell and a wooden trumpet.

TŪĀ. Baptismal rite.
Baptism.

TŪĀHU, see ALTARS.

TUATARA. A lizard-like reptile native to Aotearoa. It is the last surviving close relative of the extinct giant reptiles — dinosaurs etc., of the Jurassic period. The *tuatara* often shared the burrows of *titi* sooty shearwaters where it was believed to keep the burrow clean by eating the bird's droppings.
Eggs.

TŪHUA, see obsidian.

TŪĪ. The tūī is a native bird also known as the kōkō. The tūī was usually caught by means of snares and spears, and occasionally by a carved perch with a cord noose, which was held in the hand. On frosty nights the birds could be taken by hand as they were incapable of flying away in such conditions. Because they were small they were caught in large quantities, and counted in pairs.

The male bird could be taught to speak. It was kept in a cage, frequently by a waterfall or a noisy stream, which drowned other sounds. The same words were then repeated patiently until the tūī was able to reproduce them. They became so tame that they could be carried on the shoulder, and would greet visitors with the words they had learned. Talking tūī were famous and battles were sometimes fought over their ownership.
Birds (hunting), Rehua, Tāne.

TUKUTUKU. Ornamental lattice work which was used to fill the spaces between the upright slabs in a whare.
Reed patterns.

TŪ-MATAUENGA. The god of war and of mankind. Tū was constantly invoked throughout the lives of men. In the *tohi*, baptismal rite, boys were dedicated to him, and again before they took part in battle. He was an evil influence among his brother gods as well as amongst men.

Tū played a prominent part in two wars against Tāne, and was victorious in the conflict with Tāwhiri-mātea.
Creation, gods, gods (wars of), man, separation, Tāne, Tāwhirimātea, Tiki, warfare.

TUNA, see EELS.

TUNU, see COOKING.
Birds (preserving).

TŪREHU, see FAIRIES.

TURI. Captain of the migratory Aotea canoe.

TURUMA, see LATRINES.

TŪTĀNEKAI. The lover and husband of Hinemoa.
Hinemoa.

TUTU. A shrub or small, softwood tree, the berries of which, when properly treated, provided a refreshing drink.
Berries, fern root, poisons.

TŪTŪĀ. A commoner.
Social classes.

TUTU NGARAHU, see WAR DANCES.

TUTUKAI, see HAND GAMES, PUZZLES.

TUTUNUI. Tutunui was the name of the pet whale that belonged to the Hawaiki chief Tinirau. Tutunui was said to be the guardian of fish and shellfish.

On one occasion Tutunui is said to have assembled the sandstone people to attack the greenstone people, a legend which explains the enmity between the two kinds of stone, as sandstone grinds greenstone in the making of *toki*, adzes and other artefacts. The significance of a whale filling this role has been lost.

Tinirau.

TŪWATAWATA, see PALISADES.

U

UA, see RAIN.

UENUKU. A war god and, as well, the personification of the rainbow. A famous *ariki* of this name lived in Hawaiki. His enmity towards Turi and Tama-te-kapua is said to have led to the departure of the Aotea and Arawa canoes for Aotearoa.

Mist, rainbow.

UHA, see FEMALE ELEMENT.

UMBILICAL CORD (*iho*). The *iho* of a new-born baby was buried or hidden in a safe place, frequently on the boundary of the lands of a tribe or *hapū*. In the case of high-born children the spot became *tapu*, and was known as the *iho* of so-and-so. The cord was severed with a flake of obsidian and tied with the stem of a plant. Baptism came after the cutting of the *iho*.

Birth.

UMU, see OVENS.

UNDERWORLDS (*rarohenga*, *raro*, *reinga*). According to this late-collected tradition there were said to be a number of underworlds; some say as many as 10. The surface layer is the world of light, presided over by Tāne. The second is the top layer of soil, and is the home of Rongo-marae-roa and Haumia-tiketike, the gods of cultivated and uncultivated or 'wild' food. The third is the Raro or Rarohenga, also called the Reinga, where Hine-nui-ō-te-pō, the goddess of death, resides, reigning over this and Autoia, the fourth subterranean land where Whiro lives. The names and details of the further underworld are debatable.

Having passed through the water at Te Reinga, the *wairua* or soul entered an underground land. It crossed a river and found itself in a pleasant land, well watered, fertile, and light. The spirits of the *taro* and *kūmara* were there; once food was eaten there was no hope of the soul returning to the land of daylight.

Popular legend nevertheless contains a number of stories of living men and women who visited the Rarohenga and returned, but only in cases where they had abstained from food.

According to one legend there is a lake in this land surrounded by hills, and the souls of the dead live in bodily form on its shores. A newly arrived soul alights on the hills and stays there until it is recognised by its relatives, when it resumes its life with them.

In contrast with this simple picture, there are other confused beliefs in strange passages, mythical guardians of doors, the brooding presence of Hine-nui-ō-te-pō, and even a succession of lower worlds through which the *wairua* travelled. The *wairua* could die a second death or, if it survived the perils of the way and reached the lowest underworlds, had the opportunity of regaining the Ao-tū-roa, the world of long-standing light, having assumed the form of a moth.

Death, evil, Hawaiki-nui, Hine-nui-ō-te-pō, Hine-tītama, Reinga, souls, weaving.

UPOKO, see HEADS.

URUKEHU. Light- or red-haired. Māori with reddish hair, blue eyes, and light skins were known as *urukehu*. It was believed that they were descended from the fair-headed fairies known as *tūrehu*.

Hair, tūrehu.

URU-TE-NGANGANA. The first-born of the gods. He was the divider of day and night, and the personified form of all the light-giving heavenly bodies.

Light, stars, sun, Tāne.

URUURU-WHENUA, see OFFERINGS.

Demons.

UTU (Revenge, ransom, payment or reward). Like *muru* and *tapu*, this was one of the more important elements in Māori life. Māori believed passionately in the concept of an eye for an eye, a tooth for a tooth, and it did not always matter whose tooth was taken. Insults were never tolerated. Very small slights were often turned into an insult and used as a pretext for fighting, especially when a strong tribe wished to increase the extent of its territories.

An insult was never forgotten and although years might pass, when the opportunity came *utu* would be claimed. As in other societies it was thought that *utu*, revenge, was a dish best eaten cold. The murder by an individual of another tribe was sufficient cause for an attack against the culprit's tribe, and so long as some members of that tribe were killed, it did not matter if the real culprit escaped. *Utu*, payment, was procured by the shedding of blood. Lesser acts might be satisfied by lighter punishment but Māori were adept at devising insults and even quicker in resenting them.

One such act might lead to a chain of raids, each of increasing severity, and tribal histories consist mainly of such battle stories. Warfare for this reason was almost a constant and accounts of victories and defeats were carefully kept. It was a point of honour to avenge a defeat and so obtain *utu*, and it was better still to establish a credit balance by an extra victory. The custom of *utu* contributed hugely to the warrior ethic of Māori society.

On the positive side, the custom, which applied as much to families and to individuals as to tribes, was one of the several practices that prevented wanton contempt of law and order in the community.

Divorce, mana.

UWHI, see YAMS.

V

VEGETABLE CATERPILLARS. The *moko* caterpillar, which is normally associated with *tōtara* trees, was sometimes attacked by a fungus parasite. It then fell to the ground and buried itself several centimetres into the soil, sending up a stick-like shoot to mark the spot. This natural curiosity was gathered, burnt and the soot mixed with oil to form the deep blue-black pigment used in tattooing.

Soot, tattooing.

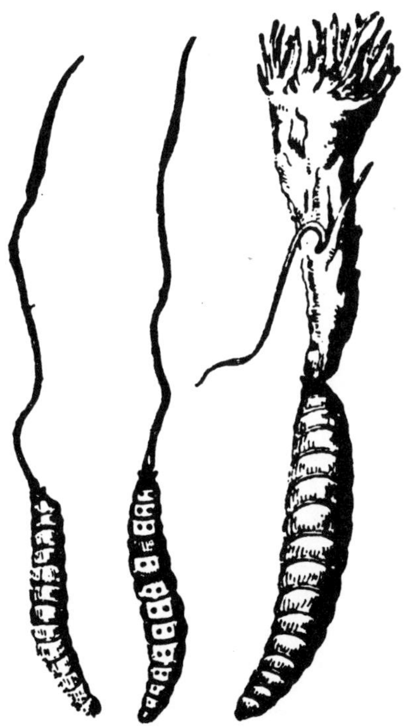

The vegetable caterpillar after it has been attacked by the fungus.

VEGETABLES. In addition to the four staple root vegetables introduced from the homeland (*kūmara*, *taro*, yam, and *hue*, gourd), the roots of the fern, *tī kouka,* cabbage tree, and *raupō*, bullrush, were also used for food. The young shoots of the king fern (*pikopiko*), the heart of the leaf base of the *nīkau* palm and the inner leaf shoots of the *tī kouka* were eaten as vegetable greens. The pith of the *mamaku* tree fern, and both the flowers and fruit of the *kiekie* were eaten as also was *karengo*, sea lettuce, a kind of seaweed. Following the arrival of the Pākehā these vegetables have been supplemented by the leaves of wild swede (*korau*), watercress (*poniu*), and sow-thistle (*pūhā*).

Berries, food.

VILLAGES, FORTIFIED, see PĀ.

VILLAGES, UNFORTIFIED, see KĀINGA.

VINES (*aka*). The name for long, thin roots of trees and plants was *aka*, and the word was used generally for vines. Together with suitable leaves such as those of the *tī kouka*, cabbage tree, flax and *kiekie* plants, they were used in innumerable ways as cordage and rope.

Swings, Tawhaki.

VISITORS (*manuhiri*). The responsibility for properly hosting guests and visitors was of enormous importance because it reflected on the *mana*, the wealth and status of the hosts. Food stores were ungrudgingly depleted sometimes to the point where starvation faced the hosts once the guests had departed, in order to provide sustenance and entertainment for honoured guests. Even chance passers-by would be invited to share a meal.

If the guests were expected, no trouble was spared in entertaining them. The visitors would march on to the *marae* led by their chiefs and would be challenged by the hosts, a procedure which occupied much time and which was conducted with detailed observation of the necessary protocols.

A very important chief might be honoured by having some of the palisades broken down in order to create a separate entrance for his use. Gifts of valued garments and weapons were a feature of ceremonial visits.

When the proper arrival formalities were finished, the visitors were greeted with welcoming cries and the hosts and their guests mingled with much weeping and mourning for their respective dead. The visitors might be shown into houses set aside for them, after which they assembled on the *marae*, and some hours might be taken up with *whaikōrero*, speeches by both parties.

During this time the food would be cooking in the *hāngi*, earth ovens, and soon the food-bearers (women, and perhaps some slaves) would come in a procession carrying the baskets of food, singing and swaying to the melody of their song.

The baskets were placed on mats on the ground in front of the visitors. Old friends might choose special delicacies for those they favoured. If the weather was cold, fires were lit in the *whare*, and at night games and songs would enliven the evening.

Challenges, feasts, water.

VOLCANOES. These are the visible sign of the volcanic fire engendered by Rūaumoko, the earthquake god.

Fire, Rūaumoko, thermal regions.

VOYAGES. The great voyages of the Māori people were the coming of the *waka*, canoes, to Aotearoa, New Zealand. There were the first discoveries of the new land by Māui and other mythical or semi-mythical explorers, followed in later centuries by Kupe and Ngāhue, Toi and Whatonga and other visitors, and then what is usually known as the Great Migration or the Great Fleet, when the various migration canoes were said to have come to Aotearoa almost in company with each other.

The Great Migration tradition has subsequently been discredited and in recent years the accuracy of the other traditional voyages has been questioned. One theory has been advanced by Andrew Sharp that the colonisation of Aotearoa originated wholly from accidental canoe voyages, and that there were no 'return trips'.

In a restatement in *Ancient Voyagers in Polynesia,* Sharp broadens his conjectures by stating that many of the traditional voyages were tales of journeys of discovery imported from other parts of Polynesia, and applied to Aotearoa.

Other scholars such as David Simmons believe that some migratory and return journeys took place wholly within Aotearoa itself.

These theories have breathed life into the debate surrounding a critical part of Māori traditional history and reawakened interest in *waka* voyaging. Several ocean-going *waka* of traditional design have been built and sailed to and from Aotearoa in recent times.

But there can be no doubt that the Polynesian ancestors of the Māori were a bold, seafaring people who were not easily daunted by the vast ocean wastes of the Pacific.

Drift voyages, Kupe, Māui, Migration (Great), Toi.

WAHANGA, see BURDENS.

WAHA NGUTU, see GATEWAYS.

WĀHINE, see WOMEN.

WĀHI POUNAMU, TE, see SOUTH ISLAND.

WĀHI TAPU. The sacred place of the village or any place considered to be of religious or spiritual significance.

Altars, tapu.

WAI, see WATER.

WAIATA, see SONGS.

Laments.

WAIORA-A-TĀNE. The health-giving waters of Tāne. This is the legendary lake of Aewa, and is also said to represent sunlight. As the moon wanes during the Hina-uri (dark Hina) phase, it sickens and goes to the Waiora-a-Tāne, where it is revived and emerges as Hina-keha (pale Hina).

Moon, Tāne.

WAIRUA, see SOULS.

WAKA, see CANOES.

Birds (hunting), canoes, tribes, troughs.

WAKA HUIA, see BOXES.

Feathers.

WĀNANGA. Learning, knowledge, especially that pertaining to sacred lore.

Baskets of knowledge, schools of learning, stones (sacred).

WAR DANCES (*peruperu, tūtu ngārahu*). The *haka taparahi,* posture dance, was performed without weapons. In the *peruperu* or true war dance the warriors held spears or large clubs, and expressed defiance in their chanting and energetic movements. *Peruperu* were performed as call and response, as this example shows:

Solo:	Kia kutia!	Close in!
Chorus:	Au, au.	Ah, ah!
Solo:	Kia wherahia!	Open out!
Chorus:	Au, au.	Ah, ah!
	Kia rere atu te kekeno	Let the seal fly away
	Ki tawhiti,	To the distance
	Titiro mai ai!	And there gaze (in fright) back
Dances.	Ā, ā, te riri.	Ah, ah, it is war.

WAR PARTIES (*taua*). A party of *toa*, warriors, could be assembled quickly because they were always in a state of readiness. Fiery speeches roused their passions and a final battle cry might be *Tokia!* (Give them the axe!)

The favoured number for a war party was *hokowhitu,* 140 (seven score). *Hokowhitu* therefore became a term for a body of fighting men regardless of the actual number. Much larger war

A famous illustration from Thomson's *The Story of New Zealand*. The warriors are armed with muskets, but the frenzy of the old-time *peruperu* is well portrayed.

parties were assembled when a great battle or siege was planned, but they were not compact, readily assembled fighting units like the true *hokowhitu*.

Peruperu, war dances, *wero*, challenges, and the sacrifice of 'the fish of Tū' – usually an unfortunate slave – were all calculated to inflame the ardour of the fighting men. The *peruperu* provided an outlet for the spirit of defiance, but there were other ceremonies to be observed.

In some traditions the *tohunga* had an important part to play in war preparations; he sprinkled the fighting men with water to consecrate them to the god of war, imposed *tapu* to enhance the importance of the war mission, and was responsible for correctly reading and interpreting the omens for the coming battle. Slaves were employed to carry food on the march, and further supplies were often obtained from friendly villages.

There was always keen rivalry amongst the warriors to capture and kill the *mātāngohi*, 'the first fish' or victim; so keen, in fact, that over-enthusiastic *toa* sometimes provided the first fish themselves.

Echoes of the warrior tradition have continued through into the modern era. For example, the inscription on the memorial arch at Whakarewarewa, Rotorua, is dedicated to the 'Hokowhitu a Tū' – the *taua,* war party, of the god of war. It commemorates the 500 men of the First Māori Contingent of World War I.

War dances, warfare.

WARFARE (*pakanga*). While Tū-matauenga was the god of men and of warfare there were many other tribal war gods, such as Uenuku and Kahukura. The causes of war were innumerable. For example, war came come about through the defence or acquisition of land; from a chief's desire for a woman of another tribe as his wife, or from her husband's resentment; from envy because of the differences in prosperity between tribes, between families and even between relatives. It could also arise over insults and slights or suspicion that such had occurred and because of sorcery. War might also start because the omens were favourable and the young men were spoiling for a fight.

More than any other cause was the influence of *mana*, *utu*, and *muru*, and its effect upon people. At times the causes of fighting seemed trivial, but warfare was an occupation, and a necessity because those who did not take part and were not highly trained made easy victims.

Young men were trained from an early age in bushcraft and in the use of weapons. These gave them great agility and made them capable of feats of endurance. The warrior life was devoted to gaining and honing the skills for the serious business of fighting. To die fighting was the most fitting end to a man's life.

Songs and dances were used to encourage the fighting men. There were songs of defiance, chants by *tohunga* who foretold the result of the coming fight, watch-songs chanted by sentries, songs of victory, and songs of derision directed at the remnants of a defeated *taua*, war party.

The garments worn in battle were a short kilt, though occasionally a coarse cloak was worn in such a manner that weapons were deflected, while leaving the wearer's arms free; most times the warrior went into battle naked.

At times acts of surprising chivalry were demonstrated, but generally Māori were fierce, vindictive, and even treacherous fighters who seldom gave quarter.

Single combat often preceded the fight and provided an opportunity for the young men to show off their skills. But in the heat of the battle there was no time to think of anything but the defeat of the enemy.

A skilled and experienced leader was able to make use of many methods of attack and defence, and to employ different strategies to deceive the enemy. A favourite formation was the wedge, where the position of honour at the point was given to the strongest and most fearless warrior. It was a coveted position.

A mass attack was called a *kawau mārō*, because the body of men was likened to a *kawau*, shag, with its neck stretched out. Another method of attack was a simultaneous assault by a number of small parties at different places, thus spreading the defences thinly. If a war party was repulsed, it would retire, but it might well be that attackers at another point had been able to smash through the defences. Combat was almost entirely hand to hand, and consequently

Hand-to-hand fighting with *mere* and *taiaha*.

a favourite stratagem when attacking a *pā* was to pretend to be repulsed and to stage a retreat, drawing the over-confident defenders from the shelter of the stockade, where they could be engaged at close quarters.

The *tohunga* who accompanied the war party took out the heart of the first victim as an offering to the god of war. He might also cut off a lock of hair or take a portion of flesh, which was laid on the *tūāhu*, altar or sacred place of the *kāinga*, village, if the *taua* returned victorious.

Although Māori were fierce fighters, there were occasions when hostilities would be settled by the gift of a woman of noble birth. There were also times when there was generosity on the part of the victors, but they were the exception rather than the rule. The usual fate of the defeated was death, the cooking ovens, or slavery. The institution of slavery was an important factor in warfare because of the need to replenish the ranks of the slaves from time to time. The children of the marriage of a slave woman and a free-born man were themselves free.

Fighting was normally a summer activity that took place between the time of planting and harvesting of crops when there was little urgent work to be done.

Bones, boys, challenges, darts, fire, gateways, gods (tribal and war), gods (wars of), gongs, mana, muru, nature, pā, palisades, peace, signals, spears, stages (fighting), trumpets, Tū-matauenga, utu, war dances, war parties, warriors, watch-towers, women, wounds.

A fight in a swamp at Rotorua, which was afterwards known as the battle of the waters of jumping whitebait.

WARRIORS (*toa*). Brave men who were good fighters were known as *toa*. But they were described in other terms as well; Ika-a-Whiro, Whiro's 'fish' for a tested fighter of experience; *arero-whero* (red tongue), a name given because of the protruding tongue in the frenzied *peruperu*, war dance; *ati-a-toa*, a young warrior yet to be tested.

Toa were trained in the art of war from an early age, in suppleness of body, fleetness of foot, skill in the use of weapons, in tactics, and in ritual

Warriors with clubs and two-handed weapons. Note the fine example of *rape* or breech tattooing on the figure on the left.

chants designed to give them the advantage over their enemies, and to enlist the aid of the war god. To become a *toa taua*, a warrior of repute, was the aim of most boys and young men.

Boys, female element, spears, warfare.

WATCH-TOWERS. At one or more strategic points in the stockade of a *pā*, tall towers were built where sentries maintained a constant day and night vigil. During the hours of darkness they chanted their watch-songs, assuring their people that they were on the alert, and warning any unseen enemy that there was no hope of taking the *pā* by surprise.

An early Pākehā visitor described one of these watch-towers in 1772:

> Inside the village, at the side of the gate, there is a sort of timber platform about twenty-five feet high, the posts being about eighteen inches to twenty inches diameter and sunk solidly in the ground. The people climb on to this sort of advance post by means of a post with footsteps cut into it. A considerable collection of stones and javelins is always kept there, and when they fear an attack they picket the sentinels there. The platforms are roomy enough to hold fifteen or twenty men.

Watch-towers on a lakeside *pā*.

Gongs, pā, palisades, songs, stages (fighting), warfare.

WATER (*wai*). Parawhenuamea was the origin and personification of water. She was the daughter of Tāne and Hine-tu-pari-maunga, the mountain girl, and therefore recognised the fact that life-giving water came from the mountains. Fresh water was called *wai māori*, salt water *wai tai*.

Water was used in baptismal and purificatory rites. A pool or stream close to the village would be reserved as *wai tapu*, or sacred water for ceremonial purposes. It was the place, not the water, that was *tapu*. That is clear from the fact that water was the purificatory element in religious ceremonies.

Water was the principal drink of Māori, and was kept in gourds. There was a graceful custom in which water given to a visitor had small fern fronds floating on the surface. The availability of drinking water was one of the principal problems in the defence of a *pā*. If a spring could be enclosed by the stockade all was well. If none was available, storage pits were dug wherever possible. In favourable situations gourds could be lowered over the edge of a cliff and filled from a stream or river, but in many cases the only method of storage was by keeping it in *hue*, gourds.

Baptism, drink, pā, Waiora-a-Tāne, war parties.

WATER GAMES. Children were thoroughly at home in the water from an early age. The youngest ones played on light rafts that were used as water wings, but they soon learned to swim, and were quite fearless in the water. Jumping (rather than diving), splashing, and ducking were all part of the fun. As they grew older they took part in swimming races and surf riding. Children were able to paddle small canoes holding one or more youngsters. Other water games included the making of tiny canoes from flax leaves and floating them on the water.

Rafts, swimming.

Surf riding, swimming, jumping, and canoeing were part of the delights of playing in water.

WAUWAU, see IMPLEMENTS, AGRICULTURAL.

WEAPONS (*rākau*). Boys were trained in the use of weapons from an early age. They were equipped with light sticks and encouraged to attack each other in mock battles. Experienced warriors trained them in proper methods of attack and defence. Sometimes, when tempers were roused, wounds were inflicted and older people became embroiled in the quarrel that followed. By the time he reached manhood, a young warrior was agile and skilled in the use of several weapons.

Because Māori warfare was characterised by close in-fighting, weapons training put much emphasis on good footwork. A great deal of time was taken during training to encourage agility. Warriors watched the big toes of their opponents in hand-to-hand fighting because a true blow, as distinct from a feint, was always signalled by the toes gripping the ground firmly.

There were three main types of weapon – thrusting, striking, and throwing. These were made of wood, stone, and bone. Many of the weapons, such as the *taiaha*, could be used for both striking and thrusting. The *mere* was used in a thrust as well as for blows with the edge of the blade. Spears were used mainly as a weapon of defence. They were not always carried by a war party, and often were used only in the first *wero*, challenge.

Clubs, darts, hoeroa, pouwhenua, spears, taiaha, tewhatewha, warfare.

WEAVING. The patroness of weaving and domestic arts was Hine-te-iwaiwa, but the woman who is credited with introducing this art to mankind was Niwareka. She was a *tūrehu*, fairy or spirit, who came from Rarohenga, the underworld, and married a mortal named Mataora. Subsequently she left him and returned to her own people.

Mataora followed her, learned the art of tattooing, won his wife's love again, and together they ascended to the Ao-mārama. Niwareka brought with her a famous garment named Rangi-haupapa, which was the prototype of woven cloaks.

Most garments were woven from flax fibre. The leaves were soaked in water, washed, scraped and dried. If a soft fibre was needed for a superior garment, the fibre was pounded. For making ornamental patterns, the fibres were bleached and dyed. The finished material was known as *muka*.

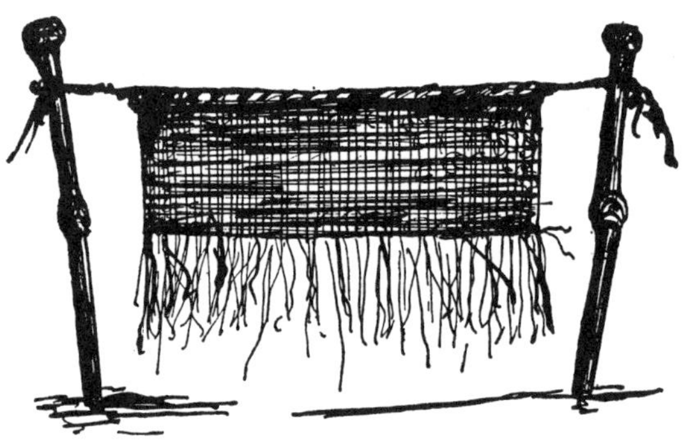

A mat in the process of manufacture.

Cord or twine was made by hand-rolling the fibres on the thigh but the preparation work was not as intensive as that required for *muka*.

Weaving was a laborious task, performed by women who had been trained by older, skilled females. There were no looms, and in fact the term weaving is perhaps a misnomer, for according to ethnologists, the product should be called downward or finger weaving, as distinct from loom weaving. The only artificial aid was two, or in the case of more elaborate garments, four upright sticks that were planted in the ground, or placed against the wall of a house. A horizontal thread was tied to the tops of the sticks, and to it were attached the many vertical threads needed to make a garment. The horizontal or woof fibres were threaded between the vertical ones, the spacing and pattern varying according to the weaver's plan and her experience.

With no mechanism to assist the weaver, the making of a fine cloak took months of work. The rare feather cloaks took even longer, as each feather was individually tied to the cloth.

Cloaks, dyes, flax, Hine-te-iwaiwa, mats, tāniko, whare.

WEIRS (*pā tuna*). Large fenced *pā tuna*, weirs, were erected in rivers and streams to catch eels and, less frequently, other freshwater fish.

Eels.

WERO, see CHALLENGES.

WĒTĀ. Large tree and cave insects of frightening appearance. Māori were especially frightened of the male insect. The giant 'tree locust' of the north was called *wētāpunga*, Punga being the personification of everything that was deformed or ugly.

Taipo.

WHAKAIRO. Decorative art of all kinds.

Art, carving (wood), painting, tattooing, weaving.

WHAKAIRO RĀKAU, see CARVING, WOOD.

WHAKAKAI, see EAR PENDANTS.

WHAKANOA. A rite to remove *tapu* from those who had been engaged in sacred tasks, or who had come in contact with *tapu* persons or things, or had been affected by ceremonial observances.

Burial, tapu.

WHAKAPAPA, see GENEALOGIES.

WHAKAROPIROPI, see HAND GAMES.

WHALES (*tohorā*, right whale; *parāoa*, sperm whale). Stranded whales provided a bountiful supply of food and were much desired for that reason. The bones were used as weapons, particularly the *patu parāoa*, whalebone hand clubs (*kotiate* and *wahaika*, and the peculiar *hoeroa*), while the teeth of the sperm whale were prized as neck ornaments.

Part of the tooth was cut away and smoothed, the pointed end was given eyes and the finished article was worn as a neck pendant.

Because it represented a plentiful supply of food and therefore prosperity, the whale often appears on the face boards of *pātaka*, food stores, but the stylised design is sometimes difficult to see because of the intricacy of the work.

Fish, food, mauri, Paikea, Tinirau, Tutunui.

WHĀNAU, see FAMILIES. The word *whānau* is also used for offspring.

Tribes.

WHAO, see CHISELS.

WHARAU. Temporary huts or shelters.
Houses.

WHARE, see HOUSES. There were many different types of houses. In the following list, some of the names are used figuratively:

whare hui: a house where all the people assembled with their guests.
whare kahu: a birth house, or 'nest house', to which mother and baby were taken the day after the birth of the child.
whare kai: dining room – a modern term.
whare kaupo: a school of tribal history.
whare kōhanga: a nest house, occupied by an expectant mother for a few days before and after the birth of a child.
whare kura: a school of learning in which the *tohunga* taught esoteric lore to his pupils. The name was sometimes applied to the common meeting house of the *kāinga*.
whare maire: a school of learning in which *mākutu*, black magic, including the killing of men at a distance and the destruction of their *wairua*, souls, was taught.
whare manuhiri: a house for guests.
whare mānuka: a name applied in some localities to a simple house with an excavated floor, no walls, and a gable roof which was probably covered with earth.
whare mātā: a hut in which bird-snaring implements were kept; used figuratively for the teaching of the skills of bird hunting. whare mate: a house of the dead, i.e. a shelter for a corpse and the closer relatives who mourned beside it.
whare ngākau: a house built specially to provide a place for discussion of some wrong or offence committed by another tribe.
whare nui: literally "big house" — another modern term to describe the largest building in a typical marae complex.
whare pora: a figurative expression for the house of weaving.
whare porukurukuru: similar to the whare maire, but usually describing a house where a *tohunga* taught a single pupil, such as his son or grandson.
whare pōtae: a house of mourning — a figurative expression only. A widow was said to remain in the whare pōtae for some months after her husband's death.
whare puni: a sleeping house, carefully built, but without carvings. It was frequently made with three layers of *raupō* on the walls and the name was given because when the door and window were shut the house was puni, closed. The name was sometimes given to the principal meeting house in the *kāinga*.
whare pūrākau: a school for the teaching of legends.
whare rangi: a storehouse erected on one or more posts.
whare rāhui: a hut built especially to house a sick person.
whare rēhia: a house of amusements: another name for the *whare tapere*. The 'arts of pleasure' were *ngā mahi a te rēhia*.
whare rūnanga: a house where important tribal discussions took place.
whare tākaha: see whare mātā.
whare takiura: a school of high-class knowledge.
whare tapere: a figurative expression for any communal building in which activities such as games, storytelling, singing, dancing were held.
whare umu: a cooking shed.
whare wānanga: the school or course of knowledge pertaining to sacred lore. See under Schools or Learning.
whare whakairo: a carefully constructed, superior house decorated with carvings.
whare whakanoho: a superior house with carefully adzed timbers.
Birth, cold, magic, overworlds, schools of learning.

WHĀRIKI, see MATS.

WHATA, see *stages*.
Storehouses.

WHATONGA. An early explorer and the grandson of Toi, whom he followed to Aotearoa. His sons were Tara and Tautoki, from whom the Ngāi Tara and Rangitāne tribes claim descent.

Drift voyages, Kurahaupo, Toi.

WHATOTO, see WRESTLING.

WHATUKURA. Spirits or celestial beings said to guard the overworlds. They are the male counterparts of the *māreikura*. They are also said to be the sacred stones brought by Tāne to the terrestrial *whare wānanga*.

Māreikura, overworlds, schools of learning, stones (sacred), Tāne.

WHEKE, see OCTOPUS.

WHENUA, see LAND.

WHETŪ, see STARS, COMETS.

WHIRO. The god of evil and darkness. He was continuously at war with most of his brothers, especially Tāne, but although Whiro was in effect the antithesis of Tāne, the latter did not embody the idea of goodness as opposed to evil. Whiro attempted to steal the baskets of knowledge from Tāne, attacking him with predatory birds and insects before being finally driven down to Rarohenga, the underworld. There he had the help of the fearful Maiki brothers.

When Rongo said, 'Let mankind be endowed with the qualities of *ihi* and *maru*' (ability, industry, benevolence and hospitality), Whiro replied, 'So be it; I shall uphold the *poautinitini*,' (disease, death, and the troubles of mankind). The *moko*, lizard, is Whiro's representative on earth.

Another Whiro, an explorer, had remarkable adventures in distant countries and is not to be confused with the god of this name.

Disease, evil, gods, gods (wars of), light, lizards, sickness, Tāne.

WHITEBAIT (*inanga*). These tiny fish were caught in great quantities as they migrated up streams and rivers. They were the juvenile stage of the species and were taken in hoop or scoop nets, being greatly valued as a tasty food. *Inanga* were preserved for future use by being spread out and dried in the sun.

Fishermen were familiar with their migratory habits and knew the time of the year when the great shoals of the fish came up the rivers on the incoming tide.

The fish were supposed to be the children of the star Rehua (Antares). When they asked their parent when and where they should migrate, he replied, 'When you observe a red glow in the sky that is the sign for you to go to your ancestor Wainui.' Wainui was the figurative term for the ocean where they spawned.

Cooking.

WIDOWS. Widows were left disconsolate at the death of their husbands and usually led the mourning, slashing their arms and upper bodies with sharp shells so that blood was drawn as a means of expressing their sorrow. It was not unknown for the widows of chiefs to commit ritual suicide. Normally a chaplet of leaves was worn as an emblem of mourning for a departed husband, and sometimes the hair was cut off, one lock only remaining. Widows frequently wore a *pōtae tauā*, or widow's cap, for a considerable period. It was made of rushes or seaweed dyed black.

Some time after the death of a husband a widow was eligible for marriage again, provided that the male relatives of her deceased husband agreed.

WINDOWS (*matapihi*). The single window of a house was placed in the front wall, and consisted of a sliding panel of wood. In the more important houses the frame was carved. Windows and doors were the only source of light, and the former often had to serve duty as an inefficient outlet for smoke.

Houses.

WINDS (*hau*). Tāwhiri-mātea is the departmental god of winds. He quarrelled with his brothers and remained with his father Rangi in the heavens, whereas the other *atua* clung to Papa, the Earth Mother.

Tāwhiri-mātea mated with Paraweranui, and their children were the winds, which were known as the *whānau puhi*, or wind children. They live in the heavens but were able to ascend and descend. They assisted Tāne in his ascent to the upper heavens when he obtained the baskets of knowledge, and fought against Whiro and his followers. But they were playful in nature, spending their time chasing the cloud children. They are said to live in the wind house where they have a number of guardians.

The different winds were given many names, with the points of the compass taking their names from the appropriate winds. *Tohunga* claimed that by means of wind charms they could exercise a measure of control over them.

Compass (points of), gods (wars of), separation, space, Tāne, Tāwhiri-mātea.

WINTER (*takurua, hōtoke*). Winter was personified in Hine-takurua, the winter wife of the sun. He lived with her for half the year. When the sun moves towards Rangi's head it is summer. Winter comes when he moves towards the Sky Father's legs.

Earthquakes, Rangi, seasons, summer, sun.

WITCHCRAFT, see MAGIC.

WOMEN (*wāhine*). As all the primal children were males they spent much time searching for the female 'element', which was eventually discovered by Tāne. He formed the body of the first woman and gave it life. An alternative myth ascribes the origin of woman to Tiki-te-pomua, the first man, who saw his reflection in a pool, covered it over and imprisoned it, then forming a woman with whom he mated.

The female organs of generation were regarded as the door of death as well as of life, and it may be for this reason that women were *noa*, or destructive of *tapu*. They were required to take part in ceremonies designed to lift the *tapu* from newly built houses, canoes, and *pā*, but were rigidly excluded from other ceremonies and feasts lest their essential *tapu* be destroyed. In spite of the condition of *noa*, women of noble birth and *mana* were regarded as *tapu*, and exercised a great influence among their people. Usually, however, they were edged about with irksome restrictions, especially before marriage, these restrictions varying from tribe to tribe.

Women wore much the same garments as men, kept their hair short, and walked with a rolling, hip-swinging gait which was much admired. Beauty among women was considered desirable, and beautiful females were renowned and much sought after in marriage.

In traditional times women's lives were tough, with their duties well defined. When engaged in hard work they discarded their cloaks, but retained the *maro* or apron. They took charge of all the preparation and cooking of meals and gathered the firewood to fuel the twice-daily ovens. The latter was an exhausting task and the carrying of huge loads of firewood contributed to the bent backs of women, helping to bring on a premature old age. The making of baskets, food platters, mats, and garments were tasks that kept them occupied all the time.

While the hunting of food was primarily man's work, women were required to work in the cultivations. Amongst some tribes, however, certain tasks in the plantation were forbidden to women. While men had the primary responsibility for hunting birds and climbing trees, women were allowed to climb the easier trees for the same purpose. Men went fishing in canoes while women netted freshwater fish and caught crayfish, etc.

The work of women – cooking, weaving, gathering firewood, working in the cultivations, washing, and pounding flax fibres.

They gathered foods such as shellfish, berries and fern root.

They also took part in warfare and infrequently accompanied raiding parties. In the absence of their menfolk they were responsible for the defence of their villages against attack, but these were not normal activities. As one proverb says, 'Fighting for men and childbirth for women.'

The tradition of motherhood was exemplified in the Earth Mother, Papa, and descended to her human daughters; but a Māori woman's life was so fully occupied that young girls often took charge of their smaller brothers and sisters.

The lighter side of life was catered for in songs and dances. Generous, hospitable women were praised, and had authority on the *marae* where food was consumed.

Babies, birth, cooking, dances, female element, garments, girls, Hina, Hine-ahu-one, lizards, man, mana, meals, men, puhi, shellfish, swimming, tattooing, weaving.

WORKING BEES (*ohu*). The *ohu* was a characteristic Māori institution. When it was necessary to clear bush to make a new cultivation, everyone joined in the working bee, which was performed co-operatively and in high spirits. There were a number of tasks that would be done by the tribe, *hapū* or *whānau* in this way. On occasions such as the making of a giant fishing net, people from a neighbouring tribe would be invited to take part, while the hosts entertained them, doing all they could to make their stay enjoyable.

WOUNDS. Wounds received in battle were cauterised with a fire stick. If they resulted from spear thrusts, the orifice was probed with the glowing end of a *mānuka* stick. The sap of the *rātā* vine was then applied to flesh wounds. Broken limbs were bound to splints of bark, or the butt ends of flax leaves; but generally speaking, nature and the power of the *atua* were relied upon to bring wounded men back to health.

WRESTLING (*whātōtō*). *Whātōtō* was a favourite sport in which women sometimes joined the men and young people. There were a number of recognised holds. The contestants spat on their hands, clenched their fists, and repeated charms before indulging in a bout.

The best wrestler in the tribe was often required to pit his skill against challengers from other tribes. Boxing was not a typical Māori form of sport.

Stilts.

YAMS (*uwhi*). The yam was introduced from Hawaiki and subsequently cultivated in the northern part of the country, but it was always a difficult plant to grow. It was neglected as a food nearly everywhere except in the Bay of Islands district. However, Captain Cook noted yams being grown at Tolaga Bay on the East Coast of Te Ika a Māui.

The yam plant.

Cultivations.

YEAR. The rising of Matariki (the Pleiades star cluster) marked the beginning of the Māori new year.

Months, seasons.